The Mystery of Acts

The Mystery of Acts

Unraveling Its Story

Richard I. Pervo

POLEBRIDGE PRESS
Santa Rosa, California

Cover and interior design by Robaire Ream

Library of Congress Cataloging-in-Publication Data
Pervo, Richard I.
 The mystery of Acts : unraveling its story / Richard I. Pervo.
    p. cm.
 Includes bibliographical references.
 ISBN 978-1-59815-012-4 (alk. paper)
 1. Bible. N.T. Acts--Criticism, interpretation, etc. I. Title.
 BS2625.52.P475 2008
 226.6'06--dc22
                                        2008040707

Contents

Preface

In the past two decades there has been a great revival of interest in the historical Jesus. Almost all that is known about that figure comes from texts produced by his followers, whose interests were more religious than historical. The book of Acts and its companion Gospel according to Luke are responsible for the general understanding of how the Christian church originated and spread. It is eminently logical for those who wish to examine the sources of information about the Jesus of history to look also—if not initially—at the forces and movements that gave birth to those sources. A good deal of those data are found, or are said to be found, in the book of Acts. As far as is known, Luke was the first author who attempted to show the bridge between Jesus of Nazareth and the community/ies that developed a world religion that appeals to Jesus as its founder. How he achieved this goal is the primary subject of this little book.

A rejected idea for a title, *Acts with Tears,* played upon an earlier practice of using "without tears" to signal to readers that the book in question would make a difficult subject accessible to the "general public." The goal is eminently worthy, and I believe that some experts should view it as an obligation. "Without tears" had a patronizing ring, implying that the general public needs to be spoon-fed, that subjects require "dumbing down" if they are to command interest. There is a difference, after all, between the lucid explication of complicated issues and oversimplification for the sake of instant intelligibility. I have long thought that one sign of mastery over a particular subject is the capacity to explain it in plain language. Any failures I have exhibited in this regard may therefore be attributed to insufficient mastery.

Specialists utilize jargon and technical terms when communicating with one another. This is no less true of orchid-growers and football fans than it is of nuclear physicists and theologians. Jargon is a useful type of shorthand. It is much easier to say "ecclesiology" or "blitz" than it is to speak repeatedly of the constitution, form, nature, and doctrine of and about the Church or to state that the linebackers charged straight for the quarterback. Technical language does crop up in this book, but a definition accompanies each unfamiliar term on its first appearance. Moreover, since not everyone reads with full concentration and careful attention from beginning to end, a glossary of names, terms and dates is appended. Items appearing in the glossary are marked with an asterisk, e.g., *Marcion of Sinope.

Instead of abundant footnotes, this book places many references within parentheses. Although this is stylistically awkward, the hope is that it will be more "user friendly." It also means that many scholars do not receive direct and immediate credit for their ideas. The lists "For Further Reading" associated with each chapter seek to compensate in part for this lack of acknowledgement. All who write, and read, about Luke and Acts have to deal with the potential confusion caused by the use of "Luke" for the implied author of both and as the name of the first book. The solution here is to use either "the Gospel of Luke" or "the Gospel," with an upper case G where there might be ambiguity.

Few disciplines have been more open to the charge of teaching their subject "without tears" than has been Christian theology, through its most numerous representatives, the clergy of local communities. Although clergy in the mainstream traditions have had to confront critical problems and have been exposed to critical methods in the course of their professional education, all too few of them share this learning in their teaching and preaching. Their reasons are pastoral, but the result is paternalism. Since many church members have encountered critical thinking in educational settings or through the media, this paternalism has become insidious. Both believers and non-believers have as much right to learn what is going on in biblical studies as they do in medicine. This book is aimed at them. Therein lies another sense of the prepositional phrase "with tears."

"The Acts of the Apostles," as it is entitled, is a crucial book in the New Testament. Many can enjoy it, but it bristles with problems—including the problem of its portrait of the Jewish people. This book attempts ruthlessly to expose those difficulties, both because they are essential to an understanding of Christian origins and because true appreciation of Acts requires an understanding of its difficulties, including the difficulties that its author had to manage. If some of the explanations or definitions seem a trifle too condescending, the hope is that this deficit will be overcome by the refusal to pull punches. For thirty years Acts has been the chief focus of my research and writing in the New Testament field, and it has been through Acts that my other academic interests emerged and developed. It is my favorite book of the Christian Bible; I love it. If some may wonder how this love can be expressed by apparently smashing Acts into pieces, I should replay that laughter follows tears, and that there can be no Easter without Good Friday.

All biblical quotations not otherwise attributed are from the *New Revised Standard Version* (NRSV), ©1989 by the Division of Christian Education of the National Council of Churches of Christ in the U.S.A. In these citations I have, for the sake of clarity, followed "lectionary practice" by supplying proper names for pronouns. These substitutions are in *italics*. Thus, instead of "He said to them," the citation will read "*Peter* said to *the disciples*." Requirements of space prevent citation of most passages to which reference is made. Ideal readers will do well to keep a Bible to hand, so that they may examine some of these references.

Thanks are due to Tom Hall, an admirable editor, and to the staff of Polebridge Press.

Richard I. Pervo
St. Paul, Minnesota
April 2008

Chapter One

A Few Basics

Introducing Introduction

Some years ago, while sampling the wares of a used book emporium, I glanced at a recent paperback of John Steinbeck's *The Grapes of Wrath*. This edition, evidently directed toward young readers, included an introduction explaining the background. There really had been a "Great Depression" in the 1930s, exacerbated by the "Dust Bowl" that caused many families to abandon ancestral farms and move west to seek their livelihoods. The perceived need to supply this information was a bit of a shock. Informing the public of the existence of "the depression" was, for a member of the generation whose parents' lives had been shaped and scarred by that era, like announcing that the sun had arisen yesterday. Contemporary persons and works may be said to "need no introduction," but the passage of time quickly cancels that claim. If appreciation of Shakespeare's four-hundred-year-old plays requires some knowledge of the social circumstances under which he wrote—for example, that women's roles were taken by boys, creating a certain amusement when boys, playing women, dressed as boys—how much more is that knowledge likely to be important for works that are five times four hundred years old?

Yet languor—some might suggest rigor mortis—has overtaken the once lively discipline of "Biblical Introduction." As many who have sought to help students learn can testify, seeking to arouse interest in the standard journalistic questions, Who, What, When, Where, How, and Why, is about as fruitful as an attempt to promote the minuet as an attractive form of contemporary social dancing. The reasons for this decline in interest are too numerous to explore here, and it must

1

be said that, if students often find "this stuff" boring, the discipline itself has become rather stale. It is tempting to relegate introductory matter to an appendix, out of fear that beginning with these basics will lead readers to set the book aside. Those who write an introduction to a single biblical book must therefore pose an introductory question to themselves: why?

One approach is to use the introduction to summarize one's views and then offer the balance of the book as justification for those opinions. This is, despite several reasonable complaints, a quite legitimate procedure. But a more artistic author will think that this is like a mystery writer telling both the reader and the detective "whodunit" on the first page, and then devoting the remainder of the story to showing how the detective reached the aforementioned conclusion. An objection to attempts at artistry is that those seeking to unravel the Bible's mysteries should not write one.

Another quite acceptable rationale for the introduction is to alert the audience to the author's presuppositions and biases, so that concerned readers may correct for these. An even more important goal is to make clear what questions the author is trying to answer and what methods s/he will use. Too many introductions leave these matters as enigmas for readers to resolve. All of the foregoing is to say that authors must decide which mysteries they will solve on the opening pages and which they will leave outstanding. What follows, then, is equivalent to information about who was killed, with what weapon or medium, and where the body was found. I propose to begin by rounding up and interrogating the usual suspects, after addressing the most basic question.

Some Answers

What is the crime? The author of Acts committed a nearly "perfect crime." Critical study of Acts suffers from the book's success. Luke, as the author of both the Third Gospel (Luke) and Acts is conveniently designated, told his story so well that all rival accounts vanished with but the faintest of traces.[1] Luke T. Johnson, no radical skeptic, puts it this way: "So successful was Luke that his narrative has become the etiological or foundational myth of gentile Christianity." The same scholar also notes that "It witnesses to Luke's literary skill that for two millennia people thought he told the story just the way it happened, indeed, had to have happened. The story of the church's beginnings need not, however, have been told at all. It might also have been told very differently."[2] I fully agree and, furthermore, have no desire to depose the myth and replace it with another.

"Myths" such as Luke's probably function more effectively when they are not confused with simple history. Behind the last statement stands the recognition that science, which provides the dominant model for our culture, sees truth first and foremost as that which can be verified by empirical method. Yet the scientific model is in itself a sort of myth. In any case it requires belief. The "truth" of a myth like Luke's myth of Christian origins can be quite valid, but it is of a different order from that of scientific truth. Members of faith communities will either recognize the coexistence of different orders of truth or develop bifurcated minds, in which scientific and religious truths are maintained in separate compartments that do not interact. These are important matters that require a book of their own. One object of the present enterprise is to enter the laboratory of the myth-maker and learn whether one may discover his secrets.

Such a project is, of course, an exercise in literary criticism, and such studies are perfectly valid. Literary studies constitute the dominant approach to the study of Luke and Acts today. This permits scholars to dispense with questions of history and focus upon the story. Readers should be aware that some who engage in literary analysis may, intentionally or not, introduce covert defenses of the historical accuracy of Acts. Literary study may seek to bypass historical problems, but it does not render them irrelevant. This short book seeks to expose the problems of attempting to derive history from Acts.

As a narrative treating the first three decades of the Christian church, Acts is unique. Canonical Christian scripture includes four "stories of Jesus" (Matthew, Mark, Luke, and John), and twenty-one works that are, or are called, "letters," as well as another unique text: the book of Revelation. The four canonical gospels, which enclose teaching and astonishing deeds within a narrative framework, give readers a sense of what a "gospel" is.

With regard to the canonical gospels, one major contribution to nineteenth-century scholarship was the development of the critical study of the historical sources that stood behind them. The assumption was that the earliest source was the most historically sound. John was viewed as the latest and historically least reliable gospel. (This judgment is no longer quite so self-evident.) The other three, Matthew, Mark, and Luke, are clearly related to one another. The effort to determine which was the earliest of these Synoptic Gospels (so called because one can arrange them in parallel columns) dates to at least the fourth century (*Augustine). Nineteenth-century research established that Mark was the major narrative source of both

Matthew and Luke, and thus the earliest. Luke and Matthew shared another source, a written collection of sayings that became known as "Q."

Research issued during the first two decades of the twentieth century destroyed the hypothesis that Mark provides an historically reliable account of Jesus' public life. Although the gospels contain things that Jesus probably said and forms of stories that he told, these texts do not allow the reconstruction of his life beyond a very broad outline, many details of which do not derive from those texts. Critical scholars are likely to posit, for example, that Jesus was probably born at Nazareth, although both Matthew and Luke state that he was born in Bethlehem. Such deductions from sources do not, to be sure, prove that those sources are historically sound. Similarly, data introduced from external sources to illuminate a text cannot be used as evidence *about* that text. These two tips may seem superfluous, but scholarship on Acts includes many instances of this bad procedure. Take, for example, Acts 12:1–23 (see below, pp. 101–5), which reports a persecution led by a "King Herod." A large number of critics equate this figure with Agrippa I (41–44 CE) and utilize this datum to assert the historical accuracy of Acts and to help determine its chronology. Acts, however, knows but one king named Agrippa (chaps. 25–26), whom historians designate Agrippa II.

Another powerful arrow in the quiver of those who defend the reliability of Acts is the invocation of coincidences between what Luke reports and what also appears in the Jewish historian Josephus. From this came a deduction: if a witness can be corroborated on some points by other witnesses, that authority should also be accepted on matters that cannot be corroborated. This principle may seem sound at first glimpse, but it is nearly worthless. The fact that Ruth Harrison claims to have seen the victim Ralph Jones drinking coffee at an outdoor café at 11:00 AM, and a waitress confirms her testimony, does not support Ms. Harrison's contention that she did not shoot Mr. Jones at 4:30. The case for coincidences has been exploded by the near certainty that Luke used Paul's letters, and the very strong probability that he was familiar with some of Josephus' works.

These observations intimate that much scholarship on Acts has lacked the critical rigor that has long characterized Gospel study. When Ernst Haenchen's commentary on Acts[3] appeared in English translation, its skepticism astonished a generation of students at "liberal" seminaries. In the middle third of the nineteenth century, some German scholars led by Ferdinand Christian Baur raised strong

challenges to the early date and historical accuracy of Acts. Their
arguments were opposed by a generation of British and German
interpreters, including Theodor Zahn, William M. Ramsay, Joseph B.
Lightfoot, and Adolph v. Harnack. By 1900 Acts appeared to have
been vindicated. With due consideration for some exaggerations and
errors, as well as allowance for the limitations of its sources, Acts had
apparently ridden out the storm of scathing criticism.

The major but almost never stated reason for reliance upon Acts
is that without it *we should have nothing else*—that is, no sustained
account of Christian origins. Everyone prefers that the emperor have
something to wear, even if the fabric and tailoring, color choice and
ensemble, fall below sartorial ideals. The following pages set out to
demonstrate that although Acts is far from naked, much of its attire
is, historically speaking, threadbare, poorly coordinated, and incomplete.

One cannot write the story of Christian origins by giving Acts a
makeover. If the story cannot be recovered, it is better to acknowledge ignorance than to build a house upon sand. Besides, Acts is not
directly interested in the story of Christian origins. Its purpose is to
show the legitimacy of the gentile mission associated with Paul. (See
also below, under "Why?") It ignores much that does not fit this
purpose: take for example the beginnings of the Christian movement
in such places as Galilee (central to Mark), most of Syria, Alexandria,
and Rome. Other facts are twisted to fit the thesis, most apparently
Luke's presentation of the harmony among Peter, James, and Paul
(for example, Acts 15). Luke's nearly perfect "crime" is not just what
he neglected to mention, but his artistry in convincing readers that
he has given them "the big picture" when what he has painted is
merely a distorted portrait of one (admittedly major) segment of the
whole.

Deconstruction provides no more than short-term rewards.
Demolition of the edifice erected by Luke is, as stated, no more than
a preliminary task. If the project of describing Christian origins can
produce no more than bits, fragments, and conjectures, the result
will be no better and no worse than what can be said of numerous
other religions and movements. Acts is a beautiful house that readers
may happily admire, but it is not a home in which the historian can
responsibly live. That is the crime. Answers to specific relevant questions follow.

Who wrote Acts? The Gospel of Luke and the book of Acts are,
like all biblical "histories," *anonymous.* Anonymity reflects neither

modesty nor concealment. Unnamed authors can serve as omniscient narrators. If, for example, the first book of the Hebrew Bible began with the statement that it was written by one Moses, who had led the people of Israel out of Egypt to the borders of the promised land, and then continued "In the beginning when God created the heavens and the earth," an alert reader might object, "How do you know that? Were you *there?*" Anonymity allows narrators to see and know all that they wish to report. In a phrase, anonymity conveys *authority*.

Not appreciating the advantages of this posture—or attributing it to divine dictation (verbal *inspiration)—readers of biblical books have, from very early times, wished to identify a human author. One basis for such identifications of anonymous authors is *tradition*, in this case, the tradition that the Third Gospel and Acts were written by a person named Luke. Traditions may be correct: it could have been known and remembered that a certain Luke had, in fact, produced these books. They may also be the product of detective work. The text of Acts suggests that the author was a gentile and a companion of Paul. Equipped with these clues, one turns to the Pauline letters in search of a suitable candidate. Those letters written by the imprisoned Paul were presumed to have been composed at Rome. In Colossians 4:10–11 the apostle sends greetings from several believers of Jewish background and three gentiles: Epaphras, Luke, and Demas. 2 Timothy 4:11, clearly written not long before the death of Paul, implies that Luke was there at the end ("Only Luke is with me") and he is therefore the single viable candidate. In this process, as in mystery novels, it is presumed that the guilty party must be among those named. Acts could not stem from an unnamed companion of Paul because God would not cheat by omitting the essential clues.

The same rationale stands behind the belief that God has planted within the Bible clues from which one can deduce when the world will end. The Almighty simply would not neglect to provide information about a topic of such vital interest to human beings. Those who hold that the Christian Scriptures are a puzzle that, when resolved, will yield answers to questions of vital interest to humanity, will probably be happier if they stop reading this book. Biblical prophets tended to provide God's answers to questions that people preferred *not* to ask, such as whether it was proper to oppress the poor, or to hedge one's bets by venerating local gods with particular specializations, such as agriculture or disease, or whether the Temple cult constituted an absolute guarantee of national security.

To return to the subject of valid evidence, it is often asserted that tradition should be accepted unless clearly refuted by indisputable facts. This claim may look reasonable, but it is without scientific basis. It is, to continue the analogy, the stance of the lazy and shallow police inspector who immediately apprehends the superficially most obvious, but actually innocent, suspect. *All* traditions are hypotheses. Good detectives understand that hypotheses purveying convenient solutions demand careful scrutiny. The tradition that Acts was composed by Luke, the companion of Paul, was most welcome to early Christian opponents of a theology promulgated by *Marcion of Sinope, who argued that Paul was at odds with the other apostles. For these writers Luke was a convenient solution to the question of who wrote Acts. Too convenient, the perspicacious detective will say.

Second-century Christian writers may well have deduced from the very passages noted above the helpful information that Luke, a companion of Paul, wrote Acts. "Granted," the police inspector may say, "But that does not prove that the deduction was wrong." Negatives are notoriously hard to prove and therefore rarely constitute a good line of investigation. In this case more can be gained from an analysis of the *quality* of the evidence. Both Colossians and 2 Timothy are among the "disputed" epistles. It is not likely that Paul wrote Colossians and quite improbable that he composed 2 Timothy. The greetings in Colossians 4:10–14 appear to be embroideries of those found in Philemon 24; that is, Philemon was a source of Colossians. Among the lists of greetings that often come toward the end of Pauline letters, those in Philemon and Colossians are unique in their similarity. In sum, the tradition could be valid, but it is suspiciously convenient, and the evidence that supports it is dubious. Furthermore, the content of Acts stands against this tradition, for it views the Pauline world from a perspective of about fifty years after Paul's death.

All that can be said about the author of Acts must be deduced from the book. This is a risky procedure. Actual authors may not have the same opinions and worldview as those of the author implied by a text, although people frequently assume that they do so, as can be seen in attributing such sentiments as "neither a borrower nor a lender be" to "Shakespeare," rather than to a fictional character created by William Shakespeare. Shakespeare, for his own part, may have thought that reasonable people might, from time to time, engage in either or both. Assuming that risk, it appears that the author of

Acts was a gentile and, from the grammatical gender of a participle in Luke 1:2, a male. Less debatable is that this person had some Greek education and was quite well versed in the language of the Greek Bible, whose content and style he could imitate. (See Chapter Five.) Another reasonable hypothesis is that the author of Acts was either a life-long Christian or had been a part of that movement for many years. That he was a companion of Paul seems quite unlikely, for a number of reasons. Positively, he was quite familiar with the region bordering the Aegean Sea, which divides modern Greece from Turkey. This matter of geography leads to another question.

Where was Acts written? The traditional provenance is Antioch, but Ephesus is more likely. The narrator is "at home" in the Aegean area, vastly more familiar with cities and routes there than those in southern Asia Minor or Palestine. Whenever the narrative moves inland the geographical details become more vague, if not simply erroneous. Ephesus also seems a more suitable basis for the geographical perspective of the author we call Luke than would be Corinth, for example, as Rome lies at a considerable distance from the narrator's eye. Ethiopia is in the far south, a perspective common to all people of the Mediterranean countries, but Alexandria (in Egypt) is also beyond his horizon, as is all that lies east of Damascus or north of central Asia Minor (modern Turkey). The latter is no more than a place to cross en route to somewhere else. More cogently, Ephesus is the high point of the Pauline mission, the subject of a lengthy and spectacular chapter (Acts 19) packed with vivid incident and crammed with adventure. Nearly one-fourth of the narrative recounting Paul's independent missionary and pastoral labors in Acts focuses upon Ephesus. Paul delivers his farewell address to the *presbyters of that community. Those leaders hear his own summary of his career, his warnings of what is to come, and his exhortation to do their duty after he has gone. Yet in Acts 19 Paul, who is the subject of the entire chapter, is no longer "on stage" after verse 10. For Luke Ephesus is the location where the battle over the Pauline legacy is to be waged.

In the first quarter of the second century, Ephesus was a center of controversy, much of which revolved about or interacted with the Pauline heritage. Other writings and teachers associated with Ephesus include the *Deutero-Pauline epistles Colossians and Ephesians, the book of Revelation, the Pastoral Epistles (1–2 Timothy and Titus), *Ignatius of Antioch, and Cerinthus (an early "*Gnostic"). Ephesus was the site of at least one Pauline "school" or circle. There, in all probability, Paul's letters were gathered into a collection. This collection, eventually supplemented with the Pastorals, together with (Luke and) Acts, became the pillars of the "*proto-orthodox" construction of the Pauline legacy. The association of Acts with Ephesus involves more than a geographical location; this provenance places Acts in the context of the battle over Paul, a struggle that began within the apostle's lifetime and endured until the third century—and beyond.

When was Acts written? Scholarly consensus has dated Luke and Acts at c. 85, with a dwindling number who place the work in the 60s and a larger minority who prefer the last decade of the first century. The consensus date is a convenient compromise that seems to demand little proof. I have argued elsewhere at considerable length that Acts belongs to the second decade of the second century (c. 115).[4] The author's use of Paul's letters and his probable knowledge of the *Antiquities* of Josephus rule out a date before 100. And whereas the Gospel of Matthew, for example, seeks to justify the existence of the Jesus movement as an increasingly gentile body, Luke and Acts justify an *existing* boundary between two religions, "Judaism" and "Christianity," the latter of which is the valid heir of God's promises. Acts is also familiar with the organization and issues of Christian groups during the first decades of the second century. The author we call Luke writes narratives like those of the evangelists (for example, Mark, John, Matthew) who told their stories for believers, but his mind is partly occupied with the questions of the "*apologists," who, from the middle of the second century onward, defended the faith against its *polytheist critics and those who they thought were betraying it. Acts is also aware of the different understandings of the Christian message that would give rise to "orthodox" and "heretical" formulations of the faith.

Acts was written after the Gospel. As much as a decade could have elapsed between the time when the author began to write Luke and the completion of Acts, but this is no more than a guess. The two volumes are related. The assumption that Luke planned to write two books at the outset of his labors cannot be proved, but it is not unreasonable. The spectrum of possibilities ranges from an enthusiastic writer who decided at one point to continue the story beyond where Mark ended (Mark 16:8) and found that this would require another roll of papyrus all the way to a careful designer who first planned the entire work and then filled in his outline. Probability lies on the side of the planner, but spectrums have many points. Chapter Two will look at the question of the relation between Luke and Acts.

Why was Acts written? The preface to Luke supplies a purpose: "so that you may know the truth concerning the things about which you have been instructed" (Luke 1:4). "You" refers to the dedicatee,

Theophilus, and, by implication, to all believing readers. A substantial majority of authorities would designate (Luke and) Acts as "legitimating narrative." "Narrative" refers to the medium, story (rather than treatise, sermon, letter, catechism, etc.). The unseemly participle "legitimating" expresses the purpose. Acts propounds the legitimacy of Christianity as a largely gentile religion and as the valid heir to the promises God made to Israel. The Roman government is not the target of the book, for Roman officials would find it disagreeable in style and obscure in content. Equally difficult to imagine is an audience of traditional Jews, who would regard much of the work as odious and its claims as highly preposterous. Luke's problem was not simply that God's fulfillment of the ancient promises led to the inclusion of gentiles. Many Jews would have agreed with this ideal, at least at one time, although most would have preferred to say "former gentiles." His task was to demonstrate that gentile Christianity was the legitimate inheritor of those old promises, and not just any form of gentile Christianity, but the fruit of the Pauline mission, which is to say, Christians who rejected Torah, the essence of Judaism.

From the market perspective, Pauline Christianity required no defense, for it was flourishing, at least in some localities, but the question of the relation of "old" to "new" remained open. If Luke and others represented a form of Christianity that hijacked the Israelite legacy along with its sacred writings and claimed them as its own, some went him one better and hijacked Paul by disowning any connection between the religion of Israel and faith in the God proclaimed by Jesus and propagated by Paul. The single well-attested representative of this trend was the above-mentioned *Marcion, who claimed that there was no link between the punitive and militant creator God of the Jewish Scriptures and the loving God of Jesus. The narratives of Luke and Acts, with their strong emphasis upon continuity in the story of salvation, are so effective as a counter to Marcion's arguments that the books look as if they could have been written, or revised, to refute him—and some have contended that this was indeed their purpose.

For those readers who think that the plot requires thickening, one may note that others built upon Paul's statements about divine wisdom and heavenly secrets (cf. 1 Corinthians 1–4) to erect a speculative theology designed to relate human destiny to cosmic mysteries. Early phases of this technique can be seen in the *Deutero-Paulines Colossians and Ephesians, as well as in the anonymous Letter to the Hebrews. Its most radical product can be found in western representatives of what is called "*Gnosis" or "Gnosticism," although others, including *Ignatius, a Bishop of Antioch c. 125, and the Alexandrian Christians *Clement and *Origen, sought to remain closer to what would become the mainstream. Others turned Paul's apocalyptic thought in the direction of the coming fiery vengeance upon evildoers. Such ideas hold a central place in 2 Thessalonians and are still vigorous in the *Acts of Paul, which appeared around the middle of the second century. Other texts welcomed Paul's epistolary method and pastoral technique without fully embracing his theology. Among these are 1 Peter, which does not mention Paul but shares some of his theological outlook, and 1 Clement, which admires and quotes Paul, but shares even less of his theological outlook. (This matter is complicated by the probability that Paul shared a number of earlier traditions with these writings—that is, that they had some common sources.) A number of early Christians made do without Paul. The Gospel of John is a canonical example of a theology that has affinities with Pauline thought but seems to have been developed independently. More or less full independence from Paul evidently endured only in eastern Syria, and what survives from this region looks heretical by western standards, as even a casual reading of the *Acts of Thomas will reveal.

Then there were those who cared for Paul not at all. Most of them fall into that ill-defined and inappropriately named bag labeled "*Jewish Christianity." The Gospel of Matthew shows great openness to gentiles, who will presently constitute a majority of the community, but its rigorous ethic views Paul's ideas as an invitation to libertinism. The author of James uses the name of one known to have had reservations about Paul and takes issue with Paul's view of how people become acceptable to God (on justification cf. Galatians; James 2:14–26). In time there would be a virulently anti-Pauline movement associated with the names of Peter and James. The *Pseudo-Clementine Recognitions and Homilies issued under the name of Clement of Rome place Paul's teachings in the mouth of the notorious Simon Magus and denounce Paul, albeit anonymously, as a renegade Jew.

The Pauline heritage (including the *Deutero-Pauline letters, Acts, and other works related to Paul, such as 1 Clement, *Ignatius, and *Polycarp) provided the major underpinnings to what is called "Early Catholic Christianity." This movement, which became the dominant form of *proto-orthodoxy, supported strong church government by bishops, presbyters, and deacons; adherence to a basic creed similar in content to the "Apostles Creed," which affirmed God as creator; Christ as God's son, who became truly human and died to redeem believers; conventional social ethics; and, in general, avoidance of speculative theologies and life-styles.

Complex as the preceding sketch may seem, it is oversimplified. What, for example, might be said of Revelation, which has some Pauline and many anti-Pauline elements? Paul was an important figure and symbol in second-century Christianity, almost as important when his name was not mentioned as when it was. Many, including those who disagreed with his ideas, imitated Paul's practice of writing letters, and others followed Luke's lead by composing Acts of particular apostles. When Luke wrote, the rockets representing various Pauline trajectories were not far from the launch pad, but the directions were plain to see. In response to these questions and issues Luke sought to demonstrate that gentile, Pauline Christianity was *the* religion (or at least a legitimate manifestation of the religion) of ancient Israel. The desired outcome was unity, or at least mutual respect, among believers. Luke, in short, was not the kind of author who presented the arguments for major viewpoints and then attempted to show which was correct.

Introductory obligations that remain outstanding are the questions *what* (that is, the literary genre/s of Luke/Acts), *from what* (sources), and *how* (Lucan methods and techniques). The third of these mysteries will be the subject of detailed attention in following chapters, while genre and sources are consigned to the Appendix. The clues that have been provided thus far strongly suggest the accuracy of the following statements:

- An unknown Christian of probably long standing wrote Acts in Ephesus or its environs c. 110–120, amidst convulsive controversies about the nature of the emergent Christian faith.

- That author, called "Luke," intended to show the continuity between Israel and the Church and the congruity among Jesus, Peter, James and Paul, in order to prove the validity of the Pauline heritage and to promote unity among believers.

Methods

All authors of non-fiction will do their readers a disservice if they fail to make their methods clear and explicit, appropriate to the subject in question, and consistent in application. The predominant methods on display here will be those known as "historical" and "literary." Postmodern study has exposed the limits and weaknesses of historical criticism, but has not dethroned it. To assert that no method is "purely objective" or value-free as an excuse for abandoning method would be like Kierkegaard's simile about a college freshman's using Socrates' admission that he knew nothing to justify abandoning study. Historical criticism attempts to interpret a text on the basis of its original milieu: those unfamiliar with the great Depression will find *The Grapes of Wrath* difficult, if not incomprehensible. Texts mean a great deal more than their authors intended, and "original meaning" can be a will-o'-the-wisp; but no study can neglect with impunity the fact that early Christian writings were composed in an ancient language that can be known but imperfectly, in cultures vastly different from those of the contemporary West, by and to persons and groups whose circumstances, needs, assumptions, questions, and lives cannot be equated with those of people today. Insofar as it is "criticism," historical criticism strives to be scientific, preferring probability to improbability, the known to unknown, causation and sequence to caprice and chaos, and, in brief, reason, logic, system, and congruity. Insofar as it deals with "history," historical criticism encounters what is particular, unique, and often enough improbable, illogical, and incongruous.

Recognition of the difficulties does not obviate the necessity of the quest. The object of historical study is to discover not only what happened but, more importantly, *why* it happened. Skepticism is one of its fundamental tools because learning is more likely to transpire through raising fresh questions than by repeating familiar answers. Doubt is not the antonym of faith; unbelief is. Doubt is an element of any faith worth holding. Well-founded challenges to received opinions should always be welcome, for they motivate researchers of integrity to evaluate their presuppositions. "Well-founded" is crucial and problematic for those seeking to communicate scholarly proposals to the general public. Far more people, for example, heard of the claims that a sarcophagus of James the brother of one Jesus had been discovered than read the eventual notices that this coffin was a hoax. (Probably even fewer asked themselves what this object would have proved, since neither the existence of James nor his eventual death have been subject to question.)

There are many manifestations of literary criticism. At its basis, especially for study of the New Testament, is the recognition of writings as just that—literary artifacts rather than a hodgepodge of isolated passages. No work can communicate to people who do not understand its genre. Those who do not accept the literary convention that people routinely deal with their personal challenges by engaging in homicide will not be able to tolerate a murder mystery, nor will those in search of a good science fiction read find satisfaction from a treatise on rocket science. Meaning comes, of course, from context. "Neither a borrower nor a lender be" may or may not be good advice. Its original literary function was to reveal the character of Polonius. For a book like Acts the essence of "literary criticism" is to look for the meaning of the whole in the part and that of the part in the whole, as well as to inquire how the whole or part functions as narrative literature, rather than simply as religious sentiment or doctrinal theory. Other methods have a great deal to offer, but because historical and literary criticism are the most appropriate tools for this project, they will dominate this book. In this instance literary criticism will most often be in the service of historical criticism, as it will demonstrate more often than reinforce, historical improbability.

An Example: Acts 19:11–12

> God did extraordinary miracles through Paul, so that when the handkerchiefs or aprons that had touched his skin were brought to the sick, their diseases left them, and the evil spirits came out of them.

Uncritical authors will take the text at face value, possibly softening its impact by appeal to psychological factors: the patients suffered from mental anxiety or psychosomatic trauma. These "transitional objects" (handkerchiefs or aprons) brought the healing message of Paul's gospel to mind, and with that recollection came emotional and spiritual relief. The historical critic is not likely to accept the report at face value and will reject the psychological explanation as obfuscating rationalization. Historical criticism is willing to accept remarkable phenomena in theory and in general, but inclines toward doubt in individual cases, especially summaries such as this. Did these materials work universally and automatically, upon believers no less than upon polytheists, for terminal cancer as well as for common colds? How long did the effect endure? For hours, days, months, decades? And so forth. Having demolished probability, the critic will turn to the history of religions, taking note of other miracles worked through relics of the second class.

At this point historical critics will be prone, with or without acknowledgement, to assume the mantle, if you will pardon the metaphor, of the literary critic; for critics of all types and stripes will note Acts 5:14–16, which describes the healing shadow of Peter, and add to that Mark 6:56, which speaks of the therapeutic fringe of Jesus' garment, with a reference also to the potent cloak of Elijah, 2 Kings 2:8. Historical criticism will thus conclude that Luke and Acts portray Elijah, Jesus, Peter, and Paul working similar wonders and explore the implications of that similarity.

Literary analysis notes not only parallels but also literary techniques: Luke *shows* continuity by telling similar stories about different figures in successive stages of salvation history. Non-critical approaches view Acts 19:11–12 as an embarrassment that requires amelioration and will thus miss its point. Rigorous criticism finds such material offensive and may do little more than say "that's what people believed in those days," possibly also missing the point. Critics with a literary sensitivity are likely to ask what the author was attempting to do by telling the story. In this example the requirements for literary sensitivity are not high. Most will see some connection between Acts 19:11–12 and the other summaries cited. Purely aesthetic literary critics may do no more than note what Luke was up to, and how. That is not, in my view, sufficient. Biblical criticism requires historical judgment and courage. If someone does not go on to point out that Paul appears superior to Jesus, since Paul's accessories could function apart from his person, whereas Jesus evidently had to be wearing the material, that critic has failed to see what the emperor is wearing.

Those who do point to these sartorial implications of Acts 19:11–12—and their number is embarrassingly small—will often be satisfied with a shot at the author: "Look at this dreadful theology, in which rags are therapeutic and Paul can do better than Jesus!" Such comments are frequently justified, but they are not the final goal of criticism, which must ask, "What is going on here?" Proposing some answers to that question constitutes the goal of this book, and, now that some basic elements of the circumstances and the terrain have been established, it is time to begin moving toward that goal. Those who know anything about thrillers will not be surprised to learn that things will have to get worse before they get better.

Note: The Titles. "The Gospel according to Luke" and "The Acts of the Apostles" are not the original titles of these two volumes. They first appear in the writings of two early Christian theologians, *Irenaeus (c. 180) and *Clement of Alexandria (c. 200). The term "Gospel" as a title for a book about Jesus may have been introduced by *Marcion. The title "Acts of *X*" may have first appeared as a designation for the *Acts of Paul*. Luke certainly did not call his second volume "The Acts of the Apostles," since its leading character, Paul, was not one of the apostles. These titles do indicate how early readers understood their subjects. Luke was a book like Matthew, Mark, and John, while his second volume related the important deeds of major historical figures.

Resources and Further Reading

A compact, accessible introduction to leading themes in the debate about Acts is Mark Allan Powell, *What Are They Saying about Acts?* Mahwah, NJ: Paulist, 1991.

Three introductions to (Luke and) Acts are:

David L. Barr, *New Testament Story: An Introduction.* 2nd ed. Belmont, CA: Wadsworth, 1995, 293–335. This is a well-written college textbook of a liberal orientation.

Raymond E. Brown, *Introduction to the New Testament.* New York: Doubleday, 1997, 225–278 (Luke); 279–332 (Acts). This is an introduction of the "classic" type, written by a popular scholar of moderate orientation.

Helmut Koester, *Introduction to the New Testament.* 2 vols. New York: Walter de Gruyter, 1995–2000, 2:310–27. This work is a masterful synthesis rather than a book-by-book introduction. Koester is refreshingly and rigorously critical.

A brief and accessible narrative analysis is Richard I. Pervo, *Luke's Story of Paul.* Minneapolis: Fortress, 1990.

More substantial is Charles H. Talbert, *Reading Acts: A Literary and Theological Commentary on the Acts of the Apostles.* New York: Crossroads, 1997.

Gerd Lüdemann, *The Acts of the Apostles: What Really Happened in the Earliest Days of the Church.* Amherst, NY: Prometheus Books, 2005. This is an accessible but detailed critical study of Acts and its presumed sources.

Endnotes

1. One symbol of this success is the principal basis of the Christian calendar: the Great Fifty Days, marked by Easter, Ascension, and Pentecost. Its other axis, based upon Christmas and the Annunciation, determined the calendar in England and its colonies until the middle of the eighteenth century. Both of these cycles derive from the Lucan writings.

2. Luke T. Johnson, *The Writings of the New Testament* (Philadelphia: Fortress, 1986), 204 and 199.

3. *The Acts of the Apostles* (trans. and ed. B. Noble et al.; Philadelphia: Westminster, 1971), ET of *Die Apostelgeschichte* (14th ed.; KEK; Göttingen: Vandenhoeck & Ruprecht, 1965).

4. Richard I. Pervo, *Dating Acts: Between the Evangelists and the Apologists* (Santa Rosa, CA: Polebridge, 2004).

Chapter Two

Enigmas of Acts

No student can read Acts without dissatisfaction: he would not have written it thus. Why does it end where it ends? Why is so much space devoted to the account of the storm and shipwreck? Why are St Paul's trials described in such repetitive detail? Why is so rigorous a subdivision imposed that we hear no more of Philip or Peter when once we have left them, except where their paths cross Paul's? If we take Acts to be straightforward history, these questions can only be answered by one of two suppressed hypotheses. The first is that St Luke was critically short of material . . . so he wrote all the detail he had heard or could remember. He did not know what happened subsequently to Paul, or Philip, or Peter; but he had been much impressed by the shipwreck and the trials. Alternatively, St Luke was critically short of sense. He could not handle more than one character at a time. The shipwreck was a good story, and deserved space. Paul's unhindered preaching at Rome seemed a good place to stop. Both of these hypotheses are better suppressed. Not only are they intolerable in themselves, but they lead on to all the notorious historical tangles which in turn cannot be resolved without making St Luke more and more ignorant and stupid.

The author of this statement, Michael Goulder, believed that Acts was written between 80–85 CE by Luke, the companion of Paul.[1] Although I am convinced that Acts appeared a good generation later (c. 110–120) and was written by an admirer rather than a companion of Paul, I quite agree with Goulder's formulation of the problem. *Read as history, Acts is unsatisfactory.* On a purely superficial level, it is evident—even to one who does not deign to point a questioning finger toward a single reputed fact—that Acts lacks balance. This statement is equally valid whether it is applied to the content of the book or to its structure. The apparent absence of balance suggests, as Goulder indicates, either that the author lacks competence or that the reader is misinterpreting his purpose.

The subject of this chapter is enigmas surrounding Acts. In addition to the problems of taking it as "straight history," these enigmas include the following:

- Why write a second volume?
- Are Luke and Acts two books or one?
- Should Acts be read in the context of the Gospels or of the Epistles?

These questions lead to a review of the critical methods applied with considerable success to the gospels, but not successfully applied to Acts. The most recent solution has been to read Luke and Acts together, without reference to other gospels or to the letters. But this option, as noted in the previous chapter, dodges historical questions. For Ernst Haenchen, who did not evade those issues, it gave birth to a two headed Luke: inept historian but excellent writer. After a brief introduction to types of narration, key points in the narrative will be scrutinized. An additional problem is the proper conclusion to the statement "Acts is the story of. . . ." Following an examination of issues regarding the structure of the book, the chapter will turn to an old problem: the relation of the Paul of Acts to the Paul of the letters, an issue that leads to a debate about the nature of Lucan theology. Opinions appear, and a conclusion is provided, but the chief purpose of this chapter is to identify, rather than to resolve, various mysteries and to demonstrate their importance.

Why Acts?

The first enigma of Acts, crisply stated, is that the book exists. Why did Luke write Acts? Why did this evangelist alone among the four (and more, when non-canonical gospels are taken into account) deem it necessary to continue the story? Merely to raise this question unleashes an unwieldy pack of gremlins. Is Acts really one big book, divided into two parts for technological reasons? Recall that, when books were written in rolls, size became a factor, as long rolls were devilishly inconvenient. If, as the contents suggest, Luke and Acts were intentionally designed as two books, then one must ask if the two are of equal importance. Is Acts a supplement to the Gospel of Luke, or is the Gospel a prelude to the "real story"? Could the author have achieved the goal of showing that the gentile mission was legitimate in a single book? The answer to that last question is probably "yes," for Matthew achieved much the same in the closing verses of his Gospel (28:16–20). Luke evidently found it necessary not only to assert the legitimacy of the mission to the gentiles, but also to tell the story of that mission in some detail.

One Book or Two?

The question of whether Acts is one book or two has rarely been explored for the simple reason that it is a recent question. From roughly the late second century until the early twentieth, Luke and Acts were normally studied in different contexts. Then, in the 1920s a great scholar, Henry J. Cadbury, coined the term "Luke-Acts" to indicate that these two consecutive books written by the same author should be studied together. The logic of this idea gradually won the day and today unification is the norm. The term "Luke-Acts" is now the title of choice for the overwhelming majority of English-speaking scholars. Few study Acts today without at least an occasional glance at the Gospel. The two books are closely related, and those who examine one without considering the other do so at their peril.

The nature of this relationship is different from that between Mark and Matthew, for example, in which Mark constituted a major source for Matthew; or the relationship between Galatians and Romans, which were written by the same author and treat some similar subjects but were not intended to be compared with one another. Matthew intended to supersede Mark, not to supplement it. Paul wrote Galatians to deal with one set of issues and Romans to deal with another, and any who read both Galatians and Romans in the 50s of the first century might have been left with some questions about the author's integrity. Luke and Acts, on the other hand, belong together. One way to frame the issue is to ask whether Luke wrote the Gospel and Acts to supersede Mark or just his Gospel to supersede Mark and Acts as a sequel to his Gospel. Strict unification theorists reject the notion that Acts is a sequel.[2] Luke and Acts are a continuous narrative.

The implication of this strict unification theory is that Luke has created something entirely novel and unique, for, although we have other gospels and Acts (for example, the *Acts of Paul*), no one else produced a work such as Luke-Acts. The logical consequence of this understanding is that Luke is not a gospel like Matthew, Mark, or John, but rather the first half of a different type of writing. Viewing Luke and Acts as a unified narrative requires the corollary that the combined books represent a single, and indeed unique, literary genre.

If Acts is, on the other hand, a sequel, it is possible that the two represent different genres. (See the Appendix.) The limits of separation are clear: treating the works as distinct books neglects the similarities between them. The corresponding difficulty is that those who view Luke and Acts as a single work will tend to overlook the differences between them. Since much of what follows stresses these differences, it is apparent that I endorse the hypothesis that Acts is a sequel but the enigmas of Luke-Acts over against Luke and Acts remain. Luke cannot "get along" without Acts and it can't get on with it.

How to Read Acts 1: With the Letters

The third enigma follows from the second. What is one to do with this book? Perhaps the most conventional and convenient approach to the question is that suggested by what is now (but has not always been) the traditional arrangement of the New Testament.[3] Acts does not follow Luke but John. This permits the four divergent portraits of Jesus to adjoin one another. Then comes Acts. How does it end? With Paul at Rome. Immediately following Acts is the letter of *Paul* to the . . . *Romans*. The *canonical* function of Acts has thus been to serve as a bridge between the story of Jesus and the story of the church, as a background and preface to the subsequent apostolic epistles. In fact, Acts also plants in the reader's mind a portrait of Paul and a view of Pauline theology and practice. When Acts appears in the company of the epistles it becomes embroiled in issues of history, in discussions about the life, teaching, practice, and so forth, of Paul. This solution *isolates* Acts from the gospel(s) and places it in the troublesome neighborhood of the letters. That enigma will receive further attention in this chapter and elsewhere. At present it need be noted only that when linked with the letters, Acts falls under the shadow of its principal character, Paul, and the accomplishment of Luke comes into collision with Paul's own writings. The more common solutions to this tension are (1) to subordinate the letters to Acts and to incorporate them within its story and (2) to reject Acts altogether as a valid source for Pauline biography and theology. Critical consensus prefers a compromise between these extremes, such as accepting the data of Acts when its account does not conflict with the primary data of the letters.

Reading Acts 2: With the Gospels

A second approach to the problem of the existence of Acts is to align the book more closely with the gospels, especially that of Luke.

When this is done, discussions revolve around the application of various critical methods. For roughly a century, c. 1875–1975, study of the New Testament narratives followed a logical course. The first requirement was the establishment of a critical *text*, because the various manuscripts of the *Synoptic Gospels—Matthew, Mark, and Luke—contained a goodly amount of contamination, in particular the introduction of material from Matthew into Mark and Luke. With a good text derived from superior manuscripts and sharpened method, it became possible to attack the *source* question. (See pp. 157–64.)

After investigation established that Mark, although the earliest, was not a trustworthy source for the life of the historical Jesus because its structure was determined by theological rather than by biographical concerns, scholarship turned to the constituent units of the gospel tradition—the origin and evolution of the individual stories, anecdotes, and other passages. This discipline, called *form criticism*, indicated that the various units that comprise the *Synoptic Gospels had been forged in the workshops of various communities, and that they were told for the purposes of instruction, edification, worship, and justification of the practices and beliefs of the early Jesus movement(s). Form criticism demonstrated that these passages ("pericopes") had evolved and that it was possible to get behind the gospel accounts to earlier stages of the tradition. This sort of gospel form criticism flourished between the two World Wars.

After 1945 a new discipline emerged. *Redaction criticism* (the study of how writers used their sources) assumed the results of source criticism and returned attention to the actual text rather than to its presumed oral and written pre-history. For source critics the evangelists were skilled in the use of scissors and paste. The less they tampered with their sources, the more helpful they were to the critic, whose task of disentangling one source from another was thereby facilitated. Form criticism, on the other hand, looked behind the detectable sources to the process of assembly. For this method the synoptic tradition was the product of *collectors* who gathered and arranged disparate materials. Collections were frequently arranged by subject, as can be seen in the grouped *Pronouncement Stories in Mark 2:1–3:6 or the parables of Mark 4:1–34, as well as in cycles of miracle stories behind Mark 4:35–8:10.

Redaction criticism recognized the role of the evangelists as editors. Rather than be content with compiling and ordering source materials, the several evangelists had edited them—by placement and alteration—to accommodate their own particular views. A useful means for discovering what Matthew and Luke were about was to observe how they had altered or supplemented Mark and their other major source, *Q.

Redaction criticism made it possible to speak of "the theology of Matthew" and "the theology of Luke." The latter phrase furnished the English title for a major contribution of Hans Conzelmann, a German scholar who brought editorial activity to the center of gospel studies. In the case of Mark (and John), however, redaction criticism is more difficult, for one must first reconstruct the source from the text itself and then attempt to show how it was altered. This problem provides a good opportunity for returning to the subject of Acts, since form criticism also depends upon editorial analysis of the conventions peculiar to the various types. If, for example, an account of the story of Cinderella introduced a fourth sister who railed against the ideal of finding a Prince Charming as the chief object of female life, and denounced high-heeled glass slippers as utterly impractical footwear, the reader would regard that sibling as an interpolation introduced by a critic of social convention. Everyone senses the propriety of the "*rule of three," and even those who do not know the story of Cinderella but have some familiarity with fairy tales would perceive that the additional sister does not "fit."

Form criticism looks for items that do not fit, with particular attention to the pre-gospel tradition. Redaction criticism does the same, with particular attention to anomalies that appear to suit the individual evangelist rather than his predecessors. For an example of the latter, one may observe how Matthew 9:17 and Luke 5:39 expand Mark 2:18–22. To put it form-critically, these changes are examples of how *Pronouncement Stories attract additional sayings;

Table 2.1: Redaction Criticism

Mark 2:22d	Matthew 9:17:e–f	Luke 5:38–39
but one puts new wine into fresh wineskins.	but new wine is put into fresh wineskins, and so both are preserved.	But new wine must be put into fresh wineskins. 39 And no one after drinking old wine desires new wine, but says, 'The old is good.'[4]

from the redaction-critical perspective, they illustrate how the other evangelists alter Mark to suit their own viewpoints:

In Mark 2:18 new views require fresh methods and practices. The old is outdated. Matthew wishes to preserve both the old and the new (cf. Matthew 13:52). Luke revises the proposal: the old is superior; the Jesus movement fulfills the ancient promises and prophecy. Both Matthew and Luke thus preserve a saying of Jesus in Mark with which they do not fully agree. Supplementation is one means for altering a sentiment.

Acts and Critical Methods

Acts, like the other New Testament narratives, was also subjected to the disciplines of textual, source, form, and editorial analysis, but with different results. Two principal editions of the Greek text of Acts survive, one of which (traditionally, and wrongly, called the "Western Text") is about 16% longer than the other. Although the critical consensus tends for good reasons to prefer the shorter text, the one represented in most modern versions, the longer text continues to have its proponents, and no comprehensive explanation of its origin has prevailed. Moreover, the text of Acts appears corrupt at a number of points, for in some places none of the manuscript readings seem to be original. In short, the lack of an original text of Acts presents another enigma.

Much the same may be said of its sources. Everyone agrees that Luke used some sources, but despite substantial efforts and no little ingenuity, their nature, extent, and contents remain an open question. (See the Appendix.) In distinction from the gospels, the sources of Acts remain entangled in questions of historicity. This exposes yet another peculiar quality about Acts and what to do with it.

Even in more conservative New Testament circles, Luke is viewed as a "gospel," that is, as a theological writing intended to set forth the meaning of Jesus' life and mission. Few would claim that Luke is "better" history (or biography) than is, for example, Mark. That Luke is often more plausible in its presentation than Mark is almost universally recognized to be the result of authorial activity. Yet when those same conservative scholars turn to Acts, historical accuracy and value become important. Such scholars are likely to defend "Luke the historian" against charges of contradicting Paul's letters, distorting facts, inventing episodes, etc. In this they are often joined by their more moderate colleagues, as well as by some who are considered "liberal." The unstated implication of this view is that Luke wrote his gospel wearing the hat of an evangelist but, when composing the second volume, donned that of an historian. But why did Luke change hats? The driving force behind this question is the dictum announced in the previous chapter: *Without Acts we would have nothing else.* Acts fills a void that no other work can replace. And yet years of patient accumulation of erudition and honing of methodical tools are not needed to enable one to see the fallacy of this argument.

The question of the earliest recoverable text remains incompletely resolved, and source criticism looks like a free-for-all, but form criticism of the traditional result raises no controversies. This is because few of the units and episodes of Acts fit into the categories (sayings, parables, anecdotes) that constitute so much of the synoptic gospel tradition. In writing Acts, Luke employed different methods from those utilized in composing his gospel. To make that statement is to acknowledge that one must look to the author rather than to the material. It is tantamount to the shift from form to redaction criticism. Redaction criticism of Acts is severely impaired by the lack of formal units with their established conventions and by the general absence of clearly identifiable sources. This difficulty would eventually set the pace for different approaches to the gospels as well, since it shifted attention from the constituent forms to the overall genre of Acts and from focus upon the composer as editor to the composer as *author*. Fifty years ago, however, this difficulty seemed to have produced a stalemate. Martin Dibelius (1883–1947), who was one of the pioneers of gospel form criticism, both exposed this stalemate in the study of Acts and pointed to a way out of it. His studies, begun during World War I, did not have a major impact until they were collected and published posthumously, in 1954.

In sum, comparison of Acts to Luke ran into difficulty because the methods that were fruitful for the Gospel did not work when applied to Acts. One result of this approach has been a tendency to subordinate the second book to the first. For example, much of the debate about Lucan theology has focused upon his understanding of eschatology, the time and nature of God's ultimate resolution of the human dilemma. This was the primary subject of Conzelmann's book on Luke. Another long-popular topic was Luke's alleged social liberalism, his concern for the poor and oppressed, including women. Yet, if Acts were taken as the basis for determining Lucan interest and thought, eschatology would not seem to be a pressing concern, while its social focus, which is oriented toward the conversion of those with wealth and status, would seem to fall somewhat short of modern liberal ideals. While the study of Acts in relation to the epistles placed it under the shadow of Paul, comparison of Acts to Luke caused it to be immersed in issues determined by the Gospel.

Luke-Acts as Narrative

In more recent years a third approach, which is a logical outgrowth of the previous, has attracted many adherents. This was introduced above as "unification." Many exegetes of this school assume that Luke-Acts, the most extensive work in the New Testament, is to be analyzed upon its own merits without frequent reference to either Mark (and John) or to the letters of Paul. "Luke-Acts" brings Acts out of the shadows. Some of these practitioners are overtly hostile to redaction criticism, while most ignore source theories. Their dominant method is narrative literary criticism—the evaluation of Luke and Acts as literature. The literary focus is upon texts as wholes, with the previously noted lack of strong interest in either the use of sources or the conflict or agreement with other texts. Although narrative study of Luke/Acts has many merits, it tends to obscure differences between the two books.

As stated in Chapter One, this approach also frees any who are so inclined from the responsibility of making historical judgments—or at least overt historical judgments. It has become acceptable to interpret Luke and Acts with the techniques developed for the analysis of modern novels, provided that the interpreter does not overuse such terms as "invention" or "fiction." The leading contemporary approach to Acts therefore deals with the question of history largely by ignoring it. "Luke the historian" has given way to "Luke the artist and theologian." The progenitor of this comprehensive literary approach to Acts is Ernst Haenchen, whose 1956 commentary raked out the debris of source criticism and then proceeded to apply consistently the insights of form-critic Dibelius to the text as it stood. For Haenchen the key question was not what Luke did with his sources but what he wished to do. He also turned his acutely critical eye upon Lucan theology, to which he gave quite sparing assent, and furthermore expressed strong skepticism about the historicity of much of the book.

Haenchen also revealed, although he did not identify, another previously mentioned enigma: Luke the highly competent narrator who is also Luke the utterly incompetent historian. This two-headed author was a logical outcome of Haenchen's critical appreciation of effective narration and his critical disdain for Acts as history. This presumably unintentional creation has led a vigorous life. Narrative analysis has, as indicated, resolved the problem by attending to Luke the writer and generally ignoring Luke the historian. Those who take exception to Haenchen's historical judgment have often gone to some lengths to defend the book's historicity while paying at best limited attention to its narrative merits. That Luke has two heads is not a problem so long as interpreters are in conversation with only one of them.[5]

In conclusion, the dominant trend in criticism seems to favor treating Acts as a continuation of Luke that may be exempted from historical study, although most would nonetheless associate it with ancient historiography. Conservatives who continue to defend the historicity of Acts with old arguments seem to be the only critics genuinely interested in the question. The debate has been going on for over a century and a half and has become stale; no one is saying much that is new. In short, most critics agree, the best thing to do with Acts is to link it to Luke and analyze its narrative, and leave history to one side.

Some Crucial Points of the Story

At this point it is necessary to reintroduce the narrator—the one who tells the story. Authors are not identical with narrators, for narrators are creations of the author. There are different types of narrator: the third person narrator limited to direct personal experience ("One fine day, as Gwendolyn was on her way to the market . . ."), the omniscient third-person narrator identified in Chapter One ("One fine day, Gwendolyn was thinking about Earnest while on her way to the market . . ."), and the first person narrator ("One fine day I was on my way to the market when . . ."), who is usually limited ("It all began one fine day when I decided, unwisely, as events would prove, to do the marketing"). Narrators begin where their creators (the actual authors) wish them to begin.

Where does Acts begin? With an account of the risen Jesus' ascension to the realm of God (Acts 1:1–11). Simply put, Jesus has to leave before the story can get going. Unlike Jesus in the Fourth Gospel, who explains the reason for his departure at some length (John 15–16), the narrator of Acts does not immediately and clearly offer such a rationale. He sees nothing wrong with a little suspense. The problem is that the Gospel of Luke, which has some relation to Acts, has already told this story—though in a different time setting and with a similar but not identical farewell speech (Luke 24:44–50, cf. Acts 1:4–8). The Ascension, it seems, is both an end and a beginning. To modern readers this juncture is rather like successive episodes of a serial, where the apparent end of one story is repeated at the start of the sequel, to bring everyone up to date, as it were, but turns out to be the basis for a fresh adventure rather than the close of what looked like a completed story. A number of attempts have been made to explain this overlap, and they will demand further attention. Nonetheless, since Luke's Gospel says that Jesus left on the evening of Easter, while Acts claims that he ascended forty days later, the beginning of Acts is troublesome.

Ends are no less important. The author may have thought that having Acts end with a summary of Paul's preaching for two years at Rome was "a good place to stop," but readers have frequently taken strong exception to that alleged judgment. They want to know what happened to Paul, for ever since chapter 13 Acts has largely been the story of Paul. Professional interpreters, who are supposed to be able to suppress mere curiosity about what happened next, have also found this ending a mystery. Historical criticism has brought forth several solutions. One is that Luke planned a third volume but was prevented from writing it by death or other circumstances. Scholars are quite familiar with "forthcoming books" (possibly including one or more of their own) that never came forth. This solution commands no support at present because conjecture is not evidence.

Two other solutions depend upon the absence of further information. One possibility is that the author was present on the scene and reported all that he knew; another is that his sources ended at that point. Neither explanation bears much weight. If it is a matter of sources, the question is simply thrown back: why did the source end at that point? The same question arises if one imagines the author to have been present. Outside of suggesting that Luke left Rome while everything was going quite well for Paul and that he had scruples against using information derived from other sources, one is left with the conjecture that the author died and left Acts unfinished. All three proposals collapse in the face of literary evidence that the close of Acts (28:17–31) is carefully crafted. At Acts 28:28 Paul announces for the third time that he will turn to the gentiles (cf. 13:46; 18:6). By the standards of the "*rule of three" this is the climactic announcement. The closing section of Acts evokes the beginning of Luke's gospel, in particular the words of Simeon in Luke 2:25–28. Paul's last sermon, like Jesus' first (Luke 4:16–30), includes a long quote from Isaiah. Jesus spoke of sight for the blind. Paul closes with the announcement of blindness for the sighted. Acts 28:28 closes the circle by speaking of "the salvation of God," looking back to the introduction of the Baptizer, also from Isaiah (Luke 3:1–6). Finally, the closing verse

(28:31) echoes the opening of Acts (1:1–3). These parallels and evo-cations eliminate the hypothesis that Acts was left incomplete.

Furthermore, the narrator is aware of Paul's death. The pastoral address to the *presbyters of Ephesus (20:17–35) is cast in the form of the last speech of a person who is about to die, and the speech looks to the time after Paul's "departure" (20:29), which is a euphe-mism for his death. (Paul was not talking about his departure from Ephesus, which took place at 20:1, nor of his departure from the East, which was announced in 19:21.) The ending of Acts is trouble-some, but its difficulties are not due to a deficit of information or inability to complete the story. The beginning of Acts exhibits some overlap and inconsistency, and its conclusion does not come at the expected point. Perhaps the middle will resolve these problems.

Middles are also important, for the mid-point of a narrative may signal the direction a story will take toward its resolution. It is not difficult to determine that chapter 15 comes at the middle of Acts. (The New Testament chapter divisions in our bibles are not original, but come from the Middle Ages; for this purpose, however, they will do.) Chapter 15 is certainly an important part of the narrative; it relates a meeting in Jerusalem at which both Peter and James gained support for not imposing the requirements of the *Torah upon gen-tile converts to the movement. The question raised by this scene is why it had to take place at all, for the admission of gentiles without requiring Torah had been settled in 10:1–11:18, where Peter, with divine guidance, had converted the gentile military officer Cornelius, together with his household, and reported the event in a speech to the community at Jerusalem which, in turn, found the action accept-able (11:18). The middle of Acts is redundant at best, anti-climactic at worst. This brief inspection leads to the tentative conclusion that it is not possible to grasp the sense of Acts by a quick examination of beginning, middle, and end.

Acts is the Story of . . .

One important contention is that Acts is *not* the story of the early church, but an account of the victorious progress of the gospel from Jerusalem to Rome. The flaw in this theory, probably not a fatal flaw but a thorn in its flesh, is that Acts does not tell how Christianity came to Rome. Paul was greeted by believers when he arrived (28:15). And Rome is not unique in this regard. Acts is equally silent about the beginnings of the movement in Alexandria. Now Alexandria and Rome were not backwoods hamlets; these were the largest cities in the empire, and both came to support important

Christian communities. Then there is Galilee, the heart and center of the Jesus movement (cf. Mark 16:7; Acts 9:31). Luke says nothing about the origin of the church there. Phoenicia, in which Tyre and Sidon were situated, appears three times in Acts (11:19; 15:3; 21:2) with no more than the barest references to the existence of groups of believers. Although Acts is the source of the information that Paul came from Tarsus (9:11), it is silent about a mission in the province of Cilicia where Tarsus was located (cf. Galatians 1:21; Acts 9:30).

Laodicea and its environs, an important center of early Christianity, and many cities in Roman Asia, including Pergamum and Smyrna, were not even on Luke's map. Equally blank is northern Asia Minor, although there were communities there, as indicated by 1 Peter 1:1 and *Marcion (who came from Sinope, on the coast of the Black Sea). Readers of Romans 15:19 are likely to be surprised by Paul's claim to have engaged in proclamation "as far around as Illyricum (roughly modern Albania)" because Acts says nothing about Illyricum. Luke's eye does not often stray from the Aegean side of the map. The point need not be belabored. Luke was not interested in covering the Mediterranean world indicating the presence of believers in Jesus or in telling how Christianity took roots in many places, including the two greatest metropolises. Luke does not draw dots that his readers might connect. He is rather a drawer of lines, lines indicating movement from east to west, from Jew to gentile, from Jerusalem "to the ends of the earth" (1:8).

It is also worth mentioning that Paul is not the only person whose fate Luke neglects to describe. The same applies to Peter, James, and John, the "pillars" of Galatians 2:9, as well as to Barnabas, Philip, and other worthies. They disappear, as Goulder observed, "except where their paths cross Paul's." There are many enigmas in Acts, but one clue to their resolution continually appears: Paul's missionary outreach to the gentiles. Rome comes into view when Paul gets there. Acts 15 is far more detailed and formal than Acts 11 because at that later meeting the *Pauline* mission to the gentiles gained approval. From chapter 13 on Acts tells the story of Paul. It does not focus upon the spread of the faith in general, but upon the "Torah-free" mission to the gentiles. Luke tells his story by reporting the actions of various characters: Peter, Stephen, Philip, Barnabas, and Paul. When each story is finished, the character is dropped. This is no less true in chapter 28 (Paul) than in chapter 8 (Philip). Luke does not wish to relate the whole story and the full story, but only one part of the story. This method is fully consonant with the purpose of legitimating the gentile mission summarized in the previous chapter.

In order to accomplish that purpose Luke had to forego recitation of the whole truth, the full truth, and nothing but the truth. That trait Luke shares with more or less every historian who has ever written, since historians must be selective if they have a theme, and there are few who will not bend the evidence, however slightly, to fit a thesis. The issue is not whether Luke omitted some information that we should like to have or adjusted some facts to achieve his object, but the quantity and quality of his deviations from "the truth." Pursuit of that question will occupy subsequent chapters. The present concern is with the general shape of the book.

Structure

The structure of Acts appears less mysterious in the light of its purpose. Martin Kähler (1835–1912) fruitfully characterized the Gospel of Mark as "a passion narrative with a long introduction." This insight could also be adopted to define Acts as the story of the Pauline mission with a long introduction. Acts is, in fact, more like Mark in its gross structure than it is like Luke. Both the Jesus of Mark and the Paul of Acts appear on the scene as adults. Only later do readers learn something of their backgrounds (Mark 3:21, 32–35; 6:1–4; Acts 22:3). It is scarcely less interesting that each ends on a note of high expectation that leaves readers dissatisfied. (Mark closes at 16:8. The later additions in Mark 16:9–20 prove that his sense of an ending was unsatisfactory to the average reader.) Although Luke found so much wanting in the Gospel of Mark that he added material at the beginning and to the ending and greatly expanded the middle, he found Mark's inadequate approach to the story of Jesus a more suitable model for his second volume.

If one tentatively accepts this analogy, a good deal of Acts 1–12 will occupy the place that the story of John the Baptizer holds in Mark, albeit at much greater length. The Pauline mission had many "forerunners" and they received substantially more attention than does Mark's Baptizer, who is on stage for fewer than a dozen verses (Mark 1:1–14a, less vv. 10–13), although his death is the subject of a later retrospective (6:14–29). To be sure, Luke had further inspiration and data from *Q, which envisioned John and Jesus as engaged in related missions (for example Luke 7:18–35), a view also found in the Fourth Gospel (for example John 1:6–8, 19–42; 3:22–36). In the Gospel story it became necessary for John's role to diminish so that of Jesus might grow. Much the same may be said of Peter and Paul in Acts. As vital as Peter is, Luke terminates his missionary work with chapter 10 (the conversion of Cornelius)—although like the Baptizer he is later the subject of a tale about incarceration and (intended) martyrdom (Acts 12:1–23). Further, Peter emerges from obscurity to make a brief speech in chapter 15, after which he returns to obscurity. From 1 Corinthians 9:5 and Galatians 2:11–14 it is apparent that Peter (and James!) engaged in missionary and pastoral travel. Luke is entirely silent with regard to the activities of James and silent concerning Peter after Acts 10. When all of the adjustments and qualifications have been duly recorded—and they are many— the author of Acts has done to Peter in Acts what he and the other gospel writers did to John the Baptizer. John's task was to summon the people to repent, baptize Jesus, and leave. Peter's task was to summon the people to repent, baptize Cornelius, and leave. A revised form of the earlier description may now be promulgated: "Acts tells the story of the victorious progress of the Torah-free Pauline gentile gospel from Jerusalem to Rome." In so doing it conforms to the general plan of Mark.

The Paul of Acts

Paul, as none need be told, is a major figure in Acts. He is also one of its enigmas. Paul is Luke's hero, but it is not likely that the Paul of Acts would be *Paul's* hero. There are many disparities between the Paul revealed in his surviving collected correspondence and the Paul portrayed in Acts. No one would expect them to be identical, for the letters were written in response to particular situations while Acts is a later narrative with purposes of its own; but the differences exceed what appears warranted by changes in time and circumstance. Credentials are one place to begin. The essence of Paul's identity resided in his calling to be an apostle, yet in Acts he does not qualify to be an apostle. Since antipathy to Paul cannot explain why he has been stripped of his primary credential in a book of which he is the hero, it is apparent that Luke had to accept a definition of "apostle" that did not include Paul. He makes up for this, so to speak, by supplying Paul with a number of other credentials. These will come into view later. (See pp. 146–48) Although the Paul of Acts is not an apostle in name, Luke and Paul agree that the missionary to the gentiles follows and identifies with his master. For Paul that means identification with the weakness, suffering, and humiliation of Jesus. For Luke, the Christ whom the subsequent leaders follow is a person of power revealed in his mighty deeds of compassion.

To reiterate, Paul is the hero of Acts. But when Acts can be compared with information derived from the *undisputed Pauline letters, there is partial or full disagreement upon most *major* points. Acts presents Paul as a Jerusalem missionary, subordinate to the community there, a Christian preacher who has not severed his connection with the Pharisaic party. In Acts Paul regularly visits Jerusalem, the mother church of all missions. Acts also presents Paul as a missionary first and foremost to the Jews who turns to gentiles (a turn that must be restated at every important juncture) only when the Jews have rebuffed his message.

Furthermore, in Acts Paul appears as a missionary fully competitive in the religious market of his day, the herald of a new god attested by great wonders and affirmed through sermons of astonishing power. Paul can convert a town within a week or two. Even his handkerchiefs work healings. He moves with ease among the socially elite, eludes plots and conspiracies, outwits adversaries, shrugs off severe beatings, and quickly stifles opposition from both polytheists and Jews.

Were Acts our sole guide to the life of Paul, we would never know:

1. That Paul ever so much as dashed off a note, let alone letters that were famous (or notorious) within his lifetime (2 Corinthians 10:9–10).
2. That he engaged in bitter controversy with *Christian* opponents (Galatians, 2 Corinthians, Philippians).
3. That the collection he raised for Jerusalem believers was intended as a sign of unity among believers.
4. That he utilized numerous colleagues and coworkers, including many women, in important roles and that Titus was one of the more important of these colleagues.
5. That he got into trouble with his churches for failing to take money, for insufficient display of spiritual endowments, and for unimpressive rhetoric.
6. That he struggled with the rejection of his message by the heirs of God's promises and attempted to come to terms with the meaning of this rejection (see, for example, Romans 9–11).
7. That he proclaimed a distinctive theology at variance with that of a number of other Christian leaders.
8. That he was executed by the Roman state.

Other points could be added. Many of these eight items are rather important. None of them is subject to more than minor qualifications, such as that Luke knew of the Collection, which he did (Acts 24:17, on which see also p. 139 below) or that he recognizes the importance of colleagues like Timothy, who are little more than lackeys in Acts. An initial reaction to these data is to think that with friends like Luke, Paul required no enemies. The portrait of Paul in Acts is comparable to an account hailing Abraham Lincoln as a great president because he was able to overcome the secession crisis by offering ironclad guarantees to slave-owners and thus preserving the union by perpetuating human bondage. For those who do not care for analogies, an aphorism is available: the Paul of Acts works miracles instead of writing letters.

One traditional way of contrasting the respective viewpoints is to speak of a "theology of glory" (Luke) versus a "theology of the cross" (Paul). The latter occasions no debate, but many find the former, "theology of glory," quite unacceptable as a characterization of Lucan thought. One reason for that view is the presumption that "theology of the cross" is positive whereas "theology of glory" is negative—in which case it becomes a red flag. In fact, a theology of glory has more than a few positive features, but that discussion belongs elsewhere. In the post-Constantinian world that has characterized Christianity since World War I anything that bears the slightest taint of "triumphalism" is gravely suspect, and numerous admirers of Luke wish to put as much distance as possible between him and that putative taint.

One is tempted to say that those admirers are doing to Luke what Luke did to Paul. There is, after all, a considerable difference between a triumphal approach when formulated by a representative of a very small and quite beleaguered sect and the posture of the Renaissance papacy. One pervasive fallacy of contemporary American culture is that its standards are often deemed to be eternal and immutable. If slavery is wrong, then Paul must either be against slavery or be unacceptable. In truth, Paul merely regarded slavery to be part of the natural order of things (1 Corinthians 11:14–15). Arguments about Lucan theology have also fallen into this anachronistic trap. If a theology of glory is bad, then Luke either did not adhere to such a theology or he is to be found unacceptable.

Nonetheless, since theologies of glory have, like the glory of God at Mt. Sinai, been under a cloud (Exodus 24:15–16), it is preferable to find other terms for comparing the theologies of Luke and Paul. To reduce the difference to a phrase, Paul tends to stress discontinuity, Luke continuity. For Paul a rupture existed between old and new, law and gospel, past and present, present and future. This rupture was justified because God brought it about, and "justification" was the word Paul used to describe it. Paul's radical successors would stress this rupture to the point of attributing creation and redemption to different gods. Some of those ideas might even have been in the wind in Luke's day. In any case, he clung to that part of Paul that acknowledged continuity and utilized it to erect a theology in which salvation history played a major part. Salvation history places a high premium upon continuity. Its core value is that God writes straight, but with crooked lines. For Paul the zigs and zags indicated that only God could write in this manner (Romans 9–11). Luke will reduce the zigs and zags to a minimum.

Irony and paradox are two of the most useful and prominent rhetorical handmaids of discontinuity. Paul was certainly paradoxical and ironic; he waxes eloquent in depicting the power of God in human weakness and the shameful cross as the instrument of salvation. Luke quite appreciated Paul's understanding of justification by faith, but he elucidates it in sentimental and romantic stories. An example of the sentimental is the story of the Pharisee and the Publican (Luke 18:9–14). To illustrate the romantic streak there is Luke 7:36–50, where a notorious woman is forgiven because of her great love. Paul and Luke agree that justification creates a level playing field. For Luke justification means that humans can do the right thing. It is primarily the gift of an opportunity for repentance, that is, for change. Paul would not wholly disagree, but he understands justification as God doing the right thing by changing people. The result is more or less the same. The theological equivalent to a sentimental and romantic perspective includes a theology of glory. More fundamentally, it reflects a different anthropology, which in theology refers to the doctrine of "human nature." Luke's anthropology is optimistic, while Paul's is pessimistic. For Paul God must blow down the door and transfer humans to the other side. In Lucan thought God need but open the door.

Luke shows no particular interest in paradox, and his irony is likely to be of the rather transparent narrative sort, such as in depicting the custodians of the law as lawless in their attempts to remove Jesus, Peter, and Paul from the scene. There is nothing paradoxical about divine power in Acts. God's will and plan are manifest in deeds of indisputable potency. The cross is a striking example of human injustice reversed by the resurrection. For his part, Luke relates a series of indisputable triumphs over bad people and bad things. All of this was to say that Luke is a "popular" theologian who communicates through stories readily intelligible to the general public. In contrast, when Paul elects to relate his accomplishments he produces a catalogue dripping with irony (2 Corinthians 11:22–33). Paul's theology is esoteric, an endless source for speculation and attempted clarification. The consistency of Pauline theology is elusive. The inconsistency of Luke's theology is patent. Occasional inconsistency did not trouble the author of Acts, who was no systematic theologian, whereas the consistency of Pauline thought must be teased out of its application to quite different situations.

Given their different situations and disparate outlooks, it should come as no surprise that the Paul of Acts is at considerable variance with the Paul who appears in the epistles. Luke evidently felt obliged to update Paul for the current situation. There is nothing novel about that. The same charge may be laid against Augustine of Hippo, Martin Luther, and John Wesley, to name but three from a lengthy catalogue of those motivated by Paul to erect fresh theological systems and launch new eras and movements. The real mystery, for those in quest of one, is why anyone has ever sought to prove that the Paul of Acts and the Paul of the letters thought and acted in similar ways. The obvious clue, a smoking gun if ever one was, is that the driving concern of this effort is not theology, but history. To the degree that Acts portrays not only Paul, but also Peter and James, in colors derived from the palette of Lucan theology, its historical value is considerably compromised.

"Compromise" is the correct term for the right and centrist approach to Acts. Borrowing a leaf from Luke's own manual, a substantial body of critics has sought to "Lucanize" Paul and "Paulinize" Acts by shaving off the rough edges of each and stressing points of similarity. Much can be said in favor of this tactic in many situations, but it does not promote advances in critical insight, most of which come from underlining differences rather than minimizing them. If it be said that I am guilty of placing too much emphasis upon differences and even that I have engaged in some exaggeration, I shall feel no embarrassment, for my object has been to make the issues as clear and inescapable as possible, so clear that they cannot be brushed aside. To appreciate Acts one must acknowledge its enigmas.

Conclusion

The first of these enigmas is that although Acts looks like a simple, unadorned chronicle of events when read as "straight" history, it exhibits profound imbalances, gaps, and improprieties. Another enigma is why the author of a gospel elected to write a further document, and this leads to the important matter of whether one should study Luke-Acts or Luke and Acts. A third is its ambiguous status: background to the epistles, a sort of "post-gospel," or the second part of an independent work that should be read without reference to others. Examination of its general structure reveals that its beginning, middle, and end are enigmatic. The greatest enigma is that Paul is Luke's hero, but is portrayed so differently from the Paul known from his correspondence that one could almost make a case that there were two different missionaries who happened to have the same name and worked in the same places.

Other enigmas could be presented, but those discussed should suffice to show that Acts is a challenge for critical scholarship, and that the challenges it raises should be of interest to all who are curious about Christian origins. After postulating some basic presuppositions in the first chapter and highlighting the mysteries of Acts in the current one, it is time to take account of the challenges faced by Luke and the stories that he told and neglected to tell in response to these challenges. Good detectives think about whether the dog barked—that is, about what is there and what is not there. Silences can be as loud and as informative as words.

Note: In discussions of the problems of the Paul of Acts, one standard alibi provided for Luke is that he did not know of the letters of Paul and therefore had no access to his thought. This alibi works only for those who do not believe that the author of Acts was a colleague, or at least a frequent companion, of Paul. This is one of the grounds for dating Acts c. 85, late enough to be at some distance from the historical events under review but not so late as to appear after the collected letters of Paul, or at least some of them, had become widely known. In fact, the alibi is ridiculous. It is impossible that someone writing about Paul who was familiar with his mission in general and at least some of the communities he founded could have not heard—or could have forgotten—that Paul wrote letters. Luke not only knew that Paul wrote letters; he made use of them. (See p. 162.) The problem of the portrait of Paul in Acts cannot be resolved by appeal to Luke's ignorance of the Pauline epistles as an assertion that requires no proof.

Resources and Further Reading

Henry J. Cadbury, *The Making of Luke-Acts*. London: SPCK, 1958 (original, 1927).

Hans Conzelmann, *The Theology of St. Luke*. Trans. G. Buswell. Philadelphia: Fortress, 1982 (1960).

Martin Dibelius, *Studies in the Acts of the Apostles*. Ed. H. Greeven. Trans. Anon. London: SCM, 1956.

Michael D. Goulder, *Type and History in Acts*. London: SPCK, 1964.

Ernst Haenchen, *The Acts of the Apostles.* Ed. and trans. B. Noble et al. Philadelphia: Westminster, 1971. ET of *Die Apostelgeschichte.* 14th ed. KEK. Göttingen: Vandenhoeck & Ruprecht, 1965.

Mikeal C. Parsons and Richard I. Pervo, *Rethinking the Unity of Luke and Acts.* Minneapolis: Fortress, 1993. (This topic is now the subject of vigorous discussion. Fortress reissued the book in 2007, with additional bibliography.)

Endnotes

1. M. D. Goulder, *Type and History in Acts* (London: SPCK, 1964), 15. Goulder's views on date and authorship appear on 14, note 1.

2. Sequels may or may not be part of an original plan. The success or failure of a particular book may motivate an author to produce a sequel. Sequels may be written much later than the original book, sometimes by a different author. *Josephus' *Against Apion* is a good example of an ancient two-volume work in which the second volume is a direct continuation, rather than a sequel.

3. Greek manuscripts usually place Acts after the Pauline epistles or following the "catholic" or "general" epistles (Hebrews-3 John).

4. See also the *Gospel of Thomas* 47, which employs the same sentiment in a series of antitheses.

5. I took a different approach to this dilemma in *Profit with Delight: The Literary Genre of the Acts of the Apostles* (Philadelphia: Fortress, 1987). See the Appendix.

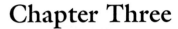

Chapter Three

How Luke Met Certain Challenges

What He Said and What He Left Unsaid

If the leading motive behind Luke's writings was to promote the legitimacy of the Pauline mission, it is reasonable to suspect that this heritage was under fire. And under fire it was, from both "left-wing" ultra-Pauline and "right-wing" anti-Pauline directions, some of which were noted in Chapter Two. That chapter also asserted that Luke wished to demonstrate continuity in the history of revelation, to show how the religion of ancient Israel became a gentile faith without abandoning its roots. He was not the only person occupied in a project of this nature. Emergent Rabbinic Judaism was also engaged in the redefinition and validation of Israelite faith in a world without a temple and with the ancestral homeland in ruins. Discontinuity looked like the order of the day, and some of Luke's Pauline opponents sought to make the most of it. Representatives of the tendencies that would flourish under *Marcion and various "*Gnostics" were burning bridges with positive relish.

The purpose of this chapter is to examine a number of discontinuities and how Luke dealt with them. Among them are the following:

1. The problem of Jesus as both messenger and object of the message
2. The conflict between the ethics of Jesus enunciated in the gospels and the views attributed to Paul
3. The question of why Luke told certain stories and overlooked others, a particular example of the latter being Paul's collection for Jerusalem
4. The contrast between the actual organization of early gentile communities and the picture given in Acts

Discovering how Luke made problems disappear will provide useful background for an examination of the means Luke used to narrate
Acts.

The Proclaimer and the Proclaimed

Many decades ago Rudolf Bultmann acutely framed one of the discontinuities confronting those who would build a bridge from Jesus
to Paul as the problem of "The Proclaimer" and "The Proclaimed."
In the Synoptic Gospels Jesus announces the Kingdom of God—
"God's imperial rule" in the apt translation of the Scholars Version.
He is thus "the proclaimer." In Paul, on the other hand, Jesus is not
the *subject* of proclamation, but its *object*, the one proclaimed as heavenly sovereign.[1] This was not a major problem for Matthew or Mark,
who narrated the mission of the proclaimer, nor for Paul and those
who revered the heavenly Christ. But it was a severe problem for
Luke, who wanted to write a sequel to the gospel. That he was able
to resolve it with considerable success is evidenced by the fact that
few who read Luke and Acts consecutively ever think to ask how it
has come about that the rather dull and sometimes cowardly disciples
of the synoptic gospels suddenly acquire such courage, wisdom, and
power. Luke's resolution of this problem begins in the final scene of
his Gospel:

> The *risen one* said to *his disciples*, "These are my words that I spoke to
> you while I was still with you—that everything written about me in the
> law of Moses, the prophets, and the psalms must be fulfilled." Then he
> opened their minds to understand the scriptures, and he said to them,
> "Thus it is written, that the Messiah is to suffer and to rise from the
> dead on the third day, and that repentance and forgiveness of sins is to
> be proclaimed in his name to all nations, beginning from Jerusalem. You
> are witnesses of these things. And see, I am sending upon you what my
> Father promised; so stay here in the city until you have been clothed
> with power from on high." (Luke 24:44–49)

In this interview the risen Jesus tells his followers that he is the
Messiah and that all of the scriptures had spoken of his fate. This
reference to the fate of Jesus as fulfillment of biblical prophecy is not
surprising to the reader because it was introduced in the previous
story of the journey to Emmaus (Luke 24:13–35, especially verses
25–27). But "messianic prophecy" was not, in fact, a major theme of
the Gospel (cf. Luke 4:16–30, where Jesus *proclaims* the fulfillment
of prophecy). The operative idea at the close of Luke's Gospel is that
his followers must study scripture to learn about the Messiah, and in
proclaiming the scriptures, proclaim Jesus as Messiah. Secondly, he

commissions the disciples to be "witnesses," that is, to testify about the saving events. The noun "witness" is important in Acts, occurring thirteen times. Included among the witnesses is Paul (26:15). This testimony will result in a universal mission. The third item is the promise of "power from on high."

The solution to the problem defined by Bultmann is that Jesus personally authorized his change of status from proclaimer to proclaimed, at which time he also authorized a mission to the gentiles ("all nations"). Jesus further announced that the witnesses would be empowered. Then . . . he took off. According to the second edition of his farewell speech, the one found in Acts, Jesus left so that the disciples might accomplish their mission. There he states that the power will come from the holy spirit (Acts 1:8). He then departs to a celestial destination. As Peter makes clear in his initial sermon, Jesus had to ascend to heaven so that *he* could dispatch the spirit: "Being therefore exalted at the right hand of God, and having received from the Father the promise of the Holy Spirit, he has poured out this that you both see and hear" (Acts 2:33). The spirit empowers witnesses to proclaim Jesus as Messiah, and the source of that gift is the heavenly sovereign.

There is more. In these final speeches Jesus does not proclaim the kingdom. He does not even refer to it. However, the disciples *do* refer to it in Acts 1:6: "So when they had come together, they asked him, 'Lord, is this the time when you will restore the kingdom to Israel?'" Jesus rebuffs this with the promise of the spirit (1:8). Luke has taken over the Pauline tendency to "replace," as it were, language about the Rule of God with statements about the holy spirit.[2] More specifically, for Paul the spirit is the *manner* in which God's futurity is now present. Luke and Acts more or less identify the coming of God's imperial rule with the *working* of the spirit. In this way Luke makes the transition—from Jesus as proclaimer of the kingdom to the object of proclamation as heavenly lord and Messiah—seem quite obvious and "natural." He solved the problem so capably that it required the insight of a Bultmann to identify it as a problem.

Evangelical and Apostolic Ethics

Ethics introduces another element of discontinuity, also noted earlier. Why does the Christian church revere the Gospels and confess Jesus Christ as its Lord and Savior, but—to the regret of many—prefer the more conventional ethics of the Pauline tradition to the robust teachings of Jesus?

Table 3.1: Jesus and "Paul" on "Family Values"

Jesus Tradition	Pauline Tradition
Jesus said "Whoever comes to me and <u>does not hate father and mother, wife and children</u>, brothers and sisters, yes, and even life itself, cannot be my disciple. (Luke 14:26) *Jesus said* "I came to bring fire to the earth, and how I wish it were already kindled! I have a baptism with which to be baptized, and what stress I am under until it is completed! Do you think that I have come to bring peace to the earth? No, I tell you, but rather division! <u>From now on five in one household will be divided, three against two and two against three; they will be divided: father against son and son against father, mother against daughter and daughter against mother, mother-in-law against her daughter-in-law and daughter-in-law against mother-in-law</u>." (Luke 12:49–53)	Wives, be subject to your husbands, as is fitting in the Lord. Husbands, love your wives and never treat them harshly. Children, obey your parents in everything, for this is your acceptable duty in the Lord. Fathers, do not provoke your children, or they may lose heart. (Col 3:18–21)

One answer to the question is that Paul won, that the Christian church was erected on faith in the proclaimed rather than on the teaching of the proclaimer. Paul's rather stodgy, "bourgeois" ethics provided a basis for communities to grow in urban society, while the proclamation of some of Jesus' more extreme utterances would have brought down the force of the law. In time Paul's ethics would become even more conventional, as reflected in the "Household Code" cited in **Table 3.1** from the *Deutero-Pauline epistle to the Colossians.

Luke deals with this problem of ethical discontinuity by finessing it. Simply stated, he largely bypasses ethics. In Acts, the risen Jesus does not tell his disciples, as he did in Matthew, to go and teach all nations whatever he has commanded (Matthew 28:19–20). Most of the ethical teaching in Acts comes through example, and money is its primary agent and symbol. Luke does not embrace the ethical norms of the *Deutero-Paulines, but neither does he have Peter and Paul instruct Cornelius and Dionysius the Areopagite (Acts 10; 17) to sell all that they have and distribute it to the poor. Nor does he report that, after circumcising Timothy, Paul instructed him to hate his mother. About certain subjects Acts is ambivalent. Women are not explicitly subordinated, but Luke does not give them leadership roles. On the subject of marriage, however, Luke represents a strengthened form of the Pauline view (1 Corinthians 7). He does not recommend it. None of the leaders has a wife, and the production of babies is absent from his narrative. Still, he includes no commands or propaganda about marriage and celibacy in Acts. (The Apocryphal Acts would more than make up for this shortcoming.)

Luke further eases potential ethical tension by his "take" on Jesus. The Galilean prophet of Luke represents the well-known social type of the itinerant philosopher who renounces wealth and comfort to function as a sort of "gadfly," whose ideas may be taken more as attempts to shock people out of their complacency than as realistic prescriptions for daily life. But Luke does no more than suggest why the ethical teachings of Jesus do not constitute a part of the apostolic message. This was a discontinuity that he could not fully resolve.

The remarkable thing, however, is the extent to which Luke was able to mask these discontinuities. Even relatively careful readers fail to raise questions about what was going on. Challenges to Acts arise through the rigorous methodological doubt and intense scrutiny of what is said but also, and often more importantly, what is *not* said. Luke has carefully protected his literary edifice from the cavils of carping critics, and any who touch it open themselves to rebuke. Who would dare to spoil such a fine story? Luke's successful handling of two major discontinuities demonstrates his prowess at making problems disappear. Detectives have their work cut out for them, and that work must be carried out against the grain of popular sentiment.

Stories Present and Stories Absent

Important clues for solving the historical issues in Acts begin with two simple questions: (1) what story does Luke tell and (2) what stories does he neglect? These are followed, of course, by an implicit third question: why? Luke wishes to describe the gentile mission, but the aims of demonstrating unity and continuity require him to make haste slowly. Haste he nonetheless does make. By verse 8 of Acts 1 Luke introduces his theme of "the ends of the earth" as the missionary goal. We are almost halfway through the book before we learn that this expression stands for the gentile mission (13:46–47), although the idea is both religiously and geographically foreshadowed in 8:26–39 when Philip converts an Ethiopian court official. It attains geographical fulfillment when Paul reaches Rome. The events of Pentecost in chapter 2 also foreshadow universalism, both through the presence of representatives from many nations and the final words of Peter's sermon, which speaks of a promise made to those who are far away (2:1–13, 39).

Before it takes us off to distant lands, Acts reveals that the Jewish leadership at Jerusalem would have nothing to do with this saving message (Acts 3–5). It was important for Luke to establish this fact because he must explain why those to whom the promise was made rejected the offer. Then, in chapter 6, a new pot begins to boil. The complaints of (evidently) Greek-speaking widows lead to the creation of a new group of functionaries, all of whom have Greek names, and the last of whom is a gentile convert from Antioch. Thereupon the story switches to the Greek world, from which it will not turn back. One of those seven officers, Stephen, engages in debate with members of Greek-speaking synagogues and thereby, to all intents, epitomizes the *Diaspora. His mission leads to serious repercussions: his murder, followed by a general persecution and the dispersion of those who spoke Greek. Into this story Luke introduces a young man named Saul whom we know as Paul. Luke weaves the beginning of Paul's adventures into the persecution aroused by Stephen's mission. That insertion—it is probably a Lucan creation—was not gratuitous.

Philip, another of the Seven, gains the adherence of some *Samaritans, an action ratified by the apostles in Jerusalem. After this is the first explicit step away from the "orthodox" path, he moves yet further by converting an Ethiopian official, a person of gentile origin whose status relative to Judaism is left unclear. In chapter 9 the narrator turns back to the counter-mission of Saul, who is converted, becomes a missionary in Damascus and Jerusalem, and is soon sent to Tarsus and disappears from the narrative. A brief summary in 9:31 is the last reference to community growth among Aramaic-speaking Palestinian Jews. At 9:32 it transpires that Peter has become a missionary to Greek-speaking Jews on the Palestinian coast. This leads to the carefully orchestrated conversion of a gentile "God-Fearer," Cornelius. (In Acts "God-Fearers" are gentiles who are attracted to the faith of Israel but have not undergone full conversion.)

With the principle of gentile acceptability established, the narrator returns at 11:19 to the refugees from the persecution set off by Stephen's work (8:1). These fugitive missionaries worked north along the paths of commerce until they came to Antioch, a metropolis and the capital of Roman Syria. There they met considerable success when they began to approach people who were evidently gentiles. As in the case of Samaria, Jerusalem learned of these efforts, apparently approved, and sent Barnabas, an early believer and benefactor from Cyprus (4:36–37) who had befriended Saul (9:27). Under Barnabas the Antiochene mission really took off. He, in turn, sent to nearby Tarsus for his friend Saul. Their work led to even greater success. Barnabas established a firm link to Jerusalem, and Saul enjoyed the support of Barnabas.

Toward the close of chapter 11 the narrator sends Barnabas and Saul to Jerusalem with money for relief. While they were in that city another persecution broke out, directed against the leaders of the Christian community. Most of chapter 12 is devoted to Peter's delivery from death. The significance of this tale will be the subject of a later discussion; at present it suffices to observe that this story brings the ministry of Peter to a victorious close. Chapter 13 returns to Antioch, where Barnabas and Saul are sent off on missionary travels. Thereafter Saul, who is presently exposed as none other than Paul, becomes the focus of the book. The narrator took some time to get to this point, but it was time well spent, for the reader has received careful assurance that the "mother church" of Jerusalem fully approved of the gentile mission and of its leaders—a thesis that is at considerable variance with the facts, as Galatians shows. After missionary work in Cyprus and southern Asia Minor (chapters 13–14), Paul and Barnabas return to Jerusalem for final resolution of the gentile question, followed by Paul's labors in the Aegean region, without Barnabas, 16–21. The Pauline mission, with or without Barnabas, always begins with the Jews, then turns to gentiles when the synagogue is not receptive. On a pilgrimage to Jerusalem Paul falls victim to false charges, as had Jesus and Stephen before him. From 21:33 onward Paul is in custody. His legal struggles, including his successful attempts to stay alive in the face of hostile plots and schemes, predominate through the end of chapter 26. Then comes the famous voyage to Rome, where Paul is able to resume his missionary life, first to Jews and, following their generally negative reaction, to gentiles.

This is, in summary, the story that Luke tells. With patient economy he shows the gradual but steady transition to the gentile mission—a shift that conformed to the clearly expressed will of God, as well as to the general but far from total failure to attract Jews into mixed communities. The role of the Jerusalem church is to provide support for this mission to others and to highlight the initial hostility of Jewish leaders—and ultimately of the Jewish public in general. This scenario is put in relief by consideration of the story and stories that Luke does not tell. It also serves as justification for the failure to tell some of those stories. The previous chapter noted a number of localities neglected by Acts. They provide a useful jumping-off point, but so do some of the places *not* neglected by Acts. In general, Luke treats missionary sites as he does his characters. Once the foundation has been described, these sites disappear from the narrative with no more than a trace. But there are exceptions—Ephesus for one and Jerusalem for another.

Acts says almost nothing about the mission to the Aramaic speaking majority (or majorities) in Jerusalem after 5:42. This was not because Luke claims that it was unsuccessful. According to 21:20, this mission has been vastly, indeed impossibly, successful. There are "myriads" of converts. Luke neglects this story because it was not his principal subject. Samaria passes out of sight at 8:25. What went on in Galilee is a blank page in Acts. A strong Jesus-movement developed there, but Luke does no more than acknowledge its existence (9:31). There were also missions of a more or less exclusive sort to Jews, but Luke was not interested in them either.

Historians would dearly like to know more about the Christian missions more or less restricted to Jews in Palestine and elsewhere, but little information—or even misinformation—exists. The fourth-century church historian Eusebius states that the believers in Jerusalem fled to Pella before the First Revolt (66–73; *Ecclesiastical History* 3.5.3). His source may have been one Ariston, conveniently of Pella. Eusebius also speaks of some relatives of Jesus who were haled before the emperor Domitian (81–96) and shown to be rustics, but he does not claim that they were leaders of the community, that is, bishops (*E. H.* 3.20). The source is Hegesippus, an earlier Christian writer. On that basis some have proposed an early Christian "caliphate" of Jerusalem leaders descended from Jesus and thus heirs of the Messiah. The evidence is extremely frail, but scholarship is obliged to propose some theories. Outside of Acts Eusebius had little information, and much of that is questionable. Eusebius was interested in the history of communities; Luke was not. To berate Luke for his omissions in the history of the early church would be appropriate only if he were writing a history of the early church, but he was not. Difficulties arise when readers assume or pretend that Luke did write a general history of Christian origins.

The Collection

Even those parts of the story that Luke chooses to tell are often incomplete. At least on some occasions that may reflect a lack of information, but this is an author who may know more than he chooses to say and may say more than he knows. A famous example of the former is 24:17, in which Paul says, while on trial before a Roman governor: "Now after some years I came to bring alms to my nation and to offer sacrifices." From this casual reference it is apparent that Luke knew of Paul's *Collection for Jerusalem but preferred to ignore it. The Collection provides a useful illustration of historical reconstruction at work. The first question, logically, is how Luke could overlook an enterprise that was so crucial for Paul. We know of the importance Paul assigned to the Collection from Romans 15:25–33. In that passage Paul also expresses his fears that he may encounter difficulties in delivering it (verse 31). From 2 Corinthians 8–9 comes evidence that Paul was suspected of raising funds under false pretenses and/or misusing them. The Collection was, therefore, controversial for two groups: the potential donors and the prospective beneficiaries.

These concerns indicate why Luke, who was quite sensitive to issues involving money, might have elected to neglect the Collection. This reasonable inference raises a second question: why, if the Collection were too hot a topic to address, does Luke appear to have Paul recall it at Acts 24:17? At this point one must resort to speculation.

The facts of this particular case are (1) that Luke knew of the Collection and (2) that he elected not to acknowledge it as the motive for Paul's final journey to Jerusalem. From these data I conclude that Luke wished to defuse the story of the Collection by relegating it to a simple act of conventional Jewish piety. That tactic was ever so much better than trying to pretend that Paul brought no money to Jerusalem. Acts chooses not to say why Paul came to Jerusalem for that final visit. Attributing this omission to the controversial nature of the Collection is a reasonable inference to explain Luke's silence, though it is not concrete proof. The proposal that Luke sought to defuse this controversial topic by his reference to "alms" in 24:17 is a plausible piece of speculation that is also incapable of proof. The best test for such inferences and speculations is whether Luke appears to

engage in similar tactics elsewhere. If this method of handling problems can be shown to be rather typical, part of a pattern, the weight
of probability will grow, but it can never become certainty.

The word "silence" may raise a red flag. In modern thought
"arguments from silence" are suspect—and with reason. A pertinent
example of a dubious argument from silence would be the assertion
that Luke's silence about the Collection demonstrates that he had
never heard of it. But silence proves only *that* writers were silent
about some matter, not why. While silences can be useful clues to
investigate, they rarely in themselves constitute arguments. The present argument has juxtaposed Luke's silence to Paul's emphasis and
thereby sought to explain that silence on the grounds that Acts 24:17
refutes the claim that Luke had not heard of the Collection, a claim
that is quite improbable to begin with. This brief detour to elucidate
a subject about which Luke seems to know more than he says was
intended to provide some illustrations of scholarly method and to
seek to resolve an historical issue. *None* of the important data comes
from Acts: the historical question arises when Acts is compared to
Paul's letters. In short, Acts is not narrating history in this instance,
but it is creating problems for historians.

Note: The Fate of the Collection. Romans 15:25–33 reveals that Paul
had fears about the reception of the Collection. This concern,
followed by Luke's avoidance of the issue, suggests that the
leaders at Jerusalem rejected the Collection. Opponents of Paul
may well have claimed that he attempted, like Simon in Acts
8, to purchase the apostleship. One hypothesis is that Paul, in
response, *did* attempt to introduce gentiles into the temple,
acting out Zechariah 14:16 in a symbolic gesture like that of
Jesus (Mark 11:15–17). Any explanation needs to account for
both Luke's silence and the arrest of Paul on this occasion,
coupled with the remarkable failure of Jerusalem believers to
come to his defense.

Community Officers

Acts 14:23 introduces a complicated subject about which Luke says
more than he knows and about which historians would like to know
a great deal more than Luke says. Chapters 13–14 recount the tumul-
tuous "first missionary journey." (The phrases "First/Second/Third
Missionary Journey" come from the nineteenth century. Luke does
not distinguish separate "journeys.") At the close of this description
the narrator states that Paul and Barnabas retraced their route, in the

course of which, "after they had appointed elders [*presbyters] for them in each church, with prayer and fasting they entrusted them to the Lord in whom they had come to believe."

Readers of Acts have usually understood this verse to describe an ordination, the ceremony by which church officials are formally authorized and spiritually endowed to exercise their functions. But in this instance Luke was saying more than he knew, although he may well have felt justified in assuming that Paul ordained presbyters because that was what had "always been done." The origin and development of the Christian ministry is a subject of historical and ecumenical interest to which Acts contributes very little. Luke might have meant that the apostles began the practice of appointing presbyters and that claim may well have been erroneous, but it would explain the origin of the institution. That such theories were quite possible, witness *1 Clement*, probably written a decade or so before Acts:

> The apostles were given the gospel for us by the Lord Jesus Christ, and Jesus Christ was sent forth from God. Thus Christ came from God and the apostles from Christ. Both things happened, then, in an orderly way according to the will of God. When, therefore, the apostles received his commands and were fully convinced through the resurrection of our Lord Jesus Christ and persuaded by the word of God, they went forth proclaiming the good news the kingdom of God was about to come, brimming with confidence through the Holy Spirit. And as they preached throughout the countryside and in the cities, they appointed the first fruits of their ministries as bishops and deacons of those who were about to believe, testing them by the Spirit . . . (44:1). So too our apostles knew through our Lord Jesus Christ that strife would arise over the office of the bishop. For this reason, since they understood perfectly well in advance what would happen, they appointed those we have already mentioned . . . (*I Clement* 42.1–4; 44.1–2, trans. Bart D. Ehrman, *The Apostolic Fathers*, 1:109–111; 113).

The letter sets forth a clear order of succession: God, Christ, apostles, the "bishops and deacons" whom they appoint, and the persons who shoulder the burden after the death of those appointees. Acts makes no such clear statements. At the beginning Peter assumes leadership of the community. This may seem reasonable enough, but Luke does not say how or why he obtained this position. The first order of business, following the departure of Jesus, is to bring the number of apostles up to twelve. These men, it transpires, are the leaders of the community. When, in 12:2, the execution of James the brother of John is reported, no replacement is called for. Fifteen verses later, Peter, who has been delivered from a death sentence, asks his listeners to relate the story of his escape to "James and the believers." This is the first explicit reference in Acts to James (apart from anonymous inclusion among other siblings of Jesus, 1:13).

James vaulted out of near non-existence in the Gospel to a place in community leadership just beneath that of the apostles. In chapter 15 James has the final say, despite the presence of Peter and "the apostles," while in chapter 21 he has the only say and his wishes have become commands (21:18–25). Peter and the other apostles have disappeared; James is in charge. Luke says nothing about how these crucial developments came about. James has become a prime minister without a cabinet that he must consult.

Acts describes the creation of just one new office, although it must be said that none of the office-holders is ever guilty of carrying out his assigned duties. When an administrative crisis arrives in chapter 6, "the Twelve"—a term not used elsewhere but doubtless referring to the apostles—call upon the community to select seven assistants to take over distribution of food. The seven are duly nominated and inaugurated through prayer and the imposition of apostolic hands. To Luke's readers and those of later times this account could serve as the foundation story for the Order of Deacons.[3] The only blemish upon this edifying picture is that Luke never calls these persons "deacons." The two whose careers do receive attention, Stephen and Philip, are not subordinate ministers but highly successful missionaries. There is but one suggestion of a different status. In 8:14–17 Peter and John make their way from Jerusalem to Samaria to bestow the holy spirit upon Philip's converts. That event, which became the proof text for episcopal confirmation in Western Christianity, is, however, unique in Acts.

Then there are those presbyters installed by Paul and Barnabas in the cities of the "First Journey." This is the first anyone has heard of such officials. Luke says nothing of their duties. From the charge given to the Ephesian presbyters six chapters later, at 20:17–35, it is apparent that they exercised pastoral leadership. To make matters more complicated, there are also presbyters in Jerusalem, mentioned several times in chapter 15 and at 21:17. These persons would seem to have a somewhat different function, serving as members of governing board, much like the analogous word "senator," which comes from the Latin equivalent of "presbyter." The narrator seems to assume that the implied reader understands these various offices. In any case, he does not attempt to explain them.

In the course of the second century two developments came into gradual predominance. One of these was the gradual emergence of a single head of each urban community, called the bishop, from a Greek word for an overseer. That leader was assisted by a number of assistants, known as "deacons." In addition there was a body of presbyters, who advised bishops and might deputize for them. From the earliest descriptions of this three-fold ministry found in *Ignatius of Antioch, where it is often more of an ideal to be attained than a reality in place, it is evident that behind Ignatius' system were two models, one of the Bishop/Deacon, and another of Presbyters. These two systems had been or were being merged, although far from uniformly or simultaneously. Moreover, some writers use "presbyter" and "bishop" more or less interchangeably. One such writer is Luke. What sort of church organization would the author of Acts see, were he to remove his eyes from the page for a moment and gaze about at the ecclesial world? What he would have seen a few years later in the neighborhood of Ephesus appears in Ignatius' letter to the Ephesians. There were quite probably different Christian groups in Ephesus, but it is difficult to believe that Ignatius does not address the largest of these. The martyr-to-be has met the bishop, one Onesimus, as well as a deacon, Burrhus (1.3; 2:1), and urges subjection to Onesimus "and to the presbytery" (2.2; cf. also 20.2). The latter is the council of presbyters, the merits of which are considerable, as its relationship to the bishop is like that of strings to a harp (4.1–2). This image of a leader surrounded by his silent—until plucked—and supportive council is familiar to Luke, for he reproduces it in 2:14 where Peter, "standing with the eleven," speaks; and in 21:18–25, in which James appears, surrounded by a group of presbyters. Whether Luke thinks that this model should be normative in the church is an entirely different question. He sees what Ignatius saw and desired, but Luke's desire is somewhat different. His Paul appoints presbyters in communities, but no bishop. Acts uses the word "bishop" but once, in the plural (20:28), which implies that "presbyters" and "bishops" exercise the same responsibilities. In general Luke tends to prefer words that describe ministerial functions, which are distributed among different offices only when necessity requires, as in Acts 6:1–7. Ideally, all officers exercise all of the functions of ministry (Luke 17:7–10; 22:24–30). It may well be that Luke is familiar with the single, "monarchical," bishop and does not fully approve of the idea.

Another normative feature began to take formal shape from around the middle of the second century, the idea of accreditation through valid succession. Succession arose in disputes about correct teaching. Christians, like the Rabbis, took over this idea from the philosophical tradition, in which it was argued that the correct current source of the teachings of Plato, for example, could be found in the legitimate head of Plato's "school," the Academy. Trustworthy leaders could trace their official lineage back to the founder. *Ignatius of Antioch, that vigorous proponent of the one bishop with his deacons and a supportive presbytery, says nothing about succession. *1 Clement* (above) links succession to legitimacy, although not explicitly to teaching authority. *Irenaeus of Lyons, building upon some predecessors, notably Hegesippus, who had made lists of bishops in various cities, propounded the doctrine of Apostolic Succession in its mature form around 180. For Luke, however, the apostles are successors of Jesus in so far as they take up his earthly functions, but they are not identified as such; and although the Seven are authorized as assistants, they function as missionaries, but not as successors to the apostles.

The Paul of Acts viewed the elders as his successors (Acts 20:17–35), but he was not a successor of the apostles, and his authority was, like theirs, of divine origin. Luke seeks to explain neither the origin of Christian officers nor the succession of leadership in a clear and cogent fashion. These failures may stem in part from a lack of knowledge, but it is also possible that the author of Acts did not wish to give divine sanction to the ideas of organization that were in the process of taking shape. He may have preferred things as they had been—leadership by a body of presbyters—but it is equally possible that he wished to uphold the notion that authority was, with important qualifications, charismatic, that is, authenticated by spiritual gifts (not all of which need be "supernatural"). This is not to suggest that one can simply place Luke on the side of spiritual power in opposition to institutional authority. With regard to the organization of Christian communities, then, it may also be said that Luke knows more than he says and says more than he knows.

Conclusion

This chapter has sought to demonstrate that Luke had to deal with some major discontinuities, most notably those between Israel and Christianity and between Jesus as radical moral teacher and the Church as a body that worshipped and proclaimed the heavenly Lord. It was his success in managing these difficulties that made his "myth of Christian origins" the normative story. Luke's story has some notable restrictions because the driving force behind it was to legitimize the gentile, Pauline mission. Although that story may seem to occupy less than two-thirds of the book, it was the goal from the beginning. As a corrective to the view that Acts is the story of the early church, the definition of Acts as "the story of Paul with a long introduction" has merit, though that definition is far from adequate.

What Comes Next

Through a review of two important historical subjects, Paul's Collection for Jerusalem and the development of some features of community organization, I have attempted to subject Acts to the stringencies of historical method and show how the author addresses several matters of vital concern for church historians. But our detective suspects that Luke is not an early church historian at all. Next, using clues found in his literary techniques, she will attempt to discover what kind of historian he is, or whether he is, indeed, an historian at all.

Resources and Further Reading

A popular introduction to Deutero-Paulinism is J. Christiaan Beker, *Heirs of Paul: Paul's Legacy in the New Testament and in the Church Today*. Minneapolis: Fortress, 1991.

The views on the origin and development of the ordained ministry summarized in this chapter are strongly influenced by some of the essays of Hans v. Campenhausen, *Ecclesiastical Authority and Spiritual Power in the Church of the First Three Centuries*. Trans. J. A. Baker. Stanford: Stanford University Press, 1963 (1953), and *Tradition and Life in the Church*. Trans. A. V. Littledale. Philadelphia: Fortress, 1968 (1960).

Endnotes

1. Bultmann's statement about the relation between the proclaimer and that proclaimed is found in his *Theology of the New Testament* (Trans. K. Grobel. 2 vols. New York: Scribner's, 1951–55), 1:33–37.

2. Paul does use the "Kingdom of God" seven times in his undisputed letters, usually with reference to the future, but he speaks far more often of the spirit. Luke may have grasped this shift by hearing and reading the letters, but it is at least equally possible that it was part of the heritage of his community.

3. Acts 6:1–7 was one of the required liturgical readings for diaconal ordinations until the late twentieth century and remains an option.

Chapter Four

How Acts Tells Its Story I

Characters, Repetitions, Parallels

Introduction

The investigation has thus far revealed a good deal about Luke. He gives the impression of knowing a bit more than he does while concealing important clues from our eyes. He dispatches some problems with such ease that they do not look like problems at all. Others he deals with in a manner that keeps the reader from noticing their existence. Yet it would not do to insinuate that Luke knows nothing beyond the arts of concealment and the generation of enigmas. When Luke wishes to deposit a clue that even the most inattentive and desultory reader will not miss, he knows how to do so. That is one literary function of the miracles in Acts. In 5:1-11, for example, we read that Peter's mere indictment of Ananias and Sapphira's financial chicanery causes them both to die, and only four verses later (5:15) his shadow is enough to cure the sick. The odd juxtaposition of events does nothing to detract from their meaning, but these examples recall another feature of Acts: the narrator prefers to tell the story by focusing upon the words and deeds of its leading characters.

This chapter will review a number of Luke's literary techniques, including characterization, narrative pace, repetition, reiterated repetition, the function of miracle stories, and parallel accounts. The popular character of these devices will be illustrated through examples from ancient novels. In terms of the general thesis of this book, it is apparent that these literary techniques detract from the historical value of Acts. Narrators may be artistic, but history is messy.

55

Colorful Elements of Lucan Characterization

No profound insight into the riches of psychology or the depths of ethical ambiguity is required to tell the good characters in Acts from the bad. The narrator comes equipped with a large supply of those black and white hats that are so useful for preventing confusion. This is not to deny that a bit of suspense is artfully employed, or even that there are some gray berets scattered throughout the plot, or that one color may be exchanged for the other. Saul makes his debut in a dark little cap that is traded in for a menacing sombrero of the inkiest hue within a few verses, but that item of gruesome headgear is in turn slated for early retirement. Likewise, Simon of Samaria first appears as the most blasphemous of creatures whose pretensions are overcome by the superior power of Philip. In the end, however, it turns out that Simon wanted no more than a taste of power, in return for which he was prepared to offer a reasonable consideration. Still, he is left dangling and unforgiven (8:9–24). Did Luke know more about Simon than he lets on? Historians wonder.

Some officials, among whom are the Roman governors Felix and Festus, give an initial impression of impartial integrity, but turn out to be greedy and weak (Acts 24–26). These exceptions liven a story in which the bad guys are very bad and the good guys very, very good. "Black" and "white" tip the hand. The characterization in Acts is, like much of the plot, melodramatic.

Narrative Pace

Popular narrative tends to move at a lively trot, and Luke needs no instruction in the techniques of rapid narration. Acts 9:1–30, in which Saul/Paul changes hats, is a good example. The first two verses suffice to describe how the infamous persecutor took his show on the road. In verses 3–9 he is overcome by a blinding light, learns that the one whom he has been persecuting belongs to the divine realm, is blinded, and finally led by the hand to Damascus, from which he had planned to drag shackled believers to Jerusalem. While he languishes without nourishment for three days, the Lord appears to one Ananias and importunes him to visit Paul. In the course of that dialogue the reader is informed of Paul's future mission and fate (9:10–16). Two and one-half verses later Paul has received healing and baptism.

By 9:20 the former persecutor has become a potent herald of the new faith, and by 9:23 he himself has become the target of persecution. After craftily eluding a dire plot, the convert heads for Jerusalem, where only Barnabas is willing to buy his story (9:23–27).

Thereafter he becomes an associate of the apostles, engages in disputes with the same group that had opposed Stephen (of whose murder Saul had approved, 8:1a), and becomes, like Stephen, the target of yet another attempt on his life. To elude it he departs for distant Tarsus (9:28–30). That is a lot of action compressed into little more than two Greek pages. In Acts, this is far from unusual.

Repetition

The conversion of Paul will serve another Lucan purpose, that of repetition. Luke evidently believed that anything really important warranted being told three times. The most famous of his "threepeats" is this very story, told in chapter 9 in the third person and repeated twice more by Paul in first-person form (chapters 22 and 26). The differences among these accounts pose a challenge to those who labor to demonstrate the strict historical accuracy of Acts. Three-fold iteration establishes this event as fundamental, and this is no surprise in a work devoted to showing the legitimacy of the Pauline enterprise. According to the *rule of three the final account should be climactic, and so it is. Through the several retellings Luke transforms this story of the punishment and conversion of an enemy into an account of the call of a prophet-philosopher. Repetition assures not only that readers will "get the point," but that they will "get it right."

Paul's experience is not the only conversion story that Luke relates on three occasions. The conversion of Cornelius (10:1–48; 11:1–18; 15:7–11) is another. Since Cornelius was the first explicitly gentile convert, this repetition will come as no surprise in a work devoted to showing the legitimacy of the gentile mission. The conversions of Paul and Cornelius share the same narrative outline: a believer (Ananias, Peter) reluctantly and at divine direction visits a candidate who has also received a vision, speaks to him, and then authorizes baptism. What took nine and one-half verses in the case of Paul occupies forty-eight verses in the story of Cornelius (Paul: 9:10–19a; Cornelius: 10:1–48). Luke, who can produce narration of machine-gun rapidity, also knows how to slow the narrative down. This is most apparent in Acts 20–26, which relates Paul's final journey to Jerusalem and his captivity there and in Caesarea. (Caesarea "Maritima" was the coastal capital of Roman Palestine.) The story of Cornelius also develops with considerable leisure. In this case the slow pace both increases suspense for readers who can anticipate (if they do not already know) the outcome and, more importantly, adds weight. One does not expect a competent narrator to devote about 5% of the entire story to a trivial matter.

Why does Luke utilize so much ink on the first account of Cornelius' conversion but deal with that of Paul so economically? It will not do to claim that Luke's source about Cornelius was much more detailed and that he used all of it, whereas the story about Paul was rather briefer. One must ask, then, whether the story of Cornelius was more important than that about Paul. To this question one may reasonably answer, "Yes, in some ways, but in other ways, no." The acceptance of gentiles was a decisive moment in salvation history. Paul was the principal agent in implementing this change. The story of the gentile mission will occupy most of Acts. The first convert, Cornelius, leaves the stage at the end of chapter 10 after appearing in one lengthy act. In investigating answers to this question of relative importance the interpreter kisses historical investigation goodbye, for this immediately becomes a literary and theological investigation that must focus upon what Luke wished to do and to say rather than upon "what actually happened." Here is an obvious but most important point: attempts to understand Acts lead again and again away from historical concerns toward identification of the author's object. Repetition of this fundamental observation will quickly become tedious. Once alerted to the issue, readers will be able to address it without constant prompting and develop interesting observations and interpretations of their own.

Cornelius' story, like Paul's, is recounted twice thereafter in speeches. The first comes immediately after the event, in 11:1–18, where Peter recounts the incident from his own point of view to an assembly in Jerusalem. The argument was persuasive. The third account was also delivered to an assembly in Jerusalem, one at which Paul himself was present, but is quite brief:

> After there had been much debate, Peter stood up and said to them, "My brothers, you know that in the early days God made a choice among you, that I should be the one through whom the Gentiles would hear the message of the good news and become believers. 8 And God, who knows the human heart, testified to them by giving them the Holy Spirit, just as he did to us; 9 and *in cleansing their hearts by faith* he has made no distinction between them and us. 10 Now therefore why are you putting God to the test by placing on the neck of the disciples a yoke that neither our ancestors nor we have been able to bear? 11 On the contrary, *we believe that we will be saved through the grace of the Lord Jesus, just as they will.*" (Acts 15:7–11, emphasis supplied)

Just as Paul's third account of his conversion was decisive, so here Peter gives the definitive interpretation of the events at Cornelius' home. In the two earlier renditions the basic issue was association with the unclean (chapter 10) and uncircumcised (chapter 11). Peter's statement in chapter 15 deals with the abolition of *Torah in general rather than with questions of purity. The Law is unbearable for Jews and gentiles alike. None can be saved except by faith through grace. This language is at the center of Pauline soteriology. (Soteriology is the area of theology that treats how people are saved, delivered from the powers of evil.) Peter appeals to the admission of Cornelius into the community, an action ratified by the spirit, as proof of what Paul taught—that is, the Pauline doctrine of justification by faith as Luke chose to understand it. Although Cornelius was characterized as a pious and moral individual who was therefore amenable to religious instruction, Acts 10:1–11:18 does not appeal to or even mention the power of faith. This new slant implies that the first gentile convert, won by Peter at divine behest, had entered the body of the faithful on the same grounds as had all those converted by Paul. This reinterpretation is no minor matter. The two well-known "threepeats," which treat the same subject in the same manner, suggest that the more Luke repeats something, the more it changes.

But these are not the only types of repetition in Acts. Another triplet involves Paul's three-fold repetition of his decision to turn to the gentiles (13:46; 18:6; 28:28), since "the Jews" have rejected the message. These announcements are distributed over three crucial geographical areas: "Asia," Greece, and Italy. Rome is, in every way, climactic. Those who know something about Paul the apostle to the gentiles may find this repetition troublesome. For Luke it is a schematic presentation of a basic thesis: Paul always went to the Jews first. In nearly every place this obligation had to be acted out concretely. A mission to the synagogue meets some success and more opposition, and Paul is left with no choice but to proclaim his message to gentiles. Another "threepeat" is the "Apostolic Decree," regulations that allow Jewish and gentile believers to engage in table-fellowship, that is, celebrate the eucharist together (15:20, 29; 21:25). These rules illustrated the distance between the faith favored by Luke and the stance of Paul's more radical followers, who would not have accepted such restrictions.

Luke makes his point by telling stories, stories that are simple, clear, and altogether innocent of subtlety: no sympathetic reader will fail to observe that Paul did everything in his power to bring the word to his own people. This technique also points to another Lucan predilection: a fondness for stereotyped episodes, for certain basic patterns repeated, with elegant variation, over and over. That practice will require additional attention, but readers will need to exercise some patience, for there is yet one more illustrative triplet to place upon the table.

Until they come to chapter 21 readers of Acts might reasonably conclude that prison is a good place for missionaries to visit, but not one in which they would choose to live. Although apostles are often tossed into the slammer, they are just as often sprung. On three occasions these releases seem wondrous to behold. In 5:19–20 an angel leads all twelve incarcerated apostles out of the prison in which they are awaiting trial and probable execution. Acts 12:6–12 describes in considerable detail an angel's rescue of Peter from impending execution. The third and most elaborate rescue benefits, among others, Paul (and Silas) at Philippi, 16:25–40. The religious significance of these deliverances is not unduly arcane. Ancients were familiar with stories about divinities who rescued their loyal followers from prison. These stories show which side God is on.

A Miraculous Digression

This is an appropriate point at which to introduce a principle from the history of religions: the nature of a god is displayed in the kind(s) of miracles the god works. Those in need of healing might turn to Asclepius, for example. Healing was something that he knew how to achieve and was most willing to perform. Liberation from bonds was associated with Dionysius, the "liberator." Through the gift of wine he delivered people from the tedium and monotony of daily life. Modern cant would say that Dionysius freed people from their hang-ups and repressions. Among those especially interested in such emancipation were women. Indeed, some forms of Dionysiac worship were "ladies only" events.

The fifth century BCE playwright Euripides tells the story of the Dionysiac mission to the famous city of Thebes in his play *The Bacchants (Bacchae)*. His priest led the local women into the wild, where they quite literally let down their hair and abandoned themselves to ecstatic and not altogether ladylike revels. Although this might come as a great shock, it transpired that the men of Thebes disapproved. Faced with the unpleasant challenges and duties of daycare and housework—not to mention fears of what their good wives might do in the company of satyrs and such—the men summoned the authorities, who promptly imprisoned the women and had them securely chained. In the middle of the night the god caused an earthquake that toppled the prison walls, caused the shackles to fall off, and released the devotees to return to the woods and resume their uninhibited worship. To find out what happened next you will have to read the drama.

Meanwhile, back in Philippi,

About midnight Paul and Silas were praying and singing hymns to God, and the prisoners were listening to them. Suddenly there was an earthquake, so violent that the foundations of the prison were shaken; and immediately all the doors were opened and everyone's chains were unfastened (Acts 16:25–26).

The similarity between this account and the tale told by Euripides strikes everyone who knows both stories. Yet, if anything is certain, it is that Paul was neither a worshipper of Dionysius nor was he rescued by that god. What is going on here? In the later Hellenistic and early Roman eras, from c. 200 BCE onward, the pressure of cosmopolitanism, a kind of early "globalization," motivated religious diversification. Just as contemporary shops once specializing in muffler replacement suddenly reappear as providers of a complete line of automobile services, or producers of colas begin to offer non-carbonated beverages, so some ancient gods responded to a competitive market by assuming functions once reserved to other deities. Gods who engaged in such diversification—most did not need or choose to participate—were likely to be angling for the status of universal and/or supreme god. The popular side of the intellectual affirmation of a single high god, "philosophical monotheism" as it is called, was the deity who could offer something approximating "one-stop shopping."[1]

The moment has arrived for another axiom of the history of religions: new gods stand in particular need of miracles. The Dionysiac myth utilized by Euripides is a good example. Dionysius was attempting to break into a new market. Older gods like Zeus had been around for a long time. Their existence and cults were well established and of proven value. A reflex of this view is the claim of Classical Evangelical theology—a view shared for some time by Augustine—that miracles belonged to the early age of Christianity, which required a spiritual jump-start to get going, after which gospel or church could more or less manage and grow without such introductory offers or flashy inducements. When a writer like Luke wished to show those of polytheist background that the god of the Christians was, indeed, "Lord of all" (cf. for example, Acts 10:36), it was appropriate to show that god as the source of a range of miracles from different elements of the traditional repertoire. "Our god can do it all!"

The first comparative religious axiom, that particular miracles show what kind of a god is performing them, requires additional comment. Early Christians were no less aware than are contemporary Westerners of the difficulty of individual healings and benefactions: Why did Jesus heal her and not me? Is it "fair" to cure some sick people and raise a few from the dead while leaving myriads mourning and in misery? The evangelists already understood these deeds as signs and symbols, indicators of what Jesus was all about. For an authority they could appeal to Jesus himself, who viewed his exorcisms as signs of the irruption of God's reign, as indicators of the defeat of evil (Luke 11:20). Only in the end would all devils be banished, every infirmity relieved, and each tear wiped away. For Luke, among others, the deeds of Jesus, Peter, and Paul showed that Satan had been defeated—not abolished, to be sure, but *defeated*, so that the devil no longer retained an irresistible grip upon humanity. Deliverance from prison was a potent symbol of deliverance from the bonds and shackles of wickedness and death. People patronize the gospel writers when they regard their miracle-stories as no more than crudely literal propaganda. The evangelists certainly believed that these events had "happened," but they also believed that their meaning extended far beyond the lives of those immediately affected. James the brother of John was among those liberated in Acts 5, but nevertheless he was murdered shortly thereafter (Acts 12:2), while Peter was rescued twice. Luke had more in mind than suggesting that James was expendable.

The first of these three stories of release from prison, Acts 5:19–20, is both the shortest and the least enduring. It could be removed from the narrative without any damage, since the apostles were promptly rearrested and brought into court no more than an hour or so after the originally scheduled time of the hearing. Actual deliverance came not from an angel but from Gamaliel, whose warning saved the day (5:34–40). The modern interpreter is therefore likely to conclude that the apostles were rescued by entirely human means and that the gratuitous story of their escape from prison is a bit of fiction that Luke would have been wise to delete.

Much the same can be said, and with even greater probability, of the story in Acts 16:25–40. Trouble had broken out in Philippi after Paul had exorcised a slave who had been turning a good profit for her owners by providing oracles, but had, without instructions or notice, suddenly become a prophet for the god proclaimed by Paul and Silas. Paul, who disdained such advertising, expelled the evil spirit. Her owners, chagrined by the loss of revenue, promptly arraigned the missionaries before the authorities on trumped-up charges. Beating and incarceration resulted (16:16–24). In response to these prisoners' prayers came the earthquake and removal of the fetters. Everyone knows what will come next: all of the imprisoned will head for the hills. But that does not happen. Paul's reassurance that they will not escape and thus incriminate the jailer leads to the conversion of the officer and his family. The next morning brings orders from the authorities that the two be released. Paul is a bit miffed by this whitewash of a false arrest and imprisonment, but in the end he and Silas are shown to the city border. Once more the rational reader will exclaim, "Aha! The miracle is meaningless. Paul was freed by normal and natural means. You could cut from verse 24 to verse 35 without difficulty."

So you could, but much would be lost. The miracle is far from meaningless. It not only affirms the power of prayer but also symbolically anticipates their coming liberation—and that of the jailer. Moreover, the scene exhibits Paul and Silas as good citizens, who, even in the face of rank injustice and police brutality, calmly await official justification. In the technical jargon of biblical exegesis this is known as "having your cake and eating it too." In the same vein one may add that this story has something for everyone. Nonetheless, the questions raised by the accounts in chapters 5 and 16 stand unanswered. The rationalist is still able to say: "Cut out the miracle and the true story will be found." Such criticism could learn from Sherlock Holmes' dictum that after every impossible element has been eliminated, the remnant, however improbable, is the truth. Rationalists do begin by excising the impossible, but this is not always helpful, especially in the matter of miracles. The strict modern definition of "miracle" identifies its subject as an event that violates the laws of nature. Our understanding of these laws comes from the eighteenth century, when they were formulated by such stalwart defenders of traditional religion as I. Newton and J. Kepler.

Ancients saw things differently. They began with the concept of epiphany, the manifestation of a god. Wine, for example, was a kind of epiphany of Dionysius and a needed rainfall was hailed as a gift from Zeus. To explicate this understanding they might tell a story, such as the transformation of water into wine. The miracle is a story (or myth) that celebrates what the god means. In the Hebrew Bible the first and chief miracle is *creation*. The deity celebrated is identified in Psalm 136:4–10: ". . . who alone does great wonders . . . who by understanding made the heavens . . . who spread out the earth on the waters . . . who made the great lights . . . the sun to rule over the day . . . the moon and stars to rule over the night . . . who struck Egypt through their firstborn. . . ." This hymn of praise moves seamlessly from creation (formation of the universe) into history (the Exodus). Luke shares this orientation. It is most apparent in Acts 14:8–18.

That story opens with Paul healing a cripple in Lystra, a town in what is now south-central Turkey. The locals spring to the conclusion that Paul and Barnabas are the gods Zeus and Hermes in human form. In an effort to avoid repeating a famous instance in which they had overlooked a visit by those very divinities (cf. Ovid, *Metamorphoses* 8.611–724; similar stories are numerous), the locals make haste to offer sacrifice to the gods in their midst. The missionaries attempt to thwart this effort with a sermon:

> Friends, why are you doing this? We are mortals just like you, and we bring you good news, that you should turn from these worthless things to the living God, who made the heaven and the earth and the sea and all that is in them. In past generations he allowed all the nations to follow their own ways; yet he has not left himself without a witness in doing good—giving you rains from heaven and fruitful seasons, and filling you with food and your hearts with joy. (Acts 14:15–17)

The argument is clear enough: God, the creator of all, has left evidence of his existence in the gifts of nature. This is called "natural theology," an expression needing no explanation. The argument is clear, but to us it makes no sense. What does the claim that God is both responsible for and discoverable within creation have to do with healing a cripple and demonstrating that Paul and Barnabas are not Zeus and Hermes wearing different hats? It does make sense, however, if creation is viewed as the chief miracle and this healing a reminder of that fact. Luke does not set "miracle" against "nature." They belong to a continuum.

"Fine," the reader may say at this point. "That resolves an interesting mystery, but what does it have to do with prison miracles?" Good question. In answer Luke would say, "Your definition of miracle is too small." Acts views the entire working of divine Providence, from seasonal regularity at the macro level to the intervention of Gamaliel (5:34–40) at the micro level, as miraculous. Miracle is what God does. It is almost impossible to understand the book of Acts if one does not grasp this equation. For the narrator of Acts, Gamaliel's surprising last-minute intervention was no less a "miracle" than was the angelic intervention of the previous evening. Both in Acts 5 and in Acts 16 the "supernatural" events are, as in chapter 14, clues toward the recognition of the divine hand behind the deliverance of the several characters.

Repetition, Again

The foregoing survey of some triplets in Acts has taken lengthy detours to provide "background" material by exploiting the immediate and ostensible subject. This was intentional, based upon the presumption that such questions are better addressed in the context of specific instances rather than as abstract paragraphs in a chapter devoted to "Lucan theology" or the like. The exposition may now return to its course. Luke uses repetition, as any would expect, for emphasis. If you say it three times, they will get the point. Repetition also serves plot development. There is a tendency for the third occurrence to be a climax. Mere repetition will do, especially when continuity is important, as in the three-fold declaration by Paul that he is turning to the gentiles. Most of the repetitions exhibit variation. This may be artistic, as in the prison escapes, but it can, and often does, result in a new interpretation. Paul's conversion becomes, by the third occurrence, a prophetic call, and the acceptance of Cornelius serves to illustrate a key Pauline doctrine when Peter summarizes its meaning for the final time in Acts 15.

Like many authors, Luke tends to provide a full description in the first instance and a brief summary thereafter. Acts 3:1–8/9 tells how Peter (and John) healed a cripple. 5:12–16 is a summary of numerous healings and exorcisms. Two principles are operative. Summaries assure the reader that what has been related in full detail is but one example of many such incidents. Those who wish to do so may fill in the details for themselves.

Had Luke given full accounts of fifteen or fifty healings, each of which would naturally be quite similar, the effect would be stifling. All authors know this. Who would want to read a mystery that gave a verbatim transcript of every fruitless interview conducted by the detective? Authors will be more likely to say something like, "Other than Mrs. Jones, none of the neighbors had seen or heard anything of interest" or "I had rung every doorbell without learning anything, until I came to the last house on the block . . ." In recounting prison deliverances, on the other hand, Acts reverses things. The first account is extremely short. Not until chapter 12 does the reader have opportunity to savor every detail of angelic rescue. Formulas are important in narrative, but narrators will do well to vary their content and order and slip in an occasional surprise. Luke employs that sort of narrator, a fact that historical criticism, with its passion for order, regularity, and consistency, can too readily overlook. Such lapses are evident in the arguments of both those who defend the historical accuracy of Acts and those would demonstrate the opposite. Literary criticism is essential to a coherent understanding of Acts.

The prison escapes introduce another function of repetition in Acts. These stories have different leading characters, notably Peter in 12 and Paul in 16, as well as the entire body of apostles in chapter 5. The effect of this repetition is patent. These stories show, rather than assert, continuity and "equality" between Peter and Paul. What Peter experienced Paul also underwent. Paul therefore belongs on the same level as Peter, for these preeminent and representative missionaries suffered similar misfortunes and enjoyed the same kinds of divine favor. Their stories also portray continuity, in particular continuity between the chief exponents of the Christian mission. Luke often prefers "showing," especially through narration, to "telling."

Literary criticism has tended to prefer "showing" to "telling." An example of the latter is "Sebastian was a scumbag." The narrator "tells" the reader about characters and events, issuing judgments and blocking alternatives. Readers will expect nothing good from Sebastian. "Showing" works by description and evocation: "Sebastian arose one fine morning, threw on, without washing, the clothes worn yesterday, and proceeded to slip into the room of his crippled grandmother, from whose purse he removed ten dollars. After eating the breakfast prepared for his younger brother, he left in quest of heroin." Readers will draw their own conclusions about Sebastian's character. Like most writers, Luke uses both methods, but he favors "showing." He never says, for example, "Now Paul was every bit as good as Peter" (or vice-versa). He shows this by narrating their respective stories. Luke is especially fond of corresponding incidents, outlines, and adventures. This fondness has long been noticed. It is called "Parallelism."

Parallels

Parallelism of various sorts can be seen within the Gospel of Luke, within Acts, and between Luke and Acts. Critics have adduced abundant parallels, and although these are not of equal weight, the existence of so vast a quantity cannot be denied or attributed to accident. Oscar Wilde said, "History does not repeat itself. Historians do." One facet of this useful half-truth is that it underscores the uniqueness of every historical event. Another is its venomous reminder that historians attempt to extract meaning from the past by noting analogies, identifying recurrences, adducing kindred circumstances, and forcing patterns upon events that quite possibly lack them. In so doing they commit no crime. Data have no meaning without organization, and organization demands some criteria. A history of red-haired monarchs, for instance, would strike most as a bit odd, but, were it written, we should expect the writer to produce some kind of a thesis, such as that red-haired monarchs have tended to bring prosperity, or its opposite.

Chronology is a case in point. By itself chronology is a very useful device. The absence of a fixed system makes reckoning difficult, as Luke 3:1–2 indicates. (See Chapter Seven.) An accidental result of the current calendar system is that people seek to find meaning in centuries and even decades. Rare is the movement that began 1 January 1901 and expired 31 December 2000, but this does not stop attempts to squeeze history into forms determined by a decimal system. (The dubious are invited to reflect upon the phenomena that attended the advent of the year 2000.) The pertinent question to put to the author of Acts in this regard is whether his quest for nice parallels is a case of an historian who may repeat himself a touch too often or whether his fondness for parallelism is quite corrosive to history. The latter seems rather more likely, but readers will have to judge for themselves.

One place to begin is where the last section left off. Acts 14:8–11a records the healing of a cripple by Paul, accompanied by Barnabas, at Lystra, in the proximity of a temple. In 3:1–8/9 Peter, accompanied by John, heals a cripple in the vicinity of the temple at Jerusalem. The two accounts are similar in form and content, and they display a number of close verbal similarities. Commentators do not neglect to point out the resemblances, together with a conclusion. Just as Peter healed a cripple following the inaugural sermon of Acts 2, so Paul heals a cripple following his first sermon (Acts 13). For more than a few critics such nicety is too good to be true. There is more. Healing stories are grist for the form-critical mill. These two accounts are *prima facie* candidates for inclusion in a folder reserved for older traditions utilized in Acts. (Traditions, please recall, are not necessarily historically "true," but they do come from a source.) If there were but one healing story like this, that view would go largely unchallenged. The presence of two is a problem. It is reasonable to hypothesize that Luke composed one of them to provide a parallel to the other, and the more common hypothesis is that the story about Paul is modeled upon that featuring Peter. Still, if Luke could invent one story, he might also invent two, basing the story of the Jerusalem cripple upon an account of a healing by Jesus. The presence of these two stories casts the shadow of suspicion upon both. Suspicion is not conviction, but, once it has entered the room, it is difficult to expel.

An illustration of a different sort emerges in the parallels between the trials of Jesus in Luke and the trials of Paul in Acts. In Luke 22–23 Jesus appears before the Sanhedrin, Pilate, Herod and Pilate. In Acts 23–26 Paul appears before the Sanhedrin, Felix, Festus, and Agrippa. Each has four legal hearings. These include one before the Sanhedrin, the presumed Jewish governing body, two by a Roman governor, and one featuring a member of the Herodian family. That is not all. There are many detailed correspondences in theme and vocabulary. Each of the accused is the beneficiary of three (!) declarations by a Roman official that he is innocent, while raging Jewish mobs demand the execution of both. (See Chapter Six, **Table 6.1.**)

The arch of this parallelism is not within Acts but between Luke and Acts. The major source of the Gospel of Luke is Mark. Mark does not relate four trials of Jesus. In this case it is therefore arguable that Acts has influenced Luke, that the author could have possessed data about four trials of Paul and adjusted the Gospel narrative to conform. Since Acts was written after Luke (see p. 9) this solution is unlikely, although it remains possible. In any case, the existence of these duplicate patterns has a certain dampening effect upon claims of historical accuracy. The most important result of identifying these parallels in the trials of Jesus and Paul is that the parallelism is not between Peter and Paul but between *Jesus* and *Paul*. Many, not least those of Protestant Christian background, will applaud when the apostle to the gentiles is jacked up to the same level as the Prince of the Apostles, but comparison of Paul to Jesus seems to be entering upon risky ground.

Before venturing onto such ground, one must attend to some other details and concerns. Although there is no need here to enumerate and evaluate all of the proposed parallels within Acts, it is desirable to mention a few more in order to illustrate the extent and range of this device. In addition to the prison escapes already discussed, one may note that both Peter and Paul, each with a companion, confront a practitioner of exploitative religion ("magic"): Acts 8:9–24; 13:6–12. Both raise a believer from the dead (Acts 9:36–43; 20:7–12). Each must fend off an attempt at divine honors (Acts 10:25–26; 14:13–15). In 8:14–17 Peter bestows the Spirit by the imposition of hands; Paul does this in 19:1–6. And this chapter has already called attention to the role of speeches as parallel and repetitive phenomena (Acts 22 and 26; 11 and 15).

Similarities among the various speeches help pull Acts together and give it a unity of theme and thought. The most striking orations are the inaugural addresses of Peter (2:14–37) and Paul (Acts 13:16–41), already noted. These two sermons display numerous instances of overlap. Each also preaches to a polytheist audience, although the circumstances are different (Peter: Acts 10:34–43; Paul: 17:22–31). Peter and Paul proclaim the same message. Investigation will reveal further links between the sermon of Paul in Acts 13 and that of Stephen (Acts 7), as well as affinities with the inaugural sermon of Jesus in Luke 4:16–30 and its narrative setting.

This examination, partly in detail and partly in summary, is sufficient to demonstrate that the careers of Peter and Paul follow similar paths and that each can do the sorts of things that Jesus did, as well as arousing similar opposition. The idea of "parallel lives" is not unique to Luke. Around the time that he was writing, Plutarch, the most famous of ancient biographers, also issued a series of "parallel lives." These compared famous figures from Greek and Roman history, such as the orators Demosthenes and Cicero and the great conquerors and founders Alexander and Caesar. In one sense there is something similar in these respective products. Like Luke who wished to show that Paul was the equal of Peter, Plutarch probably wanted to note that there had been a famous Greek or two in the past, some of whom may have made contributions comparable to those of the more recent Romans. Conversely, he may have wished to remind his fellow Greeks that the Romans had produced great men.

Otherwise there is no real comparison, as it were. Plutarch does not go out of his way to make the pairs in this series identical. His subjects do not lose so much of their particularity as do Luke's. Alexander crosses the Euphrates but not the Rubicon. Plutarch also comments upon similarities and differences between his characters. Luke's project called for homogeneity rather than for particularity, for similarity rather than distinctiveness, for implicit comparison rather than for authorial comment. His "great men" face the same problems in similar if not identical ways, and say very much the same thing. It is quite difficult to resist the conclusion that Luke sacrificed the integrity of such historical records as he had to the stronger demands of his literary plan. Like all good detectives, Luke does not view coincidence as accidental. Readers were not expected simply to note and appreciate his many parallels and deduce from them conclusions about such individuals as Peter and Paul. The very existence and number of these remarkable similarities deals a strong blow to the quality of Acts as history. In "real life" things do not work out quite so neatly time after time after time.

Novel Harmony

When dealing with literature, critics tend to explain such coincidences by reference to omnipotent narrators, who can make things happen as they will. Everyone knows that truth can be stranger than fiction, but not all appreciate that this is precisely why people often prefer fiction. Those who seek literary parallels to Acts will do well to examine later epics, such as Vergil's *Aeneid*, with its "fearful symmetry," but there are also less elevated examples closer to hand in the romantic novels of the Hellenistic and, especially, the Roman eras. If nothing else, these works show what attracted readers of that day—both those of limited education and the elite in their less exalted moments. An essential feature of "popular" or consumer-oriented literature is that it provides the public with what it wants, rather than what its betters believe it ought to be reading for its cultural and moral elevation.[2] The time has come to shift—briefly, mind you—from mystery to romance.

Only five Greek romantic novels survive in full, although there are fragments of others. The majority of these novels were written within a hundred years of Acts, most during the second century. To illustrate the genre authorities often turn to *An Ephesian Tale*, which is anonymous but has come down to us under the name of one Xenophon of Ephesus. This novel is quite short, so short that critics often suspect that at least some parts of it have been abbreviated. At first reading it appears to lack any sophistication or subtlety of plot, style, theme, or characterization. *An Ephesian Tale* is the story of Anthia (girl) and Habrocomes (boy), teenagers with clueless parents cast against the cruel wiles of a heartless world. Both hero and heroine are very young and quite inexperienced, deeply in love, and equally subject to the slings and arrows of outrageous fortune. Soon separated, they, like most of their compatriots in the romantic novels of the day, undergo adventures that propel them hither and thither about the Mediterranean world. The map of their adventures will call to mind those charts derived from Acts that depict the missionary travels of the Apostle Paul.

Among the surface narrative devices and techniques utilized by this "Xenophon" and other novelists are the very ones that have been identified in Acts: duplications and parallelism. One narrative technique quite congenial to such stories is called "interlacement," the shift of focus from one person or place to another and then back. (Interlacement underlies the kind of plot in which the wicked villain, suitably garbed in black hat and cloak, has just finished securing the innocent maiden to the railroad tracks as the speeding train appears on the horizon, at which point the narrator intervenes to announce, "Meanwhile, back at the ranch. . . .") This simple back and forth rotation creates retardation of the plot, which brings suspense, for those reading about what happened at the ranch are unlikely to have forgotten about the screaming girl on the tracks.

The thrust of Luke's plot requires that much of the first part of Acts concentrate upon Peter and Jerusalem, while the second follows Paul "to the ends of the earth," but within these limits he makes effective use of interlacement. Acts 8:1 and 4 state that all except the apostles were put to flight because of the persecution following the murder of Stephen. In 8:5 the narrator turns his attention to Philip. Not until 11:19 does the narrator return to the activities of other refugees. Acts 18:19 reports the arrival of Paul in Ephesus, his most important missionary center. To the reader's surprise, he promptly leaves to engage in a pilgrimage to Jerusalem, followed by a leisurely land journey across Asia. Since no ancient reader would suppose that this journey had consumed less than several months, those waiting for Paul to return to Ephesus and go into action would have felt more than a little strain in this delay.

Retardation is at its strongest in two related parts of the plot. The over-arching component is Paul's voyage to Rome. He announces his plans in 19:21: ". . . Paul resolved in the Spirit to go through Macedonia and Achaia, and then to go on to Jerusalem. He said, 'After I have gone there, I must also see Rome.'" Nearly one third of Acts will elapse before he reaches that goal in 28:14. Enclosed within this interval is the trip to Jerusalem. Luke, who had devoted less than a verse to Paul's last visit to Jerusalem and propelled him to Antioch in the same verse (18:22), then whisked him across Asia with five words (19:1b), utilized fifty-five verses to narrate the last journey to Jerusalem (20:1–21:17). For the voyage to Rome no fewer than fifty-eight verses would do (27:1–28:14). The parallel with the Gospel is instructive. Luke 9:51 announces the beginning of Jesus' journey to Jerusalem. He reaches his destination at 19:45. That is a long delay, but the reader feels no pressing suspense, for the trip is without adventure, so much so that the narrator must periodically remind the reader of both the fact of the journey and of its goal (13:22; 17:11; 18:31; 19:38).[3] The journey of Jesus in Luke is filled with teaching;

Table 4.1: Interlacement

Acts	An Ephesian Tale
6:8–8:60. Stephen, a "Hellenist"	2.3–8. Habrocomes
(7:58) 8:1, 3. Paul	2.9–11. Anthia
8:4. Some "Hellenists"	2.12. Habrocomes
8:5–12. Philip	2.13. Anthia
8:14–25. Peter	2.14–3.3. Habrocomes
8:26–40. Philip	3.11. Anthia
9:1–30. Paul	. . . etc.
9:32–11:18. Peter	
11:19–30. Some "Hellenists," Barnabas, Paul	
12:1–17. Peter	
13:1–14:31. Paul and Barnabas	

Paul's journeys in Acts are replete with gripping incidents. **Table 4.1** compares Luke's intermittent use of interlacement with the generally consistent alternation of *An Ephesian Tale*.

Table 4.2 and **Table 4.3** illustrate Xenophon's predilection for repeated incidents and for parallel experiences involving his two leading characters. Those who consult *An Ephesian Tale* may object that some of these parallels are a bit strained. In 2.13, for example, Anthia is to be sacrificed to Ares, a procedure that featured being run through with javelins while hanging from a tree. Although the essence of crucifixion is hanging the condemned upon a tree (cf. Acts 5:30), this looks more like target practice. In 4.6 she is incarcerated in a pit (with two large dogs) rather than in a conventional jail. These objections do not obviate the parallels. They rather show how important they were to the author, who was willing to go to considerable lengths to have his characters enjoy—surely an inept verb—similar experiences. Identical parallelisms are boring.

Table 4.2: Duplications in *An Ephesian Tale*

Pirates or Bandits	1.13; 2.11; 3.8; 4.4
Rescue by the divine Nile/Isis	3.11; 4.2; 4.3 (cf. 5.15)
Rival Lovers	1.5; 2.3; 2.11; 2.13; 3.11, et al.

Table 4.3: Parallelism in *An Ephesian Tale*

Event	Anthia	Habrocomes
Crucifixion	2.13	4.2
Shipwreck	2.11	3.12
Incarceration	4.6	4.2–3

Note: To avoid duplication in *this* book, two of the items in **Table 4.2** that could be included in **4.3**, rivals and bandits, are omitted. Neither list is complete. They are illustrative rather than exhaustive.

One test of authorial ingenuity, therefore, was to make these parallels recognizably similar but not *too* similar. Those who are alert to the game will respond to Peter's encounter with Simon (8:9–24) in part by asking, "Now how is he going to match this in the story of Paul?" Acts 13:6–12 supplies the answer. Conversely, after reading about Paul's handling of Elymas/Bar-Jesus in 13:6–12, the reader who is not in on the game will say: "Aha! Peter also cursed a nasty oaf who practiced magic!" In both Acts and *An Ephesian Tale* the use of parallels bears a message. That of Acts has received some attention. A key point in *An Ephesian Tale* is that both lovers undergo the same types of ordeals. Anthia does not languish at home waiting for her lover to return from war or quest, nor does she passively await rescue. They are in this together. Note also that except for bandits, the adventures and experiences are of kindred types.

This excursion into the realm of the romantic novel has attempted to support the thesis that the recurrence of similar episodes in Acts does not strengthen the case for viewing it as a valid chronicle. Rather, the devices of duplication and parallelism, as well as the technique of interlacement, have a corrosive effect upon the reading of Acts as pure history. The narrative exhibits some artistic elements that were dictated by literary and theological concerns rather than by the probable sequence of historical facts. The parallels from Pseudo-Xenophon do not, of course, prove that Acts is a novel. They do, however, suggest that Luke made use of methods also employed by the authors of popular fiction and that people who enjoyed *An Ephesian Tale* might also find some things to enjoy in Acts. It would not be unreasonable to suggest that these two books were written with similar audiences in mind.

Having delved into this matter and consulted some of the literature to see if there were similar cases, it is now time to turn to more detailed examination of some larger components of the plot structure.

Resources and Further Reading

A general and accessible study of the use of parallel incident and structure in Luke and Acts is Charles H. Talbert, *Literary Patterns, Theological Themes, and the Genre of Luke-Acts.* SBLMS 20. Missoula, MT.: Scholars Press, 1974.

A valuable discussion of the subject is Susan M. Praeder, "Jesus-Paul, Peter-Paul, and Jesus-Peter Parallelisms," *Society of Biblical Literature Seminar Papers* 1984, ed. K. H. Richards. Chico, CA: Scholars Press, 1984, 23–39.

For a one-volume translation of *An Ephesian Tale* and other ancient Greek novels see Brian P. Reardon, ed., *Collected Ancient Greek Novels.* Berkeley: University of California, 1989.

Endnotes

1. Greco-Roman polytheism nonetheless remained a market of almost innumerable boutiques, managed by local and single-function proprietors.

2. An analogy: From roughly the mid-1950s onward, the three major networks developed nightly news programs. These featured what the network news chiefs believed people ought to know, with a concentration upon world and national events. (Local newscasts included sports and weather with local news and some features.) Cable television and the Internet vastly expanded the horizon. People could view such news as they chose. Large numbers have elected sources that agree with their viewpoint (for example, the Blogosphere), but an even larger number prefer entertainment, gossip about celebrities, and much that the old network news program would have viewed as trivia. News is no longer determined by our "betters." Similarly, one hears people talk about books they once read because they were required in school. Freed of that burden, they choose popular literature, if they read at all.

3. Although the "Passion Predictions" (Luke 9:43b–45; 18:31–34) provide foreboding, they do not create much suspense because they are quite explicit about what will befall Jesus in Jerusalem.

Chapter Five

How Acts Tells Its Story II

Cycles, Stereotyped Scenes,
Mimesis

This chapter continues the examination of some Lucan literary techniques by exposing his tendency to compose narrative cycles building toward a climax, the use of stereotypes or "cookie-cutters" for composing scenes, and the ancient (but by no means exclusively ancient) propensity for imitating the style and content of "classic" writings. These techniques are no less literarily useful than those described in the previous chapter, and scarcely more conducive to inspiring confidence in the historical accuracy of the book.

Defining the motive force of the plot of Acts requires but a single word: opposition. For those who prefer entire sentences the following two will do: Missionary activity achieves success, which leads to opposition, frequently including persecution. In response the mission changes direction, either to a different place or to a different audience, leading to still greater success. Even J. S. Bach would have been hard pressed to produce as many variations upon so simple a theme as did Luke. He works these variations upon a theme that characterizes a variety of ancient writings about the expansion or foundation of a religion:

1. Missionaries of a new god or movement appear on the scene.
2. Their message is well received, often among the more marginal, such as women, foreigners, slaves, or other "outsiders."
3. The powers that be become jealous of this success, sparking opposition.

4. Said opposition takes the form of persecution and punishment, including arrests, beatings, executions, other legal actions, riots, and lynchings.
5. The movement is vindicated by what believers regard as a miracle.
6. The opponents are defeated, punished in their turn, and may, in the end, join the movement.

This outline does not imply a rigid scheme. The order may vary, and not all of the elements appear on every occasion; this is a list of typical features rather than necessary components of a fixed sequence. Chapters 3–28 (less chapter 15) pulse to the beat of missionary success, opposition, and vindication. Persecution drives the plot. Luke sets up this pattern in Acts 3–7, working variations upon the following pattern:

1. A miracle, which draws attention and a crowd
2. Teaching addressed to those so attracted
3. The arrest of the missionary by jealous Jewish officials
4. A subsequent trial of the missionary
5. Miraculous vindication of the mission

Table 5.1 illustrates the use of this pattern in three narrative cycles.

Other important elements complement these cycles. As well as notes on numerical growth at 2:47, 4:4, 5:13–14, and 6:8, Luke includes material about the life of the community in 2:42–46, 4:32–5:11, and 6:1–7. By interlacing comments about quantitative and qualitative growth Luke shows how ineffective the opposition was. Indeed, opposition is the agent of growth, an idea eventually immortalized by *Tertullian's famous dictum: "The more you mow us down, the more we spring up; Christian blood is seed" (*Apology* 50.13). Although his scheme is so simple that it verges upon the primitive, Luke has so effectively varied it in length, arrangement, and characters that readers find it anything but monotonous. Through the use of crescendo Luke turns these episodes into a three-act drama. Each section recounts the increasing violence of the frustrated officials, who first warn, then whip, and finally murder. Through each cycle the circle widens, from two apostles, to all twelve, and ultimately netting the "Hellenists." Cycle 1 describes an orderly trial following a night of detention. Cycle 2 does the same, but adds a thrilling escape. Death was threatened there—indeed, the extinction of the apostolic body—until Gamaliel intervened. The narrator has put the fear of death into his readers.

Table 5.1: Patterns in Acts 3–7

Cycle 1 Peter and John	Cycle 2 All the Apostles	Cycle 3 Stephen
A. 3:1–11. Healing of cripple at Temple gate. A crowd gathers. B. 3:12–26. Missionary address by Peter. C. 4:1–3. Chief of temple police and Sadducees interrupt the speech to arrest the alleged miscreants, who are brought to D. 4:5–21. Trial. Accusation of magical practice. Disciples act like philosophers. E. 4:21–31. Pair released with a warning. A God-sent earthquake affirms their cause.	A. 5:12–16. Miracles reported in summary form. B_1. 5:12b. The apostles teach in the temple, like philosophers. C_1. 5:17–18. The High priest and the Sadducees arrest them. But E1. 5:19–20. An angel engineers a Miraculous release, leading to B_2. 5:21a. Continued teaching. Meanwhile, back in the courtroom, D1. 5:21–25. The Trial aborts for lack of accused. This is presently remedied by C2. 5:26–27a. The re-arrest of the accused, so that D2. 5:27b-39. The trial resumes. The threat of death is forestalled by Gamaliel's appeal to leave the matter in God's hands. In a compromise that leaves no doubt about the Deity's stance, E2. 5:40–41. The twelve are whipped, then released; they return to teaching. Gamaliel has saved the day.	A. 6:8. He works Miracles (summary) B. 6:9–10. Stephen Teaches (summary—for content of his teaching see 7:2–53). This leads to his C. 6:11–12. Arrest and arraignment before the Sanhedrin. D. 6:13–7:57 is a full-length report of the Trial. E. 6:15; 7:55–56, 59–60. Vindication marked by signs of divine approval and heavenly recompense.

The smooth order of Cycle 1 and the confused order and thwarted plan of Cycle 2 give way to unmitigated rage in the final cycle, where there is no juridical deliberation and not even the pretense of due process. Stephen, hauled in off the street to face a Sanhedrin already seated and thirsting for blood, has the opportunity to deliver the longest speech of the book, a defense that amounts to more than plot retardation, since his audience responds not by throwing rotten fruit but lethal missiles. To justify this lynching the authorities had to resort to the concocted evidence of shameless perjurers.

As the church gains followers and exhibits a wondrous form of communal life, officialdom descends from the bumbling issuance of hapless threats into the dark pit of tyrannous insanity. While the community lives out an ideal of the philosophers (as well as the Hebrew Bible, 4:32–35), and its leaders teach like philosophers (5:12), the Jewish leaders shed every last vestige of authenticity. Five times followers of Jesus blame the authorities for the death of Jesus. Although the ruling forces do not wish to accept that blame (5:28), they confirm it through their wish to kill the twelve (5:33), a wish finally fulfilled in the case of Stephen.

The narrator includes one of nearly everything within this cycle: one exemplary healing (3:1–8), one punitive miracle (5:1–11), a transfiguration (6:15), and a gripping epiphany (4:31). There is one missionary address (3:12–26), one judicial debate (4:5–21), and a single full-length defense speech (7:2–53). This is quite a recipe, and the dough does rise in the form of community growth, violence, and suspense. From a few scraps of tradition, possibly including the healing in 3:1–8, and more possibly a brief notice about the death of Stephen, Luke has created a marvel of his own. The quantity of history in Acts 3–7 will satisfy only those who can survive on a very thin diet of the same: the followers of Jesus continued the movement and faced resistance; their group included some who spoke Greek, one of whose leaders was executed. The climax of this cycle of cycles is the martyrdom, not of Peter, James, or John, but of Stephen. At the point of his death the narrator introduces a new character: Saul. Luke has arranged this material so that it culminates in a small circle of the faithful and the person chosen to carry out the gentile mission. Luke does utilize cycles, but his plot is far from cyclic.

Following this sequence comes Peter's work outside the traditional bounds of "orthodox Judaism." His labors opened with the confrontation of a "magician" and climaxed in the conversion of a gentile (8:4–10:48). Paul's work beyond the community in Antioch began with his defeat of a "magician" and climaxed in the conversion of gentiles (13:6–49). After Acts 5, however, Peter experiences no opposition to his mission. Hostile Jews or alarmed polytheists do not seek to disrupt his work in Samaria or in the coastal cities. The same may be said of Philip, who worked in the same regions. All opposition in Palestine is based in Jerusalem. In so far as Acts reports, only Saul/Paul attempted to export persecution (9:1–2). After the death of Stephen persecution in Acts is, chapter 12 excepted, a "Pauline privilege," as it were.

Some examples will suffice to illustrate the pattern. The success of Paul's message in Pisidian Antioch among gentiles motivates some Jews to engage in political intrigue that leads to their expulsion. The missionaries move on to Iconium (14:50–52). There both Jews and Greeks respond to the message, but unresponsive Jews engage in political intrigue that eventuates in an attempt to stone the missionaries, who set their course for Lystra (and Derbe, 14:1–7). An unduly successful healing in Lystra leads to a fearful climax when Jews from both Antioch and Iconium irrupt onto the scene and stir up the mob to stone Paul (14:8–19). Then there was Philippi where polytheists started the trouble, and Thessalonica where hostile Jews once more took the lead, promptly followed by a fracas in Berea where Jewish instigators from Thessalonica showed up to make trouble, propelling the missionary onward to Athens.

In the capital of Greek culture Paul could enjoy a break of sorts, but he did not escape a trial by the world's most famous court. No judgment issued from that hearing, but Paul did return to the road, moving on to Corinth, where he remained for an unusually long stay that culminated in an unsuccessful effort by his Jewish antagonists to arraign him before the Roman governor. In Ephesus Paul once more separated from the synagogue. His stupendous success eventually precipitated a massive outbreak of urban disorder, in which the missionary had no personal involvement (Acts 16–19). These stories are all different, but each follows the same plot line. If the thesis that opposition drives the plot of Acts has not yet been accepted, no amount of additional argument will suffice.

The scheme looks artificial. No reasonable person doubts that Paul had his full ration of problems, but those which his letters detail are problems *within* the community, whereas Acts devotes page after page to issues aroused by opposition from outside. At this point it is appropriate to unveil an important but obscure psychological principle: everyone would prefer that his or her problems be caused by others. One element of maturation, however, is the sad realization that most of our problems stem from our own behavior. With regard to groups, the view that all of their problems are due to the enmity and actions of others is a typical characteristic of minorities (or those with a minority self-understanding). In the sociology of religion, unfortunately, the attribution of difficulty to external forces is an habitual characteristic of sects. Nascent Christianity was thoroughly sectarian, and it is not surprising that Luke would take this view of the source of difficulties.

Those who seek to reconstruct church history should, however, scrutinize such claims with acute care. Not all opposition comes from blind prejudice. The adolescent boy who comes home drunk at 4:00 AM after wrecking the family car and is subsequently grounded may feel that he is being persecuted without warrant, but this is not the only possible interpretation of the situation. The same conflict of interpretations applies to writings like Acts, which contends that Paul was harried from place to place in the Mediterranean world by enemies who were usually envious Jews or their dupes. Luke's narrative implies, "Yes, we are persecuted, but the sorts of people who harass us and the methods they employ prove that we are right. People with enemies like ours deserve to be your friends. Moreover, God's view of this situation becomes apparent when you understand that persecution not only failed to quash the message but actually contributed to its continual expansion."

The artificiality of this scheme is apparent in the conclusion to the "first journey" in Acts 13–14. After being successively driven out of Antioch, Iconium, and Lystra, Paul and Barnabas swing back through that circuit in 14:21–23, visiting each community in turn without the slightest indication of any opposition, without the emergence of a single diligent soul who cries out, "Omygods, they're *back!*" and summons the populace to swing into action. The narrator of Acts has a reservoir of persecution that can be turned on and off at will. This is a useful instrument, and some might envy Luke's possession of it, but the use thereof does not enhance the estimate of Acts as a historical record. The summary of 14:21–23 just cited is a convenient introduction to another technique. As Acts recognizes, Paul and/or his colleagues visited many sites on more than one occasion, but the narrative nearly always concentrates all of the action into a single visit, normally the first, touching upon others in highly terse summaries.

Corinth is an apt illustration of this "pooling" technique. From the Pauline correspondence it is apparent that Paul the apostle made a number of visits to Corinth. Luke mentions two, the second in a summary (20:2), while all of the detail appears in 18:1–18. That passage is not without gaps and confusions. For example, the living arrangements are difficult to unravel. In 18:1–4 Paul lives and works with Aquila and Prisca, then shifts to the residence of Titius Justus at verse 7, for reasons that are not clear. One might wonder whether he broke with the couple, but when Paul left for Syria, he traveled with Priscilla and Aquila (Acts 18:18). In verse 17 one Sosthenes is identified as the head of the synagogue. Readers might presume that he had replaced Crispus, who had become a convert, but the narrator does not say so. It is possible that Luke had different sources about Corinth (including 1 Corinthians) and combined them all into this one report. The tradition is patchy and quite possibly not unified.

This practice of concentrating detailed narrative about a particular site is not difficult to observe, but, as John C. Hurd noted nearly forty years ago, most of those who attempt to construct a history of Paul's missionary activities pay limited attention to this phenomenon. The strong consensus of the critical tradition is to date Paul's founding visit to Corinth during the governorship of Gallio—a date that is known from an external source—without considering whether Acts 18 might have fused more than one visit. Another aspect of this cornerstone of Pauline chronology deserves a moment's notice. The edifice in which this cornerstone is located (Acts 18:12–17) is a legend. Legends always communicate some truth, but that truth does not always take the form of simple facts.

A conventional practice involves probing for the "historical kernel" of a legend. In this case that kernel would be some sort of encounter between Gallio and Paul, while the narrative itself is a disposable husk. This interpretation may be valid, but it is worth remembering that legends do prefer to feature prominent and suitable people. The declaration, "Father, I cannot tell a lie" is not, after all, venerated as an utterance of the youthful Richard Nixon. Proper modesty would direct the historian to conclude that, presuming that Paul was brought before the Proconsul Gallio, he would have been in Corinth in 51/52, although that incident may not have occurred during his initial visit.

In sum, Luke's literary methods are in strong tension with the requirements of history. His use of stereotyped scenes, preference for dramatic development, routine assignment of all incidents to a single visit, and his tendency to blame all problems upon Jews or socially undesirable types do not inspire confidence. This does not mean that everything he says is erroneous, but that much of what he says has been squeezed into his formulas, packed into a single envelope, or selected on the grounds that it suits his purposes; and therefore that considerable caution is advised. This survey of Lucan methods has made substantial contributions to an understanding of why his story has become *the* story of Christian origins while raising considerable doubts about the general and particular accuracy of that story.

Michael Goulder, whose words served as an epigraph for Chapter Two, sees an extensive network of types behind the composition and plan of Acts. Although I am not prepared to endorse his interesting case in full, two passages in Acts to which he, and others, attribute symbolic significance merit consideration. These passages, which will be taken up in the following chapter, are evident examples of the imitation of biblical models, a type of mimesis.

Mimesis

"Mimesis" is a Greek word meaning "imitation." It has become a hot topic, and for two reasons. One of these is the current understanding of "intertextuality," which has vastly expanded the once prevalent understanding of source criticism and allusions. Standard source criticism operates mechanically with the notion of an author who selects a particular source, then revises, abridges, expands, or otherwise appropriates and modifies the material. Allusions are likewise intentional artifices that seek to underscore a point or contribute a bit of elegance: "Sebastian was scarcely the glass of fashion and the mould of form." This is a nicely manageable model, concrete and linear. Intertextual theories explode it.

These theories acknowledge that both authors and readers approach no texts in the sterile environment of a laboratory, but rather in the context of exposure to many words, written and spoken. From an intertextual angle it is even possible to speak of the influence of James Joyce upon Shakespeare, for example, a proposition that traditional source criticism would dismiss as ridiculous, for Shakespeare indisputably preceded Joyce by centuries. Yet, those familiar with Joyce's *Ulysses* will not be able to expunge from their minds its comments and debates about Shakespeare and the relation of father to son, etc. Joyce *does* influence Shakespeare.

In composing the preceding paragraph I had to choose specific examples, and probably selected Shakespeare and Joyce because of the likelihood that this comparison will resonate with more readers than would, say, the example of T. S. Elliott and Lancelot Andrewes, about whom even more apposite observations might be—and have been—made. The example selected thus also illustrates the complicated web created by authors in search of allusions that are pertinent and recognizable. Intentional allusions—and intertextual theory attends to unconscious allusions as well—present authors of literature with the sorts of problems detective writers have with clues. Some should be apparent to every reader and others will elude all but the most astute.

The second contemporary propellant of mimesis is the product of perfectly traditional criticism. To describe a contemporary piece of music, art, or literature as "imitative" is to pay it little, if any, compliment. "Influence" is different, for influence implies learning from one's predecessors and building upon their work. During the Roman Imperial era the adjective "imitative" would have been complimentary, but it was rarely used, for "mimesis" was expected. Authors employed mimesis for many reasons, including learning, evocation, and the conveyance of some emotion or effect. Mimesis exercises a very strong tug in cultures and eras devoted to the exaltation of former glories and/or any context in which there is a ruling sense of what is "right" or "correct." The cultivation of mimesis was a leading element of Greco-Roman education. One learned by imitating the masters, and people demonstrated their education by making (and recognizing) apt allusions in the course of their writing and reading.

This mimesis included both what we call "imitation" and that realm labeled "influence." Since the Romantic Movement that began around 1800, originality has been highly prized. People of his time (1685–1750) did not castigate Bach for ripping off Vivaldi; they were more likely to compliment the composer for what he had done with his predecessor's work, if they were aware of it, a possibility that was less likely in an era that rarely listened to earlier music. Similarly, ancients did not attack Vergil for plundering the plots of the *Iliad* and the *Odyssey* rather than inventing his own. His mimesis was—and is—viewed as the product of genius. One impetus toward mimesis was the Latin adaptation of Greek models. After it had fallen under Roman rule, Greek culture also took up imitation of "the classics," that is, literature before Aristotle (d. 323 BCE).

One might choose a subject and then look for an appropriate model, as did the Jewish historian *Josephus, who wrote a history of the first Jewish Revolt modeled upon the work of the great Greek historian Thucydides. Alternatively, one might have a model and then cast about for suitable subjects. The third-century Roman author Arrian was a great admirer of the fourth century BCE author Xenophon. Arrian wrote a history of Alexander's conquest modeled upon his predecessor's *Anabasis,* using the same title, as well as a collection of the teachings of the Stoic philosopher Epictetus, corresponding to Xenophon's *Memorabilia* about Socrates. Mimesis was what writers did. Their challenge was to select an appropriate model and to use it skillfully, not woodenly. To appreciate the pervasive nature of this cultural trend we might imagine that all plays written in English at the present time would be obliged to follow the style and themes of Shakespeare, that the author of a drama entitled "Benedict Arnold," for example, would be praised for producing an up-dated edition of *Coriolanus* or excoriated for his failure to do so. Lexicons to Shakespeare would serve less to help readers understand unfamiliar words than to assist playwrights in avoiding the use of words not employed by the bard of Avon.

A somewhat related factor was a propensity for stereotyped descriptions of certain incidents. Tradition had evidently determined what incidents a proper siege should include, and writers included them. The details are probable enough—infants crying at the breasts of mothers who cannot feed them, while other babes serve as supper for parents desperate to stay alive—but the recurrence of such items with all the flourishes of rhetorical pathos will eventually arouse not only pity but also suspicion. Shipwrecks are another example, as are urban riots. Such stereotyped reports are instances of historians repeating themselves, whatever history may have done. They are useful reminders that ancient history tended to be more interested in the typical than the particular, that it did not seek to expose unique facts so much as to reveal general truths.

For Luke the object of imitation was the Greek Bible, the *Septuagint (LXX). No author in search of cultured Greek readers would select such a "barbarous" prototype. In his *Antiquities*, for example, Josephus paraphrased many of the "historical" books of the LXX to improve their style. That Luke selected the LXX as his model shows that he had different cultural ideals. By "writing like the Bible" Luke shows the continuity between the Christian movement and its Israelite predecessors. This is one aspect of his mimesis. For English speakers, an analogy would be the imitation of the language of the AV ("King James Version"). Luke knew his LXX the way most educated Greeks knew their Homer (a writer whom Luke also knew). Those who read Luke 1–2 in Greek are swept back into the times of the patriarchs and the prophets. Septuagint style lends authority to Luke and Acts. Historically, this style may seem unimportant. "Four score and seven," after all, supplies the same information as "eighty-seven," but the *rhetorical* difference is substantial.

Things become slightly murkier when the author clothes his episodes in biblical motifs. Acts 20:7–12, set in Troas, includes the story of Eutychus:

> On the first day of the week, when we met to break bread, Paul was holding a discussion with them; since he intended to leave the next day,

he continued speaking until midnight. There were many lamps in the *room upstairs* where we were meeting. A *young man* named Eutychus, who was sitting in the window, began to drift off into a deep sleep while Paul talked still longer. Overcome by *sleep*, he fell to the ground three floors below and was picked up *dead*. But Paul went down, and bending over him took him in his arms, and said, "Do not be alarmed, for his life [*psyche*] is in him." Then Paul went *upstairs*. . . . Meanwhile they had taken the boy away *alive* and were not a little comforted.

This account evokes similar stories told of Elijah (1 Kings 17:17–24) and Elisha (2 Kings 4:18–37), as demonstrated in the following sentences by the use of italics and parentheses. The Elijah story speaks of an *upper room*, and contains the expression "Let his *life* (*psyche*) return to him." The story ends with an announcement that the child is alive. In 2 Kings 4 the boy *sleeps*, then *dies*. The prophet eventually comes, *lies prone upon him*, and ultimately restores the child to his mother. Some of the details are minor and have different uses, but it is very difficult to get around the use of the word "life," for this is a Hebrew idiom. Greek readers would be likely to understand it as "soul."

Of at least equal difficulty is the physical contact, which involves more than taking the patient by the hand. (NRSV is euphemistic here. The AV is more accurate: "Paul went down, and fell on him, and embracing *him*. . . .") The options are clear: (1) the resemblances between the incident in Troas and the stories in the LXX are purely fortuitous, (2) Paul had revived a presumably dead boy at Troas and Luke or his source had conformed these to the accounts in the Books of the Kings, and (3) Luke or his source *composed* the tale on the model of the Elijah-Elisha cycle. The first, which requires pure coincidence, will not satisfy responsible historians and so need not be considered further. The issue therefore lies between the second and the third options. The second, conformity to an LXX model, points to two possible suspects: Luke or a source. If Luke was fond of assimilation to the LXX, he becomes a more likely candidate than an unknown source; and of such fondness Luke had a full measure.

The third option, the move from quotation or general allusion to the actual casting of stories in biblical form by inventing or conforming details to the heroic tradition, is a step that Luke was quite willing to make. The "Petrine Parallel" to Acts 20:7–12 is the raising of Tabitha (Acts 9:38–41) by Peter, an event that also takes place in an upper room and has several echoes of the Elijah/Elisha stories noted above. Behind the story of Tabitha stands the influence of Mark 5:38–41, in which Jesus raised a girl. Finally, there is the story of how

Jesus revived the son of the Widow of Nain, Luke 7:11–17, which amounts to a near re-telling of Elijah's miracle in 1 Kings 17. Form criticism would identify Acts 9:38–41 as a typical healing story, and thus nominate it as a candidate for an existing tradition used by Luke, but its appropriation of the story from Mark 5, coupled with Luke's proclivity to show "parallels" among the works of Elijah/Elisha, Jesus, Peter, and Paul, do not generate confidence to this claim of independent tradition. It appears at least equally likely that both the story of Eutychus and the story of Tabitha are Lucan creations aimed at achieving the goal of parallelism. Mimesis also has a chilling effect upon the quest for history in Acts.

Another proposed type of mimesis looks to both the exploitation of narrative models and allusions to the prophetic writings. Acts 8:26–39 narrates the conversion of an Ethiopian court official by Philip. This remarkable story is atypical in that it does not lead to the founding of a community. In so far as Acts is concerned, it trails off into the wild blue yonder. Ethiopia was an exotic place of considerable interest in Luke's time, the subject of fabulous tales, utopian fancies, and actual exploratory expeditions. Ethiopia would almost certainly have qualified as "the ends of the earth." That notion may not have escaped Luke. Structurally, this episode could have been included under "duplications," for it follows an outline that closely resembles Luke 24:13–35, the Road to Emmaus. Since the Emmaus story encapsulates the Gospel of Luke in a nutshell, its pattern is important. The structural similarity is set forth in **Table 5.2.**

Allusions to the Elijah/Elisha tradition are fairly thick on the ground in Luke's story of the Ethiopian official. Thomas Brodie argues that 2 Kings 5 (the story of the foreign official Naaman) is a major source. Other Lucan motifs are also found in the books of the Kings. An angel guides Philip (1 Kings 19:5–7; 2 Kings 1:3, 15; Acts 8:26), who ran to complete his mission (1 Kings 18:46; Acts 8:30), and was swept up by the Spirit (1 Kings 18:12; 2 Kings 2:11, 16; Acts 8:39). 2 Kings 2 showcases a chariot and includes a "rapture" of the prophet, as well as the observation that he was no longer visible (2 Kings 2:11–12; Acts 8:39). These parallels are difficult to overlook. Many of the other specific details can be found in the brief prophetic book of Zephaniah. See **Table 5.3.**

The initial impression is that there is a coincidental overlap of the names Gaza, Ashdod/Azotus, and Ethiopia, as well as of a few basic concepts like noon/south, desert, and foreigners bowing down before the God of Israel, all of which involve identical words in the Greek texts. Detectives are suspicious of coincidence, a quality rewarded in

Table 5.2: Emmaus and the Road to Gaza

Incident	Luke 24	Acts 8
1. Traveler meets traveler(s)	24:15	8:29
2. Question answered with question	24:17–18	8:30–31
3. Subject of conversation is the death and the resurrection of Jesus, demonstrated by scriptural interpretation	24:26–27	8:32–35
4. Invitation/request	24:29	8:36
5. Sacramental action	24:30–31	8:38[1]
6. Disappearance of teacher	24:31	8:39
7. Emotional Reaction of guests	24:32	8:39

Table 5.3: Acts 8 and Zephaniah

Acts 8	Zephaniah
26. Then an angel of the Lord said to Philip, "Get up and go toward the **south** [or **at noon**] to the road that goes down from Jerusalem to **Gaza**." (This is a **wilderness [desert]** road.) 27. So he got up and went. Now there was an **Ethiopian** eunuch, a court official of the Candace, queen of the Ethiopians, in charge of her entire **treasury**. He had come to Jerusalem to **worship**. 40. But Philip found himself at **Azotus**	2:4. For **Gaza** shall be **deserted** . . . **Ashdod's** [= **Azotus**] people shall be driven out at **noon** . . . 2:11–12. . . . and to him shall **bow down**, each in its place, all the coasts and islands of the nations. 12 You also, O Ethiopians, shall be killed by my sword. 3:10. From beyond the rivers of **Ethiopia** my suppliants, my scattered ones, shall bring my offering. (Cf. also Psalm 68:31: "Let bronze be brought from Egypt; let Ethiopia hasten to stretch out its hands to God.")

this case by the absence of any other passage in which these words occur in such close proximity. Zephaniah proclaims the joy of Zion at God's universal reign of justice, a message quite congenial to the universalistic theme of Acts 8:26–39. More concretely, there is the Greek pun upon "*gaza*," which means both a place, Gaza, and "treasure," a word play exploited, evidently, in both the LXX and Acts. Many will regard as improbable the proposal that Luke lifted these bits from Zephaniah and blended them into the chariots, officials, divine guidance, and other motifs from the story of Elijah, then poured the mixture into the mold provided by Emmaus. Still, there is no getting around the data, and the story is quite odd. Philip is in an unusual place at an unusual time heading in a strange direction and happens to meet a most unusual person who has been engaged in an irregular pilgrimage. At the very least the LXX has provided a great deal of the color and detail of Luke's story of the Ethiopian official.

Those who have studied the Lucan imitation of LXX style observe a general gradient. This imitation is strongest in Luke 1–2 and weakest in Acts 13–28. As the mission moves into the Hellenic world, the style of Acts more closely approximates that of conventional Greek prose. Dennis R. MacDonald has argued that the story of Eutychus in Acts 20 (cited above) is based upon an episode from Homer. With many others, although in greater detail, he also argues for Homeric influence upon the account of the voyage in Acts 27, and for the use of Euripides in Acts 16:25–40. (See pp. 62–63.) Luke's citations conform to these proposed allusions. Other examples abound. The proof text cited in Paul's Areopagus Address (Acts 17:28) comes not from Jewish scripture but from a Greek poet, Aratus. When he relates the story of his conversion to a cultured audience, Paul attributes to Jesus a Greek proverb ("It hurts you to kick against the goads," 26:14), found in Euripides' *Bacchants* and quite possibly taken from it. The missionary program to the Jews involves "Saul" and the Septuagint, but the Greeks are offered "Paul" and the Classics: all things to all people. This is a very clever tactic because of its subtlety. Luke shows rather than tells the processes by which he paints a picture of how a Jewish sect became a gentile religion.

Literary Models

This chapter has attempted to demonstrate that Luke's "history" is based upon models determined more by art than by nature, that his story owes much to cycles, fixed patterns, imitations, and stereotypes. To a degree such schemes may be found in other ancient (and later) writers, including historians—but not, one can confidently assert, in the quantity and quality exhibited by Acts. It can be said of the famous Latin historian Livy, for example, that he sets out to show that Rome conquered the world in self-defense. This thesis owes at least as much to apologetics as to historical fact, although it is far more faithful to the facts than would be the contention that Rome engaged in an intentional scheme of relentless expansion. *Josephus, equally apologetic, has his own little schemes for exposing the villains of the First Jewish Revolt against Rome (66–73 CE), although they are varied in origin and often mixed in motive.

The label "apologetic" may also be applied to Luke, but he makes little or no effort to convince the neutral and objective reader. Historians interested in producing more than a mere chronicle are all but obliged to look for some thematic continuity and logic, but it is not legitimate to pick an example from Livy, or even from Polybius (a Greek historian far more admired for his insight and honesty than is Livy), and then utilize that parallel to justify Luke's method. Before rushing to conclusions, critics must first compare Acts in its entirety to Livy and company as entireties. Second, if the object is the determination of historical fact and event, critics will identify and correct for the biases of *all* their sources, however reputable these might be.

An example much closer to home, in several senses, is the biblical model of "Deuteronomic History" (Deuteronomy-2 Kings), and 1–2 Chronicles. These books almost certainly served Luke as prototypes, and they exhibit, in addition to some sections of superb historiography, a number of patterns and clear theses. When rulers and people obey God's commands, things go well. The disobedient, individually and corporately, receive their just desserts. This is all quite edifying, but no one today would write a history of ancient Israel by paraphrasing the contents of these texts. In Deuteronomic history fact must often give place to interpretation so that the moral will remain clear and right prevail over wrong. The alignment of Luke and Acts to Deuteronomic History is tantamount to classifying these books as residents in the neighborhood of historical fictions—at best as moralizing narratives about the past.

These general literary observations ought and are intended to give historians of nascent Christianity grounds for the exercise of skepticism, or at least a degree of caution, in their use of this or that passage or episode from Acts. Prior to extracting a historical base from a particular passage, the historian should consider not only its form and source(s) and the extent to which the data conform to Lucan themes, but also whether the passage conforms to Lucan patterns of narration. This chapter has shown some examples of the well-known fact that Acts often exhibits formulaic writing. Narrative formulas are quite useful for the development of plots, but they are not always the best media for relating facts, which can be notoriously difficult to fit into patterns. It is difficult to fend off the conclusion that, for the author of Acts, the pattern was more important than such facts as he had at his disposal. Scarcely less difficult to evade is the recognition that Luke sought to replicate stories from the Septuagint. Mimesis serves many useful purposes, but history, in the narrow sense, is rarely one of them. "Salvation history" would be much closer to the mark.

The investigator has determined that much of the narrative of Acts has been homogenized and, in addition, that it has been arranged with considerable architectural and decorative care. This does not make the investigative enterprise any easier. Assiduous literary detectives must needs pursue not only obvious aspects of motivation but also psychological factors, including unconscious motivation. The next step of this investigation will follow a similar line: pursuit of meaning that lies beneath the surface of the story. The most important narrative material of this sort can conveniently be examined under the rubric of "symbolism."

References and Further Reading

On Deuteronomistic History see the article of that name by
A. D. H. Mayes, in John H. Hayes, ed., *Dictionary of Biblical Interpretation*. Nashville: Abingdon, 1999, 1:268–73.

For arguments that Acts makes use of the Homeric epics see:
Dennis R. MacDonald, "Luke's Eutychus and Homer's Elpenor: Acts 20:7–12 and *Odyssey*, 10–12," *Journal of Historical Criticism* 1 (1994), 5–24.
_____, "The Shipwrecks of Odysseus and Paul," *New Testament Studies* 45 (1999), 88–107.
_____, *Does the New Testament Imitate Homer: Four Cases from the Acts of the Apostles*. New Haven: Yale University Press, 2003.
_____, ed. *Mimesis and Intertextuality in Antiquity and Christianity*. Harrisburg, PA: Trinity Press International, 2001.

On sources of Acts 8:26–39 see:
W. K. L. Clarke, "The Use of the LXX in Acts," in *The Beginnings of Christianity*, F. J. Foakes Jackson and Kirsopp

Lake, eds. 5 vols. London: MacMillan and Co., 1922–1933,
2:66–105.

T. L Brodie, "Toward Unraveling the Rhetorical Imitation of
Sources in Acts: 2 Kgs 5 as One Component of Acts 8,9–40."
Biblica 67 (1986), 41–67.

Acts' propensity to place all of the information about a mis-
sion site into one passage was elucidated by John C. Hurd,
The Origin of I Corinthians. 2nd ed. Macon, Georgia: Mercer
University Press, 1983.

Endnotes

1. Acts 8:37 is an interpolation that makes the story conform to
liturgical practice of requiring believers to make a confession of faith
at the time of baptism.

Chapter Six

Symbolism

The previous chapter proposed that the evangelists were evidently prepared to understand that some of their stories might have a symbolic content—which is not to say that they did not believe these events to have happened. Exorcisms and healings are synecdoches of the reign of God. (Synecdoche is a literary *trope, in which the whole may stand for the part or, more commonly, as in these examples, the part for the whole. "Lend me a hand" is a synecdoche that has become a cliché.) Of these stories no type has more immediate and obvious symbolic application than do stories of raising the dead. The Fourth Evangelist exploits this symbolism with considerable sophistication (John 11). Two passages in Acts yield fruitful meaning when considered as narratives laden with symbolic meaning, whereas they are, from the perspective of historiography, somewhat puzzling.

Background

Among the movements preceding the Reformations in Western Europe was an attack upon the dominant tradition of scriptural interpretation, which gave primary attention to figurative meanings, resulting in a general lack of attention to the surface meaning of many biblical texts. Reformers like Martin Luther utilized the principle that scripture has one literal meaning as a bulldozer with which to knock down the entire structure of medieval exegesis. They held that scripture interpreted itself, and that every person could understand the Bible, without the assistance of professors or priests.

*"Literal interpretation" thereafter became one of the hallmarks of Protestantism and also became one of its major tools for biblical criticism. The Roman Catholic Church also gave priority to surface meaning, but without relinquishing appreciation for "deeper meaning" (*sensus plenior*). Despite the motto of "one literal sense," non-papal interpreters also found and developed a range of non-literal interpretations, not least in the parables of Jesus. This is most apparent in the christological interpretation of passages from the Hebrew Bible ("Messianic Prophecies of the Old Testament") or in such interpretations as viewing the triplet "holy, holy, holy" (Isaiah 6:3) as a proof of the Trinity.

The house of interpretation demolished by reformers of various persuasions was often viewed as a wagon with four wheels (*Quadriga*), each of which represented a layer of meaning. In the thirteenth century Augustine of Dacia wrapped this up in a mnemonic quatrain, loosely translated as:

> The letter shows what God and our forebears did;
> The allegory shows where our faith is hid;
> The moral meaning gives us rules of daily life;
> The anagogy shows us where we end our strife.

That is, scripture reveals not only history (the literal), but also doctrine (the allegorical), rules of behavior (the moral), and eschatology (anagogical). There was no general agreement about the existence of four layers of meaning, let alone their presence in every passage, but the number coincided with that of the Gospels and other universals (for example, the four cardinal virtues, the four points of the compass), so the concept of four-fold meaning exercised an appeal that influenced not only exegesis, but also art and literature, notably that of Dante.[1]

The scheme looks bizarre today. To us such varieties of meaning are not ubiquitous; they are related to types and genres, scattered among various books and chapters. Some of the Bible recounts narrative history, creedal statements are explicit, moral direction is clearly denoted as such, and eschatology can be found in those passages referring to death, judgment, heaven and hell. For example, 1 Samuel relates history, Proverbs morality, Revelation eschatology, and Hebrews theology. How did this atrocious, if not impious, four-wheeled vehicle of multiple meanings come to be manufactured and allowed out onto the road?[2]

It all began much earlier than some might think. The Christian retention of Jewish scriptures probably made symbolic interpretation inevitable. Believers lived in the time of fulfillment. Prior to that was the era of promise, to which belong the Jewish scriptures: besides being "old" they must promise the very fulfillment that believers experience. In Acts 3:18, Luke has Peter proclaim: "In this way God fulfilled what he had foretold through all the prophets, that his Messiah would suffer." The scheme of promise/fulfillment in this example is patent. The only difficulty is that not one single passage in Jewish scripture speaks of a suffering Messiah. The principle was that any mention of a just person suffering, such as that of the "servant" in Isaiah 49–53, could be taken as a reference to the Messiah. Thus Luke was not obliged to have Peter say, "Now, although none of the prophets troubled to mention the matter, the Messiah did suffer." In fact, the argument moved from fulfillment to promise. It was not so much the Messiah had to suffer, but that the scripture had to be interpreted as showing that the Messiah would suffer.

Dating Acts c. 110–120 allows time for weeds to invade the garden of faith. So we must ask whether Paul, for instance, would have said such a thing. 1 Corinthians 15:3–4 is part of a creedal statement:

> For I handed on to you as of first importance what I in turn had received: that Christ died for our sins *in accordance with the scriptures*, and that he was buried, and that he was raised on the third day *in accordance with the scriptures*. . . . (emphasis supplied)

Paul evidently learned this tradition in the 30s, during the first decade of the post-Easter Jesus movement. Luke misrepresents neither Peter nor Paul. Consider also 1 Corinthians 10:1–6:

> I do not want you to be unaware, brothers and sisters, that our ancestors were all under the cloud, and all passed through the sea, and all were baptized into Moses in the cloud and in the sea, and all ate the same spiritual food, and all drank the same spiritual drink. For they drank from the spiritual rock that followed them, and the rock was Christ. Nevertheless, God was not pleased with most of them, and they were struck down in the wilderness. Now these things occurred as examples for us. . . .

In this passage the Apostle already views the passage through the Red Sea and the nourishment in the wilderness as "types," to use the technical word, of Christian sacraments. Appropriating a bit of non-biblical tradition, the Apostle states that the rock tapped by Moses was a sort of mobile water-wagon and, relying upon a further interpretation which identified that rock with *Dame Wisdom, could say that the rock was Christ, whom Paul identifies with Wisdom (1 Cor 1:25). For believers these historical events serve as admonitions. In short, Paul focuses upon the "moral meaning" of the Exodus. Medieval interpreters could claim that they were doing what Paul had done. Furthermore the trope wilderness rock=Wisdom shows that symbolic interpretation was not a Christian invention. Pre-Christian Jews had also engaged in the practice. Among them were not only exegetes of an overtly Greek mentality, such as *Philo of Alexandria, but also those who wrote the Dead Sea Scrolls.

It is apparent that before the gospels appeared in written form believers had reflected on the relation between "the Proclaimer" and "the Proclaimed." (See pp. 40–41.) They presumed that Jesus spoke about himself and his mission. Stories that he had told about shepherds and weddings, for example, must have had christological significance. Jesus was understood as "the Good Shepherd" and as "the Heavenly Bridegroom," etc. The trajectory from Jesus' story about a shepherd seeking lost sheep (Luke 15:3–7) and his proclamation of himself as the Good Shepherd (John 10:1–16) is thus quite intelligible as Christian reflection upon the "deeper meaning" of stories that Jesus told.

Allegory and Allegorism

The parables provide the clearest data for this development. Mark 4 shows that these apparently simple stories were held to be mysterious speech that had to be unlocked by a key. Jesus himself taught not only content, such as the Parable of the Sower, Mark 4:3–9, but also method, as in the interpretation of that parable privately delivered to the disciples in Mark 4:14–20. The method there, and elsewhere, is called "allegorical interpretation" or "allegorism." Allegorism is an interpretive (hermeneutical) technique based on a conviction that the text is written in a code for which the interpreter provides the key. In the case of the Sower, the activity of sowing refers to proclamation of the message. The various types of soil represent different kinds of hearers. Allegorical interpretation should be distinguished from "allegory," a narrative *composed* in code. An example of the latter is Matthew's Parable of the Wedding Banquet, 22:1–14, in contrast to Luke's "Fancy Dinner," 14:15–24. One useful clue for revealing the allegorical nature of Matthew's version is that the story makes no sense.

According to Matthew 22, many of those invited to a royal wedding feast ignore both the invitation and a courtesy reminder. When they continue to reject the invitation, the good monarch sends additional messengers to plead for a change of heart. Those who refuse not only blithely pursue their daily routine, but, rather than be satisfied with a message of regret—most of which are the equivalent to "So-and-so regrets that he cannot accept her Majesty's kind invitation to attend the nuptials of the Prince of Wales because he plans to mow

the grass that morning"—they beat and kill the royal messengers who
have had the temerity to remind them of this festive occasion. When
the king finally takes umbrage, he sends an army to burn the city,
which is, in fact, his own capital. All of this takes place between the
preparation and eating of the meal. Meanwhile, as destruction proceeds apace, there is still the dinner, now growing cold. Other guests
are located, somehow, among the ruins. Finally, the king has a temper
tantrum because one of these refugees, and just one, was not clad in
a tuxedo—and this in a combat zone! If it all seems to be a bit much,
it was supposed to. Matthew did not want anyone to miss the point.
As the story of a royal wedding this is too unlikely for words, but as
an allegory of salvation history it works rather well: the king=God, the
city=the world, the messengers=the prophets, and so forth.

From the mid-first to the mid-nineteenth centuries, parables were
regarded as susceptible to multiple interpretations and as multilayered in meaning. The range of meaning was controlled, essentially,
by the doctrines, convictions, and principles of various religious traditions. Not until the closing decades of the nineteenth century was
the ignominy that had fallen upon allegorical interpretation in the
Reformation era extended to parables. Then it was asserted, perhaps
too strongly, that Jesus would never stoop to allegory. Reasonably
enough, historical criticism contended that the parables of Jesus were
not allegories and the allegorical texts and interpretations were the
product of the church. The object of criticism was to pluck out the
tares so that the true wheat of Jesus' teaching would remain. The
task of interpretation was to discover the single "point" of each of
these stories. Allegory and allegorism were to be avoided at all costs.
"Typology," on the other hand, in which one event was compared to
another, such as baptism to the flood (1 Peter 3:20) or the examples
from 1 Corinthians 10 cited above, was kosher and commendable.

Things have since changed. Structuralism and other recent methods have more than a little sympathy with the presupposition of
allegorical and other symbolic modes of interpretation that authentic
meaning often lies beneath the surface of the text. Parables are a
good example. They are now seen as susceptible to a variety of interpretations and as "polyvalent," multilayered, in meaning. That is a
viewpoint quite akin to the philosophy that authorized allegorical
exegesis. What has gone around has come around. (The major difference is that current interpretation looks to parables to illustrate the
world and thought of Jesus rather than, for example, to resolve the
question of whether the Holy Spirit proceeds from the Father alone
or from both the Father and the Son.)

The intellectual climate is now better disposed to consider the possibility that some New Testament authors may have written with symbolic meaning in mind. Expressions like "allegory" and "deeper meaning" are no longer anathema. The essence of this case is not, however, based upon postmodern methods. My argument is historical. The purpose of this review has been to demonstrate that the quest for and the use of symbolism in stories about Jesus and his followers antedates the origins of any of our written texts. The idea that Jesus taught in code was not introduced by *Origen or *Augustine of Hippo. It is already present in Mark, the earliest extant written gospel.

Luke and Symbolic Narrative?

A highly relevant and important objection to this thesis may be reduced to a one-word question: LUKE? Luke is not disposed toward the mysterious or esoteric. He, of all writers, is unlikely to engage in narrative symbolism. The point is apt. Luke has only a limited use for allegory and does not seem to write for those who look beneath the surface or who view the faith as a congeries of riddles needing elucidation. Yet it would not be accurate to state that Luke has no interest in symbolism. Paul's visit to Athens (Acts 17:16–34) could have been omitted for all that it contributes to the narrative in terms of community foundation and growth. Yes, it features the one full-length Pauline sermon to polytheists, but that could have been placed elsewhere (indeed, much of its thought is present in Acts 14:15–17). Luke places the full sermon here because the mission to Athens is a symbol of the meeting between the gospel and Greco-Roman culture.

A dominant symbol in Luke and Acts that achieves high narrative visibility is the preferred designation for Christianity: "the Way" (or "the Movement"). Luke views the faith as a journey, and journeys dominate both Luke and Acts. The same Greek word, *hodos* (cf. "method," "Methodist"), serves for the name of the group, for a journey, and for the path or road. Jesus teaches the way of faith on his way to Jerusalem. The theme of travel is a vital element in some of the Lucan parables, such as The Good Samaritan (Luke 10:30–35), The Prodigal (Luke 15:11–32), and The Pounds (Luke 19:12–27), and is central to two of his most important stories: the journey to Emmaus in Luke 24:13–35 and the conversion of the Ethiopian Official in Acts 8:26–39. (See pp. 86–88.) Both of these stories are good candidates for the role of symbolic narratives. The image of the Way shows Luke's interest in overarching symbols, specifically in this case, a "root metaphor." "The Way" is for Luke a root metaphor. That trope reaches back to the roots, if you will, of the Israelite story, to the formation of the community "on the way" from Egypt to the promised land. Another Lucan root metaphor is money. That trope leads to a rather compelling example of symbolic narrative in Acts.

The cogent example in mind is the description of community life in Acts 2:42–47 and 4:32–35. As often observed, Luke portrays the early believers in the light of one of the dominant ancient utopian ideals, a commonwealth in which all share their resources. Their sharing was truly miraculous but, alas, far from realistic. There is no effort by the narrator to depict this state of affairs as permanent. The emissaries who radiate out from Jerusalem do not erect kindred utopias in other places. If Paul had declaimed before the Areopagus that friends hold all in common, the Stoic and Epicurean philosophers would have agreed, but that topic was not on his agenda.

Rather than speak of the perpetuation of this common lifestyle, 6:1–7 speaks of difficulties in distribution—difficulties promptly resolved, to be sure, but blots upon any heavenly utopia. It is not likely that Luke wishes to suggest that the communal experiment failed—and thus that "socialist" ideas are unworkable—nor that the effort had to be abandoned when the community became too numerous and diverse. These are rationalizations of his silence. For Luke the life of sharing was a stimulus to and a symbol of new life. Once he had made the point that the gift of the spirit enabled the believers to realize the great ideals of the Greek and Israelite tradition, he was willing to drop it. For Luke, once symbolic narrative has communicated its message, the narrator moves on. Although in modern art and literature symbols tend to have a stable—even universal—meaning, in antiquity and the Middle Ages they were more flexible, capable of different meanings in different settings. Readers should therefore not expect all biblical symbols to have permanent and consistent meaning.

Speaking of narrators, this one has promised to discuss two important symbolic narratives, but has not yet clearly revealed what they are. One of them is the story of Peter in Acts 12. The other addresses the adventures of Paul in chapters 27–28. The core of the argument is that these are symbolic passion-resurrection stories, expositions of Easter in the life of the church. Although the meanings are similar, the narratives differ. The story of Peter's liberation (and the destruction of his adversary) is dense with symbol and allusion. The specific clues are not so thick in the case of Paul's voyage, but its structural position lends considerable weight to the hypothesis.

Since at least the sixth century interpreters have asked whether the major division in Acts should come after chapter 12 or after chapter

14. The subsequent exposition's support of the former view, it should be noted, does not beg the question, for the two chief climaxes in Acts come in chapter 12 and chapters 27–28. Luke, like many ancient writers, seems to have honored Janus (a Roman god depicted with two faces looking in opposite directions, whence "January") as a kind of patron literary deity. His transitions often look two ways and serve both to conclude one section and to introduce the next. Useful outlines of Acts will show that the narrative is fluid and often overlapping rather than rigidly compartmentalized. Structure was no more inflexible than was symbolism.

The thesis of this section is that in Acts 12 and 27–28 Luke recounts the passion, death, and resurrection first of Peter and then of Paul. Before attempting to make a case for these interpretations, it would be well to offer some comments upon the terms. "Passion" requires no particular defense. It means "suffering," and serves as a technical term for the experiences of Jesus and those apostles and martyrs who were eventually provided with suitable "passion narratives." It did not escape early Christians that the Greek word for Passover, *pascha* (a transliteration of Hebrew *pesach*), could be linked to the verb used for "suffer" (*pascho*). And it has already been intimated that more or less every use of "raise" in scriptural accounts of healing and the like could be viewed as symbols of rising to new life.

When, for example, Jesus took Peter's sick mother-in-law by the hand and *raised* her, she became well and immediately began to "serve" the company (Mark 1:30). "Serve" is Mark's word for engaging in ministry. These "resurrections" are metonymies. (Metonymy is a *trope in which cause stands for effect or effect for cause, or attribute for essence. Those who speak of "the suits" mean persons *wearing* business suits—managers and executives, that is, those in power. People who accept an offer of "a taste of the grape" will be given an alcoholic beverage. "Grape" is a metonymy, cause for effect—and "taste" is a synecdoche, part for whole.) Those raised to new life are free to serve. The emphasis is not upon the "raising," but upon its offer of new life.

In our world the distinction between "life" and "death" is rather firm, giving rise to the demand for legal and medical definitions of both. Ancient Hebrews used "death" more metaphorically of human beings than we usually do. Thus in his psalm Jonah says

> I called to the LORD out of my distress, and he answered me; *out of the belly of Sheol I cried*, and you heard my voice. You cast me into the deep, into the heart of the seas, and the flood surrounded me; all your waves and your billows passed over me. Then I said, "I am driven away from

your sight; how shall I look again upon your holy temple?" The waters closed in over me; the deep surrounded me; weeds were wrapped around my head at the roots of the mountains. *I went down to the land whose bars closed upon me forever; yet you brought up my life from the Pit, O LORD my God.* (Jon 2:2–6, emphasis supplied)

The text is quoted in full because it is germane to both of the passages to be considered. Those in great distress may poetically describe themselves as in Sheol, that is, dead, because they have experienced a symbolic "death." Compare Matt 12:40, "For just as Jonah was three days and three nights in the belly of the sea monster, so for three days and three nights the Son of Man will be in the heart of the earth." Just as the word "resurrection" is not always used in its literal sense, so "death" can be symbolic of a state. Jonah 2:6 reveals another key image: death could be depicted as bonds or as a prison (Isa 24:22; 1 Peter 3:19; Jude 1:6; Rev 20:1–3 and cf. the English "bonds of death," evidently derived from Ps 116:3). Of considerable interest for both Acts 12 and 27 are two sections of Psalm 107. One of these (vv. 10–14) uses prison imagery and will serve to introduce the next subsection:

Some sat in darkness and in gloom, prisoners in misery and in irons. . . . Then they cried to the LORD in their trouble, and he saved them from their distress; he brought them out of darkness and gloom and broke their bonds asunder. . . .

St. Peter and the Gates of Hell: Acts 12:1–23

Such ancient critics as *Philo of Alexandria and *Origen were, like modern scholars, delighted to discover anomalies in a text. Both ancients and moderns, although singing from different hymnals, viewed difficulties as clues to interpretation. For the ancients anomalies indicated that since the surface meaning was absurd or erroneous, the real meaning must lie below the surface. The anomaly here is Acts 12:17: "*Peter* motioned to them with his hand to be silent, and described for them how the Lord had brought him out of the prison. And he added, 'Tell this to James and to the believers.' Then he left and went to another place." For Peter to go into hiding was eminently reasonable, but one expects the narrator to say where, as in 9:30, when Paul was sent to Tarsus. Readers deserve to know where Peter went. They can certainly be trusted not to inform the authorities of his whereabouts.

If the text said, "he went to Joppa" (or Galilee, etc.), no one would blink (at least not just then). Moreover, the expression "go to a place" is ominous. It was last used by Peter himself in speaking of the fate of Judas (1:25). Perplexity deepens when readers discover that Peter has essentially been taken off the board. Though he will make a brief speech in Acts 15, there is no explanation of his whereabouts and actions between chapters 12 and 15, and none thereafter. Other than to remind everyone of what he did in chapter 10, Peter's part in Acts ends at 12:17. Neither Antioch nor Rome is on his itinerary. This difficulty has led some ingenious interpreters to contend that Acts 12 reports (while covering up) the martyrdom of Peter in Jerusalem. The "place" to which he went was his final resting place. This interpretation is unlikely, but it confronts the problem and contains some insights. Unlike allegories, which often seem dreary to those who do not see their meaning—and to more than a few who do, Acts 12:1–23 is a very good story, bubbling with interest and including humor, drama, suspense, and finely balanced examples of "poetic justice."

It begins with a vicious persecution launched by "Herod the King," whose name is all but synonymous with villainy. Herod executed James the brother of John, proving that he plays for keeps, unencumbered by the smooth rhetorical subtleties of a Gamaliel. Seeing his poll numbers rise, the miscreant also had Peter nabbed, but that execution would have to wait until the end of the holidays. Enter suspense. Earlier experience with imprisoned missionaries (5:17–25) leads to elaborate security measures: not only sturdy chains but also four soldiers in four shifts, with two in immediate attendance. Against these perils the faithful can do no more than pray.

On the very night before Peter's death an angel appeared, together with a great light but evidently untroubled by the fear of death, our hero slept through all this. It took a nudge of the angelic sandal (as it were) and a sharp command to arouse the apostle. The angel then supervises Peter's dressing. For the reader this is too much. Grab your belt, coat, and shoes, and run, for heaven's sake, Peter! This is no time to attend to grooming! Imagining the first head of the community being dressed as if he were a small boy would be quite an amusing cameo if his life were not hanging by a thread. Peter trails obediently after the meticulous angel, thinking that it is all a dream. The tension becomes more excruciating as the pair pass through one security gate and then another. The last barrier is the most awesome of all, an iron door! That obstacle swings open of its own accord. They go on for a block and then the angel leaves. It looks as if there had been a mix-up in orders. Instead of a mighty warrior who would endure to the end, Peter has to put up with one of the valets from the heavenly court rather than the sort of power-lifting angel needed to effect prison breaks. Still, any angel is vastly better than none.

Now at last Peter knows that it isn't a dream, but he isn't out of the woods yet. With, one must assume, alarms sounding, gongs ringing, and torches flaring here and there, Peter has to slink through town to John Mark's mother's place, a destination the narrator does not explain. There many have gathered for prayer. Now Peter must face the light for a moment, exposed to prying neighbors as he attempts to slip quietly in. He raps on the door, no doubt as softly as possible, but loudly enough to be heard. This is the last of several barriers through which he must pass. The principles that govern suspense stipulate that it will be the most difficult. In response comes a maid, Rhoda (Rose), who peeks through the spy hole, recognizes Peter, and, swept away with joy, rushes off to tell everyone the good news. A fine idea, no doubt, but it did have the unfortunate effect of leaving Peter out in the cold and in hot water, for the increasing noise from within would soon attract the attention of the most assiduously incurious neighbors. What should have been a happy ending has become an impending disaster.

This is an "evener-upper." Peter is paying the price for an earlier encounter with a different maid in another courtyard, where he had denied his master (Luke 22:56). While he stands outside knocking at the door, those inside are debating Rose's sanity. They conclude that all is over, that she has seen his guardian angel. (Guardian angels allegedly hang about for some time after the death of their charges.) There is more than one irony to savor here. Those engaged in prayer (vv. 5 and 12) seem to have had no hope for a positive response, and the reference to guardian angels evokes that guard-thwarting angel who had busted Peter out. Finally someone comes up with the exceptionally bright idea of taking a look. It *is* Peter, who, surprisingly, has no time for tea, conversation, or further prayer, but utters a few words and departs.

The narrator then abandons Mary's house for the prison, and night for the next day. Herod sends for the condemned, only to discover that he is absent. He has the guards executed and then leaves for Caesarea, Passover having ended. (Readers of today may regret that providence did not find some way to exonerate those guards for what was no fault of their own, but Luke did not concern himself about such matters.) Other problems awaited the king at Caesarea. Tyre and Sidon were eager to resolve a conflict with Herod, who controlled their food supplies.

Acts frames this episode with an account of a famine (11:27; 12:23). Believers in Antioch had collected money for those in Jerusalem. Money also featured in Herod's conflict, for the wily Tyrians and Sidonians evidently bribed one of his officials to mediate.

Peace restored, the king held a celebration on an appointed day and delivered an address, donning his regal paraphernalia for the occasion. This is the second reference to getting dressed in this passage. If Herod's outfit was considerably less humble than Peter's, so was his posturing. The crowd hailed him as a god. This is a jab at the practice of deifying rulers for routine benefactions, the "benefaction" in this case amounting to calling off the dogs. When Cornelius had attempted to venerate Peter, the apostle gently rebuked him (10:25–26). Herod did not reject this veneration, and paid for it. An angel of the Lord "struck" him, and he died of an infestation of worms—proof positive, in those days, that he was a bad guy.

The word for "struck" is exactly the same participial form used of the prod that aroused sleeping Peter (12:7). The tyrant who would have killed Peter on a predetermined day meets his own fate on another day that he had specified, and by the foot of the very kind of heavenly agent whose foot had brought Peter back from death. Acts 12:1–23 is a fine story that delivers humor, drama, adventure, tension, and a well rounded bit of vindication. The wicked ruler who had planned to kill Peter at the beginning comes in the end to a gruesome death. The stories of Peter's deliverance and Herod's death are mirror twins. That should be enough for anyone, but there is more.

Although historians often identify "King Herod" with Agrippa I (see p. 4), this murderous creature is a veritable Pharaoh, like the baby-slaying King Herod of Matthew 2. The "days of unleavened bread" (v. 4) adds suspense by evoking the death of Jesus at Passover: disciples are to follow the master's footsteps. This initial allusion establishes a paschal context. Peter's statement in v. 11, "The Lord has sent his angel and rescued me from the hands of Herod" is an allusion to Exodus 18:4 (LXX) and thus confirms the context. These explicit references authorize a search for other potential symbols relevant to Passover in a Christian context. Among these are intimations of deliverance, passion/resurrection, and the new life of baptism/community membership.

The *bonds* of v. 6 are a *trope for captivity, the opposite of freedom, the dominant example of which is Israel's bondage in Egypt (cf. Ps 107:10–14; Isa 52:2; 61:1–2, cited in Luke 4:18). Peter *sleeps*, a common symbol for ignorance, spiritual "blindness," and death. Note Luke 21:34–36 and, especially, Ephesians 5:14: "Sleeper, awake! Rise from the dead, and Christ will shine on you," evidently a fragment from a baptismal hymn and certainly a useful parallel to this passage. When Peter wakens he is freed, as the falling shackles indicate. "Prison" or "bondage" is also a trope for "death" (above).

The direction to "rise" in v. 7 is logical enough here. It is also the command given to one being raised from the dead (Eph 5:14).

The directions for dressing in v. 8 reinforce the paschal setting, for they recall the instructions about Passover apparel in Exodus 12:11. They are also rich baptismal symbols (cf. Gal 3:27 and Col 3:9–10). Easter has always been the normative occasion for Christian baptism. Peter is like "a newborn babe," who must be dressed by his nurse or mother. 1 Peter 2:1–2 describes the newly baptized as "newborn infants." Within a paschal context, the door-miracle and the passage out of prison evoke the transit of the Red Sea. Deutero-Isaiah (Isaiah 39–54), which was effectively Luke's "favorite" biblical book, developed the image of breaking open prison doors as a symbol of "conversion," mission, and liberation (Isaiah 42:6–7; 45:1–2). And v. 11 (cited above) provides the relevant interpretation from Peter's own lips. The narrator paints Peter's deliverance from prison as an "exodus," a passage from death to life.

In the context one is tempted to view the angel's sudden departure as analogous to the cessation of the Israelites' heavenly support system at the end of their journey to the promised land (Joshua 5:12). The passage certainly does not overlook life after deliverance. In v. 8 the angel says, "follow me." This is the summons to discipleship (Mark 1:17, etc.). Similarly, the instructions about clothes evoke the theme of "dressed for action" used in moral exhortation (for example, Luke 12:35; 1 Peter 1:13). The difficulties of that life are apparent in Peter's effort to pass through the final barrier, the gate to Mary's house, which returns him to the setting of Jesus' passion (above). In accord with this is the prayer of the community (vv. 4 and 12), a corporate echo of "Gethsemane" (Luke 22:39–46). Other motifs recall the resurrection of Jesus. Rhoda responds to Peter's return from the "dead" with joy, as did the disciples upon seeing Jesus (Luke 24:41). Those who believed that she had seen a ghost were astonished at the sight of Peter in the flesh, a clear allusion to Luke 24:36–41.

The return of Peter from the realm of the "dead" is a resurrection story, following his passion. Why does Luke so shape this account? His interests were more than biographical. The exodus coloration makes this account paradigmatic, a model for Christian life. By the natural link between the Christian "Passover" and baptism, viewed as the passage from dark into light, from death to life, Peter's story becomes the story of all believers. Baptism is not the end of the struggle; it is initiation to discipleship rather than to life on easy street. The devil has, however, been defeated. Clothed in the robes of salvation, believers can live a redeemed existence. The sign of that defeat here is the fate of the wicked Herod, Peter's opposite in every important way.

That is all to the better. Acts 12 is not only a good story, it also shows that believers were empowered. Other disciples could have served as a useful example here, but Luke chose Peter for the part. This is the final "Jesus-Peter parallel" in Acts. Luke concludes the story of Peter with a sort of passion and resurrection that corresponds to the fate of the founder. Peter did follow Jesus, to the brink of the grave and to new life. The literary critic will affirm that a better conclusion to the story of Peter would be difficult to devise. The historian will be less enthusiastic in issuing praise, for this was not the actual end of Peter's story. Luke knew, from Galatians, that Peter had been to Antioch, and he very probably had heard that the apostle had gone to Rome and actually died there, but he chose to conclude the story of Peter on this climactic and symbolic note. Peter must "go to his place," "die," so that Paul may rise to prominence. Some may not wish to call Acts 12 fiction, although the label is highly appropriate, but it is certainly not history.

Hell and High Water: Acts 27:1–28:14

The problem that generates reflection upon Acts 12 could focus upon a single verse (12:17). In Acts 27 the problem is too many verses. Why does Luke, who devotes seventeen verses to the evangelization of Corinth, nine to that of Thessalonica, and zero to the initial mission to Rome lavish fifty-eight on the story of Paul's voyage to Rome? This is a question that every interpreter of Acts should be obliged to answer, not least those who view Acts as a type of history. In fact the problem is worse, for it goes back to chapter 20. Why does the author devote more than one-fourth of this book to Paul's last journey to Jerusalem and its sequel? Therein also lies the answer. Chapter Four of this book pointed out a number of parallels between the Passion of Jesus in Luke and the story of Paul in Acts 21–26. In addition to the trials, there are numerous parallels between the journey of Jesus to Jerusalem in Luke 9–19 and the journey of Paul to Jerusalem in Acts 20–21. Notable among these are three predictions of the passion of Paul (20:23–25; 21:4, 11–13) that parallel those of Jesus in Luke (9:22, 43–44; and 18:31), and a farewell address in 20:17–35, corresponding to Jesus' speech in Luke 22:14–38.

Some of these are rather minor. Luke 20:27–39 presents an argument about resurrection. The Sadducees reject this doctrine; certain scribes support Jesus. Pharisees support Paul in a debate on the same subject, while Sadducees oppose it (Acts 23:6–10). Assistants of the high priest beat Jesus (Luke 22:63–64), and in Acts 23:1–2 Paul begins his trial by the Sanhedrin with a declaration of his innocence, leading the high priest to have him struck on the mouth. This is a bizarre incident. It is arguable that Luke introduces it for the sake of the parallel. **Table 6.1** shows seven types of parallel between the respective "passions."

Table 6.1: Jesus and Paul: Some Examples

Jesus	Paul
1. "Passion Predictions"	**1. "Passion Predictions"**
Luke 9:22	Acts 20:23–25
Luke 9:34	Acts 21:4
Luke 18:31	Acts 21:11–13
2. Farewell Address	**2. Farewell Address**
Luke 22:14–38	Acts 20:17–35
3. Resurrection: Sadducees Oppose	**3. Resurrection: Sadducees Oppose**
Luke 20:27–39	Acts 23:6–10
4. Staff of High Priest Slap Jesus	**4. Staff of High Priest Slap Paul**
Luke 22:63–64	Acts 23:1–2
5. Four "Trials" of Jesus	**5. Four "Trials" of Paul**
A. Sanhedrin: Luke 22:66–71	A. Sanhedrin: Acts 22:30–23:10
B. Roman Governor (Pilate): Luke 23:1–5	B. Roman Governor (Felix): 24:1–22
C. Herodian King (Antipas): Luke 23:6–12	C. Herodian King (Agrippa): 26
D. Roman Governor (Pilate): Luke 23:13–25	D. Roman Governor (Festus): 25:6–12
6. Declarations of Innocence	**6. Declarations of Innocence**
Pilate: Luke 23:14 (cf. 23:4, 22)	Lysias (Tribune): Acts 23:29
Herod: Luke 23:14	Festus: Acts 25:25
Centurion: Luke 23:47	Agrippa: Acts 26:31
7. Mob Demands Execution:	**7. Mob Demands Execution:**
Luke 23:18	Acts 22:22

The point has been made. The parallels between the passion of Jesus in Luke and Paul's experiences in Jerusalem are too numerous and too transparent to deny. But after chapter 26 this symmetry seems to collapse. Whereas the Gospel goes on to relate the crucifixion, death, and resurrection of Jesus, Acts narrates Paul's voyage, shipwreck, survival, and eventual arrival in Rome. This much remains undeniable: *the voyage and its aftermath occupy the same structural position in Acts that the crucifixion and its sequel have in Luke.* The alternatives are clear: either Luke carefully erected his parallelism between the respective fates of Jesus and Paul until he came to the end of their legal hearings and then dropped it overboard, or the existence of the parallel scheme invites critics toward further inquiry. The latter looks like the more likely option. At the very least it is worth a try.

Voyage by ship and the travail of "those in peril on the sea" provided one of the most productive narrative themes and literary symbols in ancient literature. From before Odysseus until Sinbad (and after); in Akkadian, Egyptian, Greek, Latin, Hebrew, and Arabic; through numerous writings in an abundance of tongues, sea travel constituted a staple of action literature. Evidence for this is apparent in ancient novels, where shipwreck practically becomes a routine concomitant of travel. Luke's narrative in Acts 27 gives readers what they wanted. Its status as a good story has never been doubted. Themes of such power and appeal will inevitably become vehicles for communicating a message. For Greek popular philosophers the image of Odysseus battling the aquatic elements illustrated the struggle for truth and virtue in the soul against various passions and through the turmoil of life. The image became ubiquitous, as in Ephesians 4:14: "We must no longer be children, tossed to and fro and blown about by every wind of doctrine, by people's trickery, by their craftiness in deceitful scheming."

The lyric poet Alcaeus, born in the seventh century BCE, may have coined the image of the storm-tossed ship of state, destined to endure in poetry until Longfellow ("Sail on, O Ship of State!"). The church quickly appropriated this symbol, which has given us the architectural term "nave" (from Latin *navis,* "ship") as the place of the body of the faithful. Mark locates some of the important experiences of Jesus and his disciples in a boat on the lake. If Mark 4:35–41 does not already see the boat as a *trope for the community, Matthew's edition of this story in 8:23–27 clearly does. The parallel between Paul and company in their ship and Jesus with the disciples facing storms at sea should not be overlooked, but the ships of Acts 27–28 constitute more than a political or ecclesiological symbol.

Fear of the dangers of the deep were no less common among sea-faring peoples like the Greeks than for nautically challenged people like the Hebrews, who rarely controlled coastal areas. The Psalter, to select but one portion of the Hebrew Bible, makes frequent use of wind, waves, and water as symbols (for example, 42:7, 65:7, 88:7, 89:9, and 93:4). This is the proper place to introduce another section of Psalm 107 (vv. 23–30):

> Some went down to the sea in ships, doing business on the mighty waters; they saw the deeds of the LORD, his wondrous works in the deep. For he commanded and raised the stormy wind, which lifted up the waves of the sea. They mounted up to heaven, they went down to the depths; their courage melted away in their calamity; they reeled and staggered like drunkards, and were at their wits' end. Then they cried to the LORD in their trouble, and he brought them out from their distress; he made the storm be still, and the waves of the sea were hushed. Then they were glad because they had quiet, and he brought them to their desired haven.

For the ancient Hebrews the uncontrolled might of the sea was a primary image for chaos, "Rahab of the deep" (cf. Ps 89:10). *Apocalyptic, based upon the thesis that the end will be like the beginning, envisions an ultimate devolution of creation into chaos. Luke 21:25: "There will be signs in the sun, the moon, and the stars, and on the earth distress among nations confused by the roaring of the sea and the waves." An apocalyptic background is of major importance for understanding the voyage of Paul to Rome, not least because apocalyptic imagery is also prominent in the accounts of *Jesus' crucifixion. In this voyage the end will also be a beginning. In short, the basic presuppositions supporting the search for symbolism in Acts 27–28 are the following: Acts 20–26 narrates a "passion of Paul." Where the Gospel tells of the execution of Jesus and his subsequent vindication through resurrection, Acts tells the story of the voyage. Sea-travel was a basic ingredient of ancient adventure and therefore became a favorite medium for figurative exposition, including the struggle of the individual against self and the storms of life, as well as the image of the community as a ship in distress. In Hebrew thought the sea was a primary symbol of chaos, of the forces of darkness and disorder.

Nearly all interpreters agree that Acts 27:1–28:14 has *some* symbolic meaning. By general consensus this narrative adds one more declaration of innocence to the list in **Table 6.1**: Paul is proclaimed innocent by God. That declaration is encapsulated in the final and climactic episode of the shipwreck, 28:1–6, where a lethal serpent fails to harm the hero. In other words, Paul is vindicated by the outcome of his adventures. This is an obvious, essential, and conclusive point. Just as God vindicated Jesus through resurrection, so God vindicated Paul through deliverance from death by water and by poison.

One of the first prototypes that would come to the mind of the biblically-informed reader of Acts is the story of Jonah, who like Paul was commissioned to preach repentance to gentiles. In an effort to evade this responsibility he boarded a ship headed for the opposite end of the world. Like Paul, he suffered storm and shipwreck. Both brought about the "salvation" of all on board their respective ships. Both were delivered and went on to proclaim their message at the world capital. Of course there are also strong contrasts, for Jonah was not a willing prophet and he deeply regretted the success of his mission. If by comparison Paul appears to have improved upon the model, so much the better.

Luke signals the comparison by a specific allusion to Jonah 1:5 (Acts 27:19). Jonah's three days inside a fish made comparison of him to Jesus irresistible. Although the Gospel (Luke 11:29–32) does not pursue this analogy, it is reasonable to suspect that Luke would have accepted it as one more instance of "all the prophets" speaking about the death of the Messiah. If one does not wish to pursue this suspicion, it will be sufficient to compare the fate of Paul to that delineated in Jon 2:2–6 (cited above). Both experienced "death" at sea.

In addition to the general theme of storm as apocalyptic chaos, two specific allusions are evocative of the crucifixion and resurrection of Jesus. Acts 27:20–38 is a time of darkness. With day (v. 39) comes salvation. As in Acts 12 darkness is a common *trope for death, so here light suggests life/resurrection. Just as Jesus' death was marked by a failure of the sun's light, so on the ship: "neither sun nor stars appeared for many days . . ." (Acts 27:20). Failure of sun and stars is one sign of the imminent advent of God (see Luke 21:25, cited above). Luke envelops the "deaths" of both Jesus and Paul with an atmosphere of apocalyptic finality. In both stories there is also a very friendly and decidedly non-apocalyptic centurion: in Luke 23:47 a centurion declares Jesus innocent, and his counterpart in Acts 27:43 is determined to save Paul. This conviction would be difficult to understand if the officer had assumed that Paul was guilty.

Acts 27:33–35 reports a brief meal scene. Although Paul could not "celebrate the eucharist" for polytheists, eucharistic allusions are present in the description of three of the four eucharistic actions: taking bread, blessing, and breaking. Sharing is omitted (although included in the longer "Western Text"—see p. 23), but even so this nourishment "saves" all who eat thereof. At that point Luke enumerates the company: 276 in all. Such numbers normally appear as an element of miracle stories, as in the feeding of the 5,000 (Luke 9:14). Acts 27 *is* a miracle story. (See Chapter Four.)

To pursue the model, Acts 28:1–6 is analogous to a resurrection appearance and is comparable to the reception of the returned Peter in Acts 12. Paul is a divine, indestructible being, rescued from the tomb of the sea. Presumptions of his imminent death were highly exaggerated (cf. Luke 24:5). In this case the reaction comes not from astonished disciples but from simple "barbarians," who conclude that Paul is a god (28:6). Their theological categories are inadequate, but, to give them the credit they deserve, they recognize an epiphany when they see it. (As in the matter of life vs. death, discussed above, so also on the question of divinity. In the Greco-Roman world the boundaries between human and divine were much more flexible than they are for contemporary Western people.) If bonds are a symbol of death, the "risen" Paul is, reasonably enough, no longer in bondage. The mention of a custodial soldier (28:16) notwithstanding, in chapter 28 Paul is essentially a free person, able to perform healings, arrange meetings, and carry out his mission "unhindered," which is the final word of Acts.

While Peter escaped safe and sound, Paul was the agent of deliverance for all on the ship. He can even borrow a promise from Jesus: no one will lose so much as a hair (27:34). Since that promise comes from Jesus' speech on the last things, Luke 21:18, it may be added to the list of items with apocalyptic resonance. Paul is becoming a bit of a savior figure in his own right. Whereas Peter's symbolic death and return formed the grand conclusion and effective consummation of his career, the deliverance of Paul led to a new beginning. The narrator signals this with the healings in 28:8–9, a report based upon the first account of Jesus' healing ministry. As in the matter of the healing of Peter's mother-in-law (Luke 4:38-40) and its sequel, a relative of Paul's host is healed of a fever through the imposition of hands, followed by a summary of the healing of all the afflicted. With this Jesus-Paul parallel Luke makes an important point: the story is always beginning afresh; the day after deliverance from death is the next day of the rest of your life.

Like Acts 12, Acts 27 gains a general application through its potentially sacramental dimensions. Presumably, the ship's company had first to remove their clothing and plunge into the depths in order to reach the "desired haven" of salvation. Those who prefer other typologies may remember Jonah, who was cast out of the deep onto the shore, and the corporate model of Israel's deliverance from the Red Sea, already described as a baptism by Paul (1 Corinthians 10, above). Prior to their "baptism," those on ship partook of a meal with eucharistic overtones. This experience gave the representative person "authority to tread on snakes and scorpions, and over all the power of the enemy" (Luke 10:19), that is, to defeat the Devil. Luke also understood that the medium is the message. The medium here is his root metaphor of "the way," Christian life as a voyage or journey that will include "many tribulations" (Acts 14:22). Paul's story is a paradigm, a model of the journey undertaken by each believer and by the community of faith. A look beneath the surface of Acts 27:1–28:14 makes these episodes more than a fascinating story about Paul that the narrator understandably let run on a bit longer than his scope might have suggested.

Oscar Wilde, whose acerbic comment upon historical repetition has been noted, generated numerous anecdotes. Before receiving a degree from Oxford in his day, students had to demonstrate their Anglican conformity by passing an exam on the Thirty-nine Articles of Religion. To the chaplain of each college fell this happy duty. Wilde duly arrived, far from early, and announced that he had come to be tested on "the Forty-nine Articles." Not amused by this absence of gravity, the chaplain presented him with some paper and a Greek Testament and had Wilde translate. The passage chosen was Acts 27 (which contains some of the more difficult Greek in the New Testament). The candidate proceeded to scribble away in his blue book for some time. Finally the chaplain interrupted, "Come now, Mr. Wilde, that's quite enough!" "But," objected Oscar, "This is a fascinating story about someone named Paul caught aboard ship in a raging storm, and I want to find how it ended!" The tale is apocryphal, since Wilde had earned prizes in New Testament Greek at school, but his alleged judgment was sound. The literary miracle is that it remains a really good story rather than a ponderous narrative of interest only to symbol hunters.

Still other justifications for this lengthy passage may be found. It provides a bright portrait of Paul's character. He is a vigorous, resourceful, and knowledgeable hero, the veritable master of all that he surveys, no mere pedant driven mad by much learning. Still, how often does Luke need to display the manifold traits his hero possessed? In a rather lengthy biography of Paul such attention might be defensible, but not in a work of this purpose and length.

When read as the story of Paul's vindication and as the triumph of the Christian cult, as a fulfillment of its climactic structural position in Acts, the length and content require no appeals to improbable conjectures or to other forms of apologetic. Luke devoted fifty-eight verses to Paul's voyage to Rome because it served as a major vehicle of his message, not merely because he possessed the materials for a rousing story. The best defense of this search for symbolic meaning in Acts 12 and 27 is that it solves more problems than it creates. By way of transition, it is interesting to step back from all of this more than literal reading and ask what it suggests about the narrator's perspective. The world of Acts 27:1–28:14 is an entirely gentile and polytheist world. Those may well be the dominant characteristics of the waters in which Luke envisions the ship of the church making its voyage.

This chapter has attempted to provide an understanding of two important stories in Acts. The object of the exercise has not been simply to present some interesting and attractive (or unappealing and dull) interpretations, but to shed light on "Luke the historian." If this "symbolic" approach—which is not to be confused with allegory—is rejected, the problems in these two accounts will remain. Indeed, they will be greater, for the critic must then come to negative conclusions about the historian's judgment and competence. Rather than release Peter from prison he will have locked him up much too early, and he will, like the apocryphal Oscar Wilde, have become so engrossed in the adventures of Paul as to lose all sense of proportion. By reading these accounts as individual and general stories of new life, the critic delivers Luke the author from the perils of literary catastrophe, but the historical price that must be paid for this liberation is substantial. Luke the narrative theologian receives high marks, but the question of whether Luke can be story teller, theologian, *and* historian looks more and more like a case of critics who wish to have their cake and eat it too.

Much of the investigation to this point has looked at historical problems created by the literary intentions and program of the author of Acts, as well as some generated by ideological interests. There are others of the latter type, and some difficulties that may be due to mere ignorance or other innocent causes. The detective is beginning to develop a working hypothesis. The question of whether there was an actual crime has arisen. Could the tomb be empty? In order to learn the answer to this and other questions you will have to read on.

References and Further Reading

For proposals to read Acts 12 and 27 as symbolic death and resurrection stories, note in English:

> R. B. Rackham, *The Acts of the Apostles*. 2nd Edition. London: Methuen & Co., 1904.
>
> Charles S.C. Williams, *The Acts of the Apostles*. HNTC. New York: Harper, 1957.

A more detailed analysis appears in two scholarly works:

> Walter Radl, *Paulus und Jesus im Lukanischen Doppelwerk: Untersuchungen zu Parallelmotiven im Lukasevangelium und in der Apostelgeschichte*. Bern: Peter Lang, 1975.
>
> Jean-Noel Aletti, *Quand Luc raconte. Le récit comme théologie*. Lire la Bible 115. Paris: Cerf, 1998.

On parallels between the "passions" of Jesus and Paul see Jerome Neyrey, *The Passion according to Luke: A Redaction Study of Luke's Soteriology*. New York: Paulist, 1985.

A recent collection of essays on the parables of Jesus is Edward F. Beutner, ed., *Listening to the Parables of Jesus*. Santa Rosa, CA: Polebridge, 2007.

Endnotes

1. Protestant critics did not object to symbolic interpretation as such. Their chief target was allegorical interpretation that claimed to have found all of medieval dogma in the latent meaning of biblical texts.

2. The Middle Ages did not abolish the literal meaning of the Christian Old Testament. In areas of law and purity literal application may be said to have gained ground. Usury (interest) was prohibited (and thus left to Jews). Menstruants were to abstain from the sacraments, a practice that was not uncommon a few generations ago and still exists among some Christian groups. This practice of literal interpretation of Hebrew codes had a large impact upon ecclesiastical, secular, and social history, including post-Reformation bodies that banished representative art from churches and enforced "Sabbath" rules.

Chapter Seven

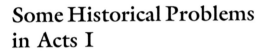

Some Historical Problems in Acts I

A Review of the Text

Introduction

Up to this point the narrator has reduced the worksheets of the patient investigator to manageable proportions, ignoring some dead ends and most false leads, selecting certain matters as representative and (one hopes) interesting examples from among numerous possibilities. The present chapter will contain a good deal less of such reader-friendly distillation. What follows is all too close in form to a catalogue. The arrangement is relatively primitive, beginning at Acts 1 and proceeding through Acts 28, yet another trip over ground that has already been partially surveyed. Cumbersome as it may seem, this catalogue is selective. Only the more choice and exotic items will be on display.

The dictum of a famous detective has already been mentioned: when you have eliminated all that is impossible, what remains must be the truth, however improbable. This works well in fiction, but in the untidy world of fact one often enough finds more than a single possibility. Historians do not live in a world dominated by black and white. Possibilities abound, and impossibilities are rather rare. The choice must be among greater and lesser probabilities. Miss Marple proposed a different sort of axiom: if a theory accounts for all of the facts, it must be correct. Lose the "must." Such theories *may* be correct, but the history of scholarship has repeatedly shown that new facts emerge and that some hypotheses that do not appear to account for all of the facts eventually prove correct. Critics of the heliocentric theory noted that it failed to account for the parallax of the stars. This was a strong point, not refuted until later astronomers discovered the great distance of other stars from the solar system.

A kind of corollary to the above-mentioned Holmesian axiom is often present in the work of those committed to demonstrating the historicity of various passages in Acts. This unstated premise proposes that if the researcher can claim something to be possible, it is therefore true. Absurd as this notion is when reduced to print, it is far from rare, and may deceive the unwary. Not all that is possible is probable, and some probabilities are greater than others. A second fallacy is a near relative of the "historical kernel" approach to legends. (See Chapter Five.) As a small child I was exposed upon several occasions to a story about Abraham Lincoln and a penny.

> The future president was clerking in a store. When he discovered that he had inadvertently short-changed a customer by a cent, he set out after work to return it. It was, of course, winter; the snow was deep and the wind fierce. Naturally, this customer happened to live at a distance of some miles. Lincoln made his way, on foot, to the farmer's home and returned the cent.

What, pray tell, is the "historical kernel" of this tale? That Lincoln once worked in a store? That would be irrelevant. This is a biographical legend that intends to illustrate the epithet "Honest Abe." The historical kernel amounts to a campaign slogan. In dealing with material of this nature the key task is not to ask what is true, but *what is the function of the passage*.

A variant to the dubious quest for the historical kernel appears more reasonable on the surface. This is the assumption that when one has removed from a story all that is patently legendary or false, the residue is true. One of its false assumptions is that more or less every difficult passage is a mixture of true and false. Another is that the false is readily identifiable. Attempt, if you will be so kind, to apply this approach to the story about Lincoln. Every detail of the anecdote is quite realistic; nothing in it is improbable. The story could even be quite true—in which case it would suggest an "Over-scrupulous Abe," who should have left a note that Farmer Jones was due a penny when he next came to the town store. The "truth" of this story resides in its function as Lincolnian hagiography. Neither the effort to find an "historical kernel" nor the pursuit of truth through removal of the obviously false is a *generally* valid critical technique.

Acts 16:25–26, cited earlier (p. 61), will serve as a specific illustration of the second questionable approach. The narrative reads, "there was an earthquake, so violent that the foundations of the prison were shaken; and immediately all the doors were opened and everyone's chains were unfastened." The rationalizing historian accepts the earthquake, common enough in Turkey, posits shoddy construction, ditto, and presumes that since earthquakes don't make manacles fall off, what came loose were the wooden stocks in which the prisoners' shackles were secured. If one tacitly ignores the narrative implication that this earthquake was the result of prayer by Paul and Silas and adjusts the statement about their chains, the residue is quite plausible. This procedure may seem reasonable but it is not, for it overlooks the story's clear intention to relate a miracle. Luke certainly would have been repelled by this "defense" of his narrative. All too often, rationalization tosses the baby overboard while carefully preserving the bathwater.

Indeed, the quest for a factual core not infrequently leads to a failure to address historical problems. In this case the "historical kernel" is readily identifiable and undisputed: Paul was jailed in Philippi. 1 Thessalonians 2:2 may be introduced to support this hypothesis. A probable fact has been established. Luke's object, however, was not to establish said fact. He wished to give it a positive spin and therefore spins out all of his details. Paul's opponents were representatives of the most vulgar form of religion, exploiting a poor slave girl in order to dupe the public out of their hard-earned currency. Paul, in short, was arrested for performing a benefaction. Obtaining this arrest involved the well-known devices of stirring up an excitable crowd and stampeding helpless officials into the execution of rough injustice. When things had settled down, the magistrates did the right thing. As for the jailer, the earthquake had made clear what side God was on; and Paul, even though unjustly imprisoned, demonstrated his commitment to law and order by keeping the others in custody.

The object of these paragraphs has been to point out that Luke has done all that he could to make the painful historical kernel—Paul was in trouble in Philippi—palatable. Rather than fracture an unwary tooth, that kernel will now melt in the mouth. This introduction has attempted to identify some unacceptable methods of historical research and to indicate why they are likely to yield misleading results rather than expose the historical bedrock of Acts. The methods under attack are comparable to the techniques of those primitive archaeologists who destroyed vast amounts of valuable material in the quest for presumed treasure. Archaeologists admire handsome objects, but they often find greater treasure in a datable and locatable fragment of pottery or a boring inscription. Enough space has been devoted to preparation. Now it's on to the excavation!

Acts 1–7

Chapter Five argued that Acts 3–7 is a series of cycles from which only limited historical information may be derived. In Chapter Two problems related to the beginning of Acts came into view. A basic issue is that the close of Luke's Gospel places the Ascension on Easter Day, whereas in Acts 1:1–11 it comes forty days later. This is a contradiction that cannot be resolved by the claim that Jesus ascended on the day he rose but repeatedly descended to make appearances, for his final words are the nearly the same on each occasion. This is a contradiction. Acts 1:14 notes the presence of the family of Jesus among the believers. His mother and siblings pop in without explanation. (Behind this surprise lie mysteries about which historians of the Jesus movement would love to learn.) Prior to that tidbit the narrator gives the names of eleven men whose status and role is not explained, although the catalogue closely resembles the list of "apostles" in Luke 6:13–16.

In Acts 1:15 it transpires that the community numbered about 120. The narrator does not say what drew these people, whether they are the result of missionary enterprise or leftovers from the throngs of those who had come from Galilee and/or other admirers. On this occasion Peter delivers a speech that is both problematic and revelatory. Through its anachronisms, notably the retelling of events (the death of Judas) that were both recent and well-known to the audience, as well as his translation of an Aramaic phrase—as if an Aramaic-speaking group listening to a speech given in Aramaic required a translation—the narrator shows that the speeches in Acts are not intended for the dramatic audience but for the readers of the book. Reinforcement comes from his use of the Greek Bible to establish his arguments. The import of this is not so much that the speeches in Acts raise particular historical problems, but that they are of little or no historical value for the circumstances they purport to address. From them one may make many inferences about the situation(s) envisioned by the narrator, but not about the immediate settings in which they appear. This observation consigns about 30% of Acts to the basket reserved for non-historical data. But inasmuch as both historians and other ancient authors were expected to compose the speeches they reported, this is quite unremarkable.

Peter's speech in Acts 1 presumes and demands that there be "Twelve Apostles." Luke does not say why, though the question will become important when others perish, as in Acts 12:1–2. Paul also knows of the Twelve (1 Corinthians 15:5). Luke does not explain their origin, although he is clear about their function: to bear witness to Jesus. According to Acts 1:8 that witness will extend to Jerusalem, all Judea, Samaria, and the ends of the earth. Later traditions will develop and exploit this worthy notion, but Luke is not among its advocates. Peter and John will go to Samaria, Peter to various parts of Judea, but there, in the narrative of Acts, their witness ends, leaving others to take up the responsibility for "the ends of the earth." Luke's material about the Twelve and their mission raises far more questions than it answers. While one does not want to whip a dead horse, some observations and analyses are still necessary, because Luke is a magician who sets forth his narrative in ways that discourage readers from posing questions that upon reflection seem as obvious as daylight.

To see why solving some mysteries requires concerted effort, it will be helpful to read Acts 2:1–13 with care:

When the day of Pentecost had come, they were all together in one place. And suddenly from heaven there came a sound like the rush of a violent wind, and it filled the entire house where they were sitting. Divided tongues, as of fire, appeared among them, and a tongue rested on each of them. All of them were filled with the Holy Spirit and began to speak in other languages, as the Spirit gave them ability.

Now there were devout Jews from every nation under heaven living in Jerusalem. And at this sound the crowd gathered and was bewildered, because each one heard them speaking in the native language of each. Amazed and astonished, they asked, "Are not all these who are speaking Galileans? And how is it that we hear, each of us, in our own native language? Parthians, Medes, Elamites, and residents of Mesopotamia, Judea and Cappadocia, Pontus and Asia, Phrygia and Pamphylia, Egypt and the parts of Libya belonging to Cyrene, and visitors from Rome, both Jews and proselytes, Cretans and Arabs—in our own languages we hear them speaking about God's deeds of power." All were amazed and perplexed, saying to one another, "What does this mean?" But others sneered and said, "They are filled with new wine."

The story is deservedly famous, for it accomplishes a great deal in a few exciting sentences. But just what does it say? A group of people is gathered, perhaps for devotion. Next comes *son et lumière*, the sound like that of wind and a light resembling fire, after which "they" (presumably all one hundred twenty) are inspired and speak in tongues. The meaning seems clear enough at first: this is the phenomenon called "glossolalia," "speaking in tongues." Although this noise emanates from inside a house, it somehow becomes loud enough to attract an evidently loud and certainly diverse crowd, which somehow knows that the speakers are from Galilee. The members of this crowd do not hear ecstatic speech, but a religious message in their respective native tongues, and all are astonished by this phenomenon. Rationally speaking, it means that each person would have heard someone speaking Latin or Egyptian, etc. The context demands a conversation in which one participant says to another, "Do you know what that language is? It's Phrygian," to which the companion replies, "Nah. You're crazy! That's the native language of rural Cyrene," and so forth. The narrative telescopes such conversation, leaving only the conclusion that everyone is hearing the native language of the place where he or she was reared. Some could not determine what all this meant, but others were clearly skeptical: "they're drunk." What can that mean? It is unlikely that someone from Parthia hearing words in her native language would conclude that the speaker was inebriated. That charge *would*, however, fit glossolalia, which involves unintelligible speech, but it does not suit the linguistic wonder narrated.

Just as suddenly as the arrival of the noise and fire, Peter, who is standing with his colleagues, attempts to explain matters. And just as suddenly the whole show has moved out of doors—not to a crowded street-corner in a teeming city, but to a space large enough to accommodate more than three thousand rapt and remorseful listeners. Peter neatly refutes the charge that they are "wasted" by noting that it is too early in the day to be drinking. Then he gets down to business. His speech was so successful that more than 3,000 chose to be baptized. That is a notable percentage of the population of Jerusalem, but the real problem is the business of baptism. Nowhere in Luke or Acts has it been stated that followers of Jesus are to be baptized in his name. In Acts 2:38 Peter promulgates the practice, the formula, and the benefits of this rite without any hint that this has not been a customary procedure. The truth is, of course, that for the readers baptism was customary and need not be explained. The narrative of Acts 2 is, in a word, a shambles, but Luke moves so rapidly and with such vividness that readers overlook these difficulties. Once the narrative has been taken apart, however, not even a determined critic can reassemble it.

Acts 4:2 reports that the leading officials and the Sadducees took exception to the proclamation of the resurrection and had Peter and John jailed. In v. 8, however, they interrogate the two men about the healing they performed in the previous chapter. This leads to a quandary that results in a ban on teaching in the name of Jesus, an edict that obliquely echoes the charge of v. 2. By 5:17 jealousy over the success of the movement has become homicidal. The assumption of the narrative is that the authorities can execute persons found guilty of heresy. That is not true. The Roman prefect (governor) reserved capital jurisdiction for himself, as the story of Jesus indicates.

According to 4:4 the movement had attracted 5,000 men, a figure that would entail well over 10,000 followers, not improbably 20,000, and certainly a very substantial proportion of the population of Jerusalem. For Luke the "crime" is teaching and proclaiming resurrection in the name of Jesus. That is an anachronism, referring to a considerably later period when the "name" (that is, status) of "Christian" was a possible ground for execution. Luke is clear that the Jewish leaders are jealous, frustrated, unhappy about miracles, and chagrined at being blamed for the death of Jesus; but he does not explain why the ruling elite were so strongly opposed to the followers of Jesus.

Chapter 6 raises new problems. A group known as "the Hellenists," the origin and nature of which is not explained, materializes. Presumably they spoke Greek. To resolve a conflict over food distribution, Peter and the Twelve call for the appointment of seven men to undertake this work. All seven have Greek names. What their opposite numbers among the "Hebrews" might have thought of being excluded receives no attention. Did the "Hebrews" speak Hebrew? Rather than resolve this quandary, Luke omits any further discussion of the matter, turning instead to the subsequent activities of two of the seven, Stephen and Philip . . . as *missionaries!* This is a fine mess. All of the specific information that Luke provides about the Seven (a title used in 21:8) suggests that they engaged in evangelizing people who spoke Greek. Chapter 6 also claims that Stephen was accused of attacking the Torah. Although his speech in chapter 7 does little to alleviate these charges, the narrator views them as slander. What was going on beneath the surface has been a matter of dispute for more than a century and a half.

The narrative of Acts 7 does not clarify whether the death of Stephen was due to a lynch mob or to a legal judgment. Clearly, the narrative implies that with the arrival of Stephen opposition begins to include the broader public as well as the officials. The narrator does not say, "When controversy arose about the *Torah and the temple, antagonism to the movement spread from the high priestly class to the common people." That conclusion is an inference made by historians. Then with Stephen's death, Saul enters the narrative. In 7:58 he serves as the "coat-check boy" for Stephen's assailants. Five verses later he is conducting raids into homes and hauling men and women off to jail, a leader of what has become a general persecution. This is a major and unexplained change. Luke says that the persecution moved from actions against the leadership to arrests of anyone involved in the movement, but he does not present a coherent or creditable account of this development, leaving historians to engage in informed conjecture and tortuous inference. All of the resultant historical reconstructions proceed from the assumption that such truth as is available comes from reading between the lines of Acts rather than from the clarity and completeness of its narration.

Acts 8–12

Acts 8:4–25 describe a mission to Samaria. An influx of *Samaritan Jews evidently had an important impact upon at least some sectors of the Jesus-movement. Noteworthy in this regard is John 4, especially vv. 39–42, but Luke is of no use here. He sends Philip to "the city of Samaria" (or possibly, but less likely, "a city"). In either case the information is hopelessly vague. As for the mission itself, the account focuses upon the miracles worked by Philip as a motive for conversion, as well as the encounter between Philip and a local religious figure named Simon. From the account it seems that baptism need not convey the gift of the spirit (unlike 2:38), since the believing Samaritans manifest this gift only after Peter and John lay sacramental hands upon them. No human controls the spirit in Acts. This is a sound theological principle, but the varying accounts have given theologians considerable difficulties.

The Ethiopian court official thereafter converted by Philip (8:26–39) is a figure of dubious historicity. He has learned Judaism and the Greek language, two quite unlikely accomplishments for one who lives at a great remove from the Mediterranean civilizations. His status is left unclear. One would expect him to be a gentile, but he is not so characterized. The story is included for its symbolic value. (See p. 98.) To top it off, when he rose from the water of baptism, the spirit did indeed descend, but upon Philip instead of his convert. Samaria may be a shadow land in Acts, but it boasts a detailed map in comparison to this road toward Gaza. After dropping Philip off at Azotus for a coastal mission, the narrator redirects his attention to the career of Paul the persecutor. To be sure, 9:36 does speak of believers at Joppa, but the narrator does not say how they were converted. Perhaps readers are to infer that Philip had introduced them to the faith.

According to Acts 9 there were believers in Damascus. Luke does not explain the origin of this community. Furthermore, Paul receives written authority from the high priest to seize these persons and bring them to Jerusalem. It is most unlikely that the chief priest possessed the power to interfere in the affairs of another province and have its residents extradited to stand trial for capital charges (cf. 26:10) in his court. This is a fantasy with serious historical implications. It has become the basis of the portrait of Paul the Persecutor. Paul certainly did "persecute" followers of Jesus: "You have heard, no doubt, of my earlier life in Judaism. I was violently persecuting the church of God and was trying to destroy it" (Gal 1:13; cf. v. 23). The common notion of the persecution of early Christians is well expressed in its full Hollywood form, complete with arenas, bloodthirsty mobs, lions, and a gloating tyrant. Even hard-headed scholars may succumb to this view. An example is the committee that produced the NRSV, just quoted. The phrase translated "violently" is better rendered by the "intensely" of the New International Version and the New Jerusalem Bible. Paul's persecution probably took the form of verbal harassment, debate, and efforts toward social ostracism. (Such persecution may be much more insidious and effective than the creation of martyrs around whom a cause may rally.) Luke prefers persecution of the Hollywood variety, and his picture has stuck.

According to Acts, Paul was en route to Damascus when he experienced the vision that led to a change of mind. Galatians, however, implies that he lived in Damascus at this time ("afterwards I returned to Damascus," Gal 1:17). For Acts it is important that Paul was a resident of Jerusalem, and the narrative has been adjusted to fit this conception. Acts 9:23–25 tell how Paul escaped a Jewish plot in Damascus. His enemies, determined to kill him, placed guards at all the city gates, but Paul was lowered from an opening in the wall and fled. One is justified in asking why these enemies did not ambush him in the streets or whack him in his bed. By their tactic they gave Paul free reign to continue his mission in the city until he had decided to leave. Equally justifiable is the question of why the authorities would allow members of an ethnic and religious community to post guards at these key places. In this case Acts can be checked against the plausible account of Paul (2 Cor 11:32–33), who states that he was wanted by the government. Acts 9:26 has Paul proceed from Damascus to Jerusalem. This introduces one of the most notorious

historical problems in Acts: the difference between its reports of
Paul's visits to Jerusalem and his own account in Galatians 1–2. The
major data are laid out in **Table 7.1**.

The issue is not simply that Acts gives Paul an extra visit to
Jerusalem or varies in some details. In Galatians 1–2 Paul doubtless
seeks to make the best possible construction of his case in the face
of criticism, but he vows that he is telling the truth (Gal 1:20). The
story told in Acts is rather close to the very rumors and allegations
that Paul takes such pains to refute in Galatians. Luke's account
evidently agrees with Paul's opponents in Galatians that Paul subordinated himself to the apostles in Jerusalem. There are additional
problems, one of which is the Collection. Most scholars have held

Table 7.1: Acts and Galatians

Galatians 1–2	Acts 7–15
1:13–14. Paul as zealous Jew, "persecutor" of Church.	8:3; 9:1–2; 26:9–12. Saul as member of Sanhedrin carrying out violent persecution of the Way in and beyond Judea.
1:15–17. "Converted/called" visits no one; does not go to Jerusalem. To Arabia, then *returns* to Damascus. 18. *After three years* **1st visit to Jerusalem** saw none but "pillars."	9:3–19 "Converted" on route to Damascus; instructed, baptized by believer; preaches in Damascus, then 26–29 **1st visit to Jerusalem** sees the apostles. Sent to Tarsus
21. To Syria (Antioch) and Cilicia (Tarsus)	(Acts 7:58; 22:3; 26:4–6; 9:26–30 contradict. Galatians 1)
22–24. Strong denials that that he was known to churches in Judea.	11:25–26. From Tarsus to Antioch. Mission of one-year duration.
2:1–10. Paul, Barnabas and Titus go to Jerusalem. This is the **2nd visit to Jerusalem** noted by Paul. Purpose: issue of gentiles and circumcision. Paul promises to bring assistance.	11:27–30. Paul and Barnabas make a **2nd visit to Jerusalem**. The purpose was to bring charity. 15:1–4. Paul and Barnabas (without Titus) make his **3rd visit to Jerusalem**. Purpose: issue of gentiles and circumcision.

that Luke had an alibi for these errors: he was not aware of Paul's letters, but this alibi has been discredited: Luke knew the letters. (See p. 162.)

Acts 10:1–11:18 records in great detail and with considerable gravity the first "official" conversion of a gentile. Peter is the agent, carefully directed by God, and Cornelius, a centurion, is the subject. (The modern equivalent to "centurion" would be either a major or a colonel.) It is possible that Peter converted the first gentile, although this must be weighed against the Lucan tendency to give him priority and to remove from Paul (and others) the putative stigma of approaching gentiles. Peter did it, and he was anything but willing to approach gentiles without specific commands from on high. The narrative has some glitches and arouses many suspicions, but it is generally cohesive. Chapter 11, on the other hand, raises two difficulties worthy of notice. The first is the identity of Peter's critics, literally "those of the circumcision" (NRSV: "the circumcised believers"). This means (male) Jews. The difficulty is that there were no "uncircumcised (male) believers" in Jerusalem at that time.

This is so gross an anachronism that interpreters are inclined to refer it to a party that demanded circumcision of all male converts, as in RSV: "the circumcision party." That interpretation does no more than shift the anachronism, since it is not feasible that such a party could have organized itself within a matter of days. In Acts 15 there is something like a "circumcision party," or at least some advocates of circumcision. Their views seem to have been clumsily transferred to the earlier chapter. Still, the chief issue between Acts 11 and Acts 15 is not this unsightly anachronism. It is that subsequent to Acts 11, the meeting narrated in Acts 15 was totally unnecessary. God had settled the issue. As Gamaliel had pointed out, resistance to the will of God is inadvisable (5:38–39).

Now (11:19–26) Luke goes back to those scattered at the beginning of chapter 8. These persons engaged in a mission in Phoenicia (the Mediterranean coast of Palestine) and Cyprus, eventually arriving at the Syrian capital of Antioch. Among them were some anonymous Cypriots and Cyreneans. (Cyrene, modern Libya, included some Greek cities and their environs.) Why does Luke not name these people? Acts 4:36 mentions a Cypriot named Barnabas, but according to 4:37 and 11:22 he was in Jerusalem at this time. Acts 13:1 takes note of a certain "Lucius of Cyrene." Never mind. The point is that these missionaries targeted only Jews until they came to Antioch, where they began to address "Hellenists," which here must mean "gentiles," despite Acts 6:1–7.

The narrator does not say why they undertook this momentous change. One would expect Luke to attribute it to divine direction, but he does not. He is probably following a source here, and probably also removing some names. It is plain to see that the narrative withholds this information until after it has related the official acceptance of Peter's baptism of Cornelius. Luke is fudging his sources to relate (that is, create) an orderly progression. In line with that conception, Barnabas is sent north from Jerusalem and in turn sends for Paul, who had been parked in Tarsus. The progression *is* orderly, from Jerusalem outwards. It is magnificent, but it is not history.

Acts 13–19

Acts 12, which was discussed at some length in the previous chapter, may be bypassed. At 13:4, after a solemn commissioning, Paul and Barnabas (with Mark, cf. 12:12, 25) set out for Cyprus. This mission appears to ignore gentiles, since only synagogues are mentioned. For some reason the very sketchy narrative summary makes no connection between this enterprise and the earlier mission to Cyprus (11:19), nor does it record any successes. The single specific incident is the cursing of a Jewish magician who is the spiritual mentor of Sergius Paulus, the Roman governor. When the false prophet was struck blind, the proconsul immediately converted to the faith. It is absolutely astonishing that such a coup should be handled in so blasé a fashion. There would be nothing like it for centuries. Be that modesty as it may, the mission, with the proconsul's prestige and resources, now has an excellent base. Conversions thereafter should be rapid and numerous. Even more astonishing than the narrator's nonchalance about the conversion of Sergius Paulus therefore, is the response of the missionaries. Rather than exploit this marvelous opportunity, they turn their backs upon it and sail away.

The mission to Cyprus is mysterious, but its function is clear: to establish through the one concrete incident the superiority of Paul. The balance of the "first missionary journey" deals with southern Asia Minor (sixty-nine verses as opposed to nine for Cyprus). Cyprus seems best forgotten. When Paul and Barnabas go back over the route in 14:21–23, they omit it from their travels. The major difficulty in this narrative is not the role of Cyprus, but the itinerary. Attempting to reach the interior of Asia Minor from the southern coast involves a very difficult journey over the mountains, as may be seen by consulting a relief map, examples of which are included in many Bibles. The logical way to go to Derbe, etc. would be overland from Antioch. Luke has thus outlined an improbable journey, quite unlike the travels to follow in chapters 16–21, which proceed along normal routes. The balance of Acts 13–14 has already been a subject of inquiry and requires no further attention. Chapter Five sought to show that the episodes are stereotyped or, as in 14:8–10, a parallel probably created by the author. Other than the abandoned Sergius Paulus, not one convert is named. There is a single touch of local color: the temple of Zeus before the city in Lystra, the existence of which is possible though unverified. But the narrator fails to note, for example, that both Antioch and Lystra were Roman colonies. Readers of Acts would be justified in concluding that the cities of southern Asia Minor were governed by mobs.

In 14:6 the missionaries "fled to Lystra and Derbe, cities of Lycaonia." In fact Derbe is almost twice the distance from Lystra that Lystra is from Iconium. The entire journey of Acts 13–14 raises an unwieldy bundle of historical and geographical problems. To prop up the vague and questionable accuracy of this material, there arose the "South Galatian hypothesis," which contends that Paul's letter to the Galatians targeted the localities mentioned in chapters 13–14. The arguments against this hypothesis are quite strong. It is unlikely that the proposal would have seen the light of day had Acts not occupied the place of privilege in the reconstruction of Pauline history. Luke scarcely mentions Paul's work in the area actually addressed by Galatians (the cities in the northern part of this region, including Ancyra, Gordium, and Tavium), possibly because of the subsequent controversies (cf. 16:6; 19:1).

The function of the "first journey" is *not* vague. By converting gentiles Paul and Barnabas set the agenda for the famous "council" of Acts 15. This, in turn, presents its own historical problems. One has been mentioned: it should not have been necessary to hold this meeting, because the issue had been decided long ago. Peter says as much in 15:7–11. Another is that, although Peter and "the apostles" (15:6, 22, 23) are present, actual leadership is in the hands of James. Luke assigns him no title and offers no explanation of how he came to usurp, as it were, the authority of Peter and the others. Still more problematic is the decree issued by the council, which establishes minimal criteria for gentile believers (15:22, 30, see p.162). These are provisions of which Paul was unaware, or in any case did not regard as binding, for he considers the issue of eating food offered to idols a discussable question (1 Corinthians 8–10) rather than a practice banned by apostolic mandate. That decree links Paul firmly to the church at Jerusalem and its leadership, a subordination that Paul himself rejected (Galatians 1–2).

Table 7.2: Acts (10) 11 and Acts (14) 15[1]

Item	Acts 11	Acts 15
God elects gentiles	10:44–47	14:27
Fellowship with Converts	10:48	14:28
Word comes to Judea	11:1	15:1
Visit to Jerusalem	11:2–3	15:2
Objection about uncircum-cised males	11:2–3	15:5
Arguments for circumcision	—	—
Arguments for not requiring Torah		
(1) Divine Choice	11:5–12	15:7
(2) Gift of Spirit	11:15	15:8
(3) Conforms to prophecy	Cf. 11:16	15:15
Decision to accept gentiles	11:18	15:19
Barnabas and Paul go to Antioch	11:22, 25–26	15:22, 30
Antioch mission prospers	11:26	15:35

Almost as if to emphasize the redundancy of Acts 11:1–18 and 15:1–29, Luke has each conform to a nearly identical sequence, as **Table 7.2** indicates.

The essential pattern is that of 6:1–7 and is a variant of the persecution/opposition scheme: A problem arises, whereupon the matter is promptly resolved in a church assembly, leading to greater success. Acts 15 is far more elaborate and exciting than Acts 11:1–18, but the process and result exhibit a standard and familiar problem-solving model. Note that the "decree" takes the form of a letter. Luke is aware of the use of letters in church life, but he will not allow Paul to get any closer to a letter of that nature than to accompany its official bearers. The letter deals with the conflict in Antioch and is thus addressed to Antioch and environs, but as 16:4 indicates, it applies to all gentile believers. Acts evidently endorses the notion that apostolic letters apply to all believers everywhere. The same notion of universality appears in the published edition of Paul's letters, which had to overcome the "problem of particularity": in short, "How does what Paul may have had to say to people in Corinth at one time apply to us here and now?"

Note: Attempts to overcome the particularity of Paul's letters have left traces in the manuscript tradition. Note the texts of Romans 1:7, 15 in **Table 7.3**.

Table 7.3

Romans 1:7, 15 (NRSV)	Romans 1:7, 15 (Some Manuscripts)
7. To all God's beloved in Rome, who are called to be saints: Grace to you and peace from God our Father and the Lord Jesus Christ. 15.—hence my eagerness to proclaim the gospel to you also who are in Rome.	7. To all God's beloved who are called to be saints: Grace to you and peace from God our Father and the Lord Jesus Christ. 15.—hence my eagerness to proclaim the gospel to you also.

The undoubtedly original text is that of the left-hand column. Elimination of "Rome" in the right-hand examples makes these words apply to all believers everywhere. A similar situation is apparent in Ephesians 1:1, as can be seen from the note in the NRSV, which includes the reading given in the RSV. Note also 1 Corinthians 1:2: "To the church of God that is in Corinth, to those who are sanctified in Christ Jesus, called to be saints, *together with all those who in every place call on the name of our Lord Jesus Christ,* both their Lord and ours." The italicized words were evidently added to make the address universal.

Acts 15:36–39 tells how Paul and Barnabas happened to go their separate ways. The break-up is reported to have been the result of a dispute over personnel: Barnabas wished to retain John Mark as an assistant, Paul disagreed, and in the end Barnabas took Mark anyway. Together they sailed for Cyprus and out of the pages of Acts, which has no report of their mission. (Cyprus gets fewer reported results than any other site mentioned more than once in Acts.) This scenario may look reasonable, but it is erroneous. Paul and Barnabas separated over a conflict about what Paul viewed as doctrine. Because Barnabas belonged to the prevailing side (Gal 2:11–14), Paul left Antioch and became an independent missionary, with momentous consequences for history. Luke, like many witnesses encountered by detectives, seeks to mislead the investigator here.

Only in chapter 16:1–3 does Acts report the name of someone converted in consequence of the "first journey." This is Timothy.

Whom Paul circumcises! Following the heated debate and formal conclusions of chapter 15, this action stuns any attentive reader. The motive is avoidance of trouble with local *Jews*. That makes very limited sense, and it is for good reason that the affair is quite a problem for historians, a large number of whom do not believe it. Many will think of the uncircumcised Titus (Gal 2:3), whose very existence Luke does not acknowledge. The properly circumcised Timothy replaces the uncircumcised gentile Titus in Acts. (Both were, of course, colleagues of the historical Paul.) Luke deals with the controversies about Paul and *Torah by indicating that although Paul did not *have* to obey the Law, he did so of his own free choice. The freshly circumcised Timothy replaces John Mark and serves as a proper assistant rather than as a colleague. In Acts Paul does not have collaborators; he has helpers. In place of Barnabas there now appears Silas, who like his predecessor came from Jerusalem.

Chapter Four included a review of Acts 16–19, a few additional themes and details from which will receive attention here. In Philippi Paul had a run-in with the law, eventuating in a public whipping and incarceration. With the next morning came release. Paul did not accept this exoneration lightly, contending that what had been done to Silas and himself was illegal. They were after all Roman citizens. In 16:37 readers hear of this vital political fact for the first time. Some of them may wonder why Paul did not object when his punishment was ordered. That is an excellent question, especially since the consensus of critical opinion is that Paul *did* hold Roman citizenship. The case of Silas is more difficult, so he is usually passed over in silence. This matter will require additional attention. (See Chapter Eight.) When Paul next mentions his citizenship, the situation is similar. He does so at the last second, just as torturers are about to exercise their technical skill (22:25). In Acts Paul's citizenship works as a literary device.

The close of the mission to Philippi exhibits another feature of the narrative. Paul falls into the tangles of the law, but is vindicated. The strange thing is that he promptly leaves town. In addition to Philippi (16:40), this pattern recurs in Athens (18:1), Corinth (18:18), and, with variation, in Ephesus (20:1), where Paul was not brought to trial but was the motive force behind a civil disturbance. Historians tend to become suspicious of characters who are always innocent but nonetheless grasp every opportunity for prompt relocation. Paul is never found guilty of any crime. In Judea (Acts 21–26) he is repeatedly declared innocent but remains in custody. His Judean trials also raise questions in the critical mind. Paul's engagement with governmental systems in Acts is rather like his approach to *Torah.

Although never found guilty, he regularly *chooses* to leave, until the option has been closed, whereupon he becomes the innocent and admired prisoner who, alas, cannot be released.

At the close of Acts 18 the narrator takes care to remove Paul from the stage in order to introduce Apollos. Eloquent and learned as this Alexandrian sage was, his theology proved out of date. The hitherto inactive Aquila and Priscilla set him straight and saw him off to Corinth. Given the evident tensions visible in 1 Corinthians 1–4, the dissociation of Apollos from Paul is interesting. In fact, Paul did have a personal relationship with Apollos (1 Cor 16:12); yet any difficulties regarding Apollos pale in comparison to those of the opening of Acts 19. The narrator does not report that Paul arrived in Ephesus and reestablished contact with Aquila and his good wife. Instead, we read that he "came upon some believers" (19:1), whose credentials he investigates in the next two verses:

"Did you receive the holy spirit when you came to believe?"
"Holy spirit? We've never even heard of it."
"What was the form of your baptism?"
"John's." (author's trans.)

Paul then explains the merely preparatory nature of John's baptism. These disciples immediately receive baptism in the name of the Lord Jesus, after which Paul lays hands upon them, resulting in the gift of the spirit as manifested in the appearance of tongues and prophecy. They were twelve in number. What is going on here? How did Paul encounter these men, whose presence had not become known to other followers of the Way? How can persons who apparently know nothing about Jesus be called (literally) "disciples," a word used elsewhere for Christians? Why did he ask them about the spirit? Were there really disciples of John the Baptizer in Ephesus? Would it have been possible for the existence of the holy spirit to have escaped their attention, since, within the context of Luke and Acts, John made prominent reference to the spirit's arrival? (See Luke 3:16.) With this bizarre story Luke has certainly given exegetes something to chew on. Fortunately, this investigator does not have to solve these intractable problems but only to identify them and then get back to the story.

Paul leaves these twelve to their own devices and heads for the synagogue, as if the community mentioned in 18:26 and the sheep recently extricated from the fold of John the Baptizer did not exist. After three months of confronting opposition, Paul pulled his followers out of the synagogue and began teaching in a suitable secular facility. By the time two years had passed the entire province had heard

the message (19:8–10). The balance of the chapter largely ignores
the mission in order to concentrate on Paul's impact upon the less
reputable manifestations of *polytheistic practice. As the biography
of a wonder-working hero this narrative is excellent. Rather than say,
"Paul did this and then he did that," the narrative relates some of the
effects of his work, allowing the reader to draw appropriate conclusions. (By this point the reader will be able to say: "Aha! The *trope
of narrative metonymy in action.")

This last episode is more than a little dubious, for it is not conceiv-
able that the number of believers in a city the size of Ephesus could
have constituted a visible threat to traditional religion by the middle
50s of the first century. In such a metropolis even 1,000 believers
would have been little more than a drop in the bucket, but a more
likely number would be 200. In Luke's time an impact like that
claimed in Acts 19:24–27 would fall into the realm of adventurous
hyperbole; in the time of Paul it could be no more than a deranged
fantasy. According to 19:31 some of the provincial officials (Asiarchs)
warned Paul against attempting to quell the storm. They took this
step not out of fear that he might make things worse, but because
they numbered him among their friends. Luke might as readily have
said that while in Rome Paul spent a number of evenings playing
bridge with the Emperor Nero. Asiarchs belonged to the thinnest
and finest layer of the upper crust of local society. Paul could have
made saddles for some of their households, but Asiarchs did not look
to artisans for social companionship. One or more of these worthies
might have listened to the lectures of a philosopher of humble background, but they were not likely to have become attracted to the
worship of a crucified rebel. Luke did not always see the past very
well, but his vision of the future could be remarkably astute.

Acts 20–28

Chapter 20 begins with plans for another swing around the circle,
this time through Macedonia and Greece as a preliminary to another
trip to Jerusalem. Paul had last gone to Jerusalem by himself in
18:18–23. That trip was trouble-free. This time Paul has a substantial entourage, seven in number, but ominous signs soon begin to
mount, signaled by a "Jewish plot" in 20:3. These are not extrane-
ous clues to the readers of the present book, for they have already
been elucidated: From Acts 20 onward Luke narrates a "passion of
Paul." (See pp. 107–8.) His companions were in fact the embassy
that would deliver the Collection raised for those in Jerusalem. As
noted, this is one movement in the story of Paul that Luke wished

to play on the softest of pedals. Acts 20:7–12 provides a charming interlude. Although Acts happily speaks of thousands of converts, whenever Luke envisions an assembled community, the setting is in a house (cf. 1:13; 2:2; 4:24–31; 12:12). That is how things were in the author's own time, although the larger cities had a number of "house churches," some of which were united in one way or another. Luke provides the material to refute his own statistical claims.

Acts 20:17–38 reports that Paul summoned the *presbyters of the church at Ephesus to meet him at Miletus, which is several days journey from Ephesus by foot. The major question is why Paul did not stop at Ephesus to meet with these leaders. A lesser question concerns their existence, since there has been no prior mention of such officials. Readers are evidently to infer from 14:23 that Paul ordained presbyters at all the churches he founded. The narrator of Acts seems to expect that the implied readers will be adept at making such inferences. The speech delivered to these leaders is quite atypical in that it looks toward the situation after Paul's "departure" (= death, v. 29). Paul's description of his missionary practice contains a few surprises, but the operating principle is not to judge speeches on historical grounds. It may nonetheless be worth noting that the speech at Miletus would be quite perplexing to a reader who was not aware that Paul would soon be arrested and that he would never get out of custody.

At 21:18, fifty-six verses after setting out, having received a warm welcome in Jerusalem, Paul meets James. Just as the narrator has not provided a reason for the length of the account, so also is there no reason provided for describing this meeting. With James are the *presbyters. The apostles of chapter 15 have vanished, again without explanation. As in that chapter (15:4), Paul begins by summarizing his work among the gentiles. As in 11:18, the hearers respond by praising God. Now Jerusalem has something of its own to report. Speaking in unison, James & Co. boast of the "myriads" of Jewish believers who have entered the fold. Without exception they are very observant. The punch line comes in v. 21: these people have heard that Paul promotes apostasy (that is, non-observance) among the Jews whom he has converted. For the narrator this is undoubtedly slander. About the historical Paul historians must wonder. The view taken by James and the Presbyters is that observance remains obligatory for those of Jewish origin, and their children after them. The historical Paul would not have agreed. In this story, however, he does not dispute that implicit understanding of the place of *Torah for Jewish followers of Jesus.

Having stated a problem, the leadership has a solution: Paul will demonstrate his own fidelity by a public display of both personal piety and generous charity. He is to undertake a vow with four of the faithful and pay their expenses, no small sum. The solution comes not as a suggestion but as a command. This may indeed show that Paul is observant, at least while in Jerusalem, but it does not touch upon the question of his teaching. One might expect that Paul would reply, "Of course, I'll do that. In addition, let's arrange a meeting with some of the more influential of these converts. You can tell them that these rumors are false, as shall I. Moreover, Timothy here will be living proof that the contention is false, for I circumcised him myself." That sounds like a good plan, and Paul was not averse to discussions of this—or any—nature. But the text reports no discussion; it is assumed that Paul will comply, and comply he does.

The proposed favorable testimony of James in Paul's behalf just now imagined touches upon an important point. The Jerusalem leaders assume no responsibility for dealing with these charges. That is entirely up to Paul. No solution is proposed for the basic accusation, the content of Paul's teaching. These are loud silences, and they grow louder, for in none of the accounts that follow, including four trials that extend through chapter 26, does a single one of these Jerusalem believers come forward to say that, far from bringing gentiles into the temple, Paul was purifying himself with four other observant Jews.

That testimony should have been decisive; in any case it would have challenged the prosecution to produce opposing witnesses of equal caliber. Paul could have introduced his four fellow devotees to support his claims. The opposition would have been strongly pressed to produce the guilty heathen. In short, according to the narrative of Acts, James could have destroyed the case against Paul at any moment. The implication of the narrative is not flattering to the Jerusalem community. That implication *may* not have been intended. What is clear is that the narrative is a sieve. As usual, Luke distracts readers from noting the plethora of holes by producing a flurry of rapid narrative filled with breath-taking twists and turns. Once again, good writing, but hardly good history.

That narrative begins with Paul's prompt obedience to orders. All went well until the end of the seventh and final day, when some Asian Jews started trouble. Incitement of riots appears to have been an Ephesian specialty that knew no barrier between Jew and Greek. In 21:28 these persons lay against Paul the charges that had earlier been made against Stephen (6:13), adding the claim that he had brought gentiles into the sacred precincts. The life of any gentile who entered the temple was forfeit. Laws about any who aided and abetted this activity are not known. The crowd here seeks not to lynch the putative goyyim, but Paul. He was delivered from certain lynching by the arrival of the Roman commander and some soldiers.

Just as he is about to be carried into the fortress (to be questioned under torture), Paul asks if he can say a word. The officer is astonished that Paul spoke Greek, for he had assumed that Paul was an Egyptian rebel. It is good that the tribune had not pursued a career in law enforcement, because this was almost as improbable as a deduction could be. To this inquiry Paul makes his famous proud reply ("a citizen of no mean city"). Awed, the officer allows him to deliver a public oration (21:37–40). The earlier observation has been confirmed, for there is nothing in the Crime Stopper's Handbook that recommends allowing the freshly arrested to deliver an oration.

At first Paul is able to calm the unruly mob with words, but when he speaks of a vision in the temple commanding him to go to the gentiles (22:21), the crowd becomes more frenzied than ever. Forget introducing gentiles into the temple. The very word "gentile" makes them scream for his blood. In the end the tribune decides to go by the book: Paul will be tortured into telling the truth. Just as they were about to wield the lash, Paul reveals his Roman citizenship. That revelation quashes the third degree tactic. Trying a different mode of investigation, the far from inflexible tribune summons the Sanhedrin to look into the matter on the next day. This hearing is no more than a farce. After an exchange of words and a slap in the face, Paul attempts to split the council (which contains both Sadducees and Pharisees) by proclaiming his faith in resurrection (a belief repudiated by the former party). That turns the august body into a mob from which Paul must once more be extracted. Evidently, the justification for his rhetorical ploy is the belief that the Sanhedrin would condemn him to death. In fact, logic would suggest an inquiry related to the charge that Paul introduced a gentile into the temple, or attempted to do so. That subject does not even come up (23:1–10). Improbability is being piled upon improbability.

Next comes a dire, fanatical, terrorist plot to assassinate Paul under the color of judicial interrogation. Thwarting this leads the tribune to reduce his forces to a dangerous minimum in order to provide security for Paul. He sends 470 soldiers of various arms to convey Paul some distance from Jerusalem, from whence a mere seventy horsemen were sufficient to escort him to the provincial capital to be held pending the arrival of his accusers. Acts 23:12–35 provides a fine opportunity to show that the Romans held Paul in high regard and believed him innocent, but the story would be more at home in an adventure story for boys than in a work of history.

The narrative then jumps ahead five days, when the accusers, now revealed to be the high priest and some of the elders, appear equipped with a Greek orator to lay their charges. The orator does just that, after which the many-talented Paul speaks in his own behalf. No evidence is examined. Felix, the governor, postpones a decision pending the arrival of Tribune Lysias (the arresting officer). Felix' inclinations become evident when the restrictions upon Paul are relaxed and he turns to the prisoner for theological conversations. When these take an unpleasant turn Felix ends them and begins to look for monetary rather than spiritual consolation. Lysias disappears from the picture, while Paul is left to languish in custody. Chapter 24 is, to say the least, difficult. The governor ought to have arranged a proper hearing, including witnesses and other evidence. Failing that, he should have issued orders to Lysias to appear forthwith. Readers can gain consolation from knowing Lysias' positive views about Paul and the apparent disinclination of Felix to buy the prosecution's story.

Chapter 25 brings a new broom to a floor badly in need of sweeping. Festus, the newly appointed governor, visits Jerusalem within three days of his arrival. Naturally, the case against Paul was his top priority. The Jewish officials asked that for the sake of convenience the miscreant Paul be sent to the holy city. The trip would be a splendid opportunity for an ambush. Festus, unaware of the Jewish leaders' proclivities toward terrorism, suggests that any accusations may be made in Caesarea, and takes up the case of *Jerusalem Leaders v. Paul* the day after his return. This hearing amounts to a replay of chapter 24, which the narrator need only summarize. Having shown who was boss, Festus is now prepared to be generous. He asks Paul whether he would accept a change of venue: trial at Jerusalem, but with himself presiding. The answer is obvious: "No thank you." Instead, Paul makes a stunning demand. He appeals to Caesar! The only ground for this is that he stands before Caesar's bench. That would also be true in Jerusalem, of course, if Festus were in the chair. His citizenship does not enter the picture. After receiving proper advice, Festus pompously accepts the appeal.

The case is out of his hands, but Festus does not know what to say in his brief to the imperial court. Fortunately King Agrippa strolls in, accompanied by his famous sister Bernice. Since he is Jewish, there is a chance that he may be able to shed light on the case. One may wonder why his being Jewish matters, for, if the charge is temple desecration, that is a relatively simple and not unfamiliar matter. Many temples had regulations about who could enter their bounds. The reason one is not inclined to question this illogical suggestion is that Luke has managed to shift the issue to matters of Israelite law and belief. The charge against which Paul has to defend himself is belief in the resurrection, a charge that did not carry the death penalty in any law book of that time. Be that as it may, Agrippa could have interrogated Paul, had notes taken, and drafted a sketch for Festus' brief from those data.

The format selected was a bit different: another public address, attended with a great deal of pomp and circumstance. Paul tells his story once more, with the predictable result. He may have some weird ideas, but they are not dangerous. Had he not appealed to Caesar, he could have been released. At this point, the reader is desperately anxious to usurp the role of the narrator, push Paul forward, and have him pronounce the ancient equivalent of "I herewith withdraw my appeal." In Acts, however, the appeal to Caesar is immutable. Paul cannot withdraw his appeal, although he made it under the most obscure circumstances for reasons that cannot be fathomed. After six chapters devoted to the issue, the legal situation of Paul has become utterly obscure. One need not argue that from the perspective of history, Acts 21:27–26:32 is deficient. For Rome Paul is destined (cf. 19:21) and, to take a leaf from the book of Festus, to Rome he will go.

Tribune Lysias is but one of many actual or potential witnesses who has evaporated from the narrative. When cases went to Rome, both parties, with all of their witnesses, documents, accomplices, and legal assistants, had to appear in the capital. Acts makes no more reference to such opposing delegations than it does to the ensuing trial. "When it was decided that we were to sail for Italy . . ." (Acts 27:1) reads like a fresh decision. The narrator does not say, "Since Paul had appealed, he was transferred to the custody. . . ." Except for Julius the Centurion, who had become fond of Paul, the soldiers treat the prisoners as condemned persons. The presumption of guilt is strong (27:42). In and of itself Acts 27 could just as well be an account of condemned prisoners sent to Rome for execution, rather than for trial. The reasons for this possible interpretation vary, ranging from over-reading and careless narration to the use of a first-hand account with many stages in between; but the observation is interesting, for it just may correspond to the facts. In any case, this is another historical difficulty of Acts.

Chapter 27 is justly famous. Concerning the voyage itself and its general difficulties the account is both vivid and apparently accurate.

Shipwreck was not a rare phenomenon. Prior to this occasion the historical Paul had been involved in three wrecks at sea (2 Cor 11:25). The leading difficulty in this story is that Paul, although one of a number of prisoners among 276 persons on board, is a V.I.P. His advice in verses 9–10 was unfortunately disregarded in favor of the views of the pilot and the ship's owner. At 27:21, when things are at their worst, Paul rises to make a speech "in their midst." This is the same phrase used of Peter's speech in 1:15 and of Paul's address to the Areopagus in 17:22, and is thus quite proper for an orator. The only difficulty lies in summoning up the imagination to envision someone assuming this role on a battered ship at the mercy of a raging storm. His pep talk concludes with the prognostication that they must needs run aground on an island (27:21–26). When, against all odds, this grounding occurs and some of the sailors attempt to sneak off in the boat, Paul alone notices their flight and alerts the centurion (27:30–32). In the next verse he is once again addressing the entire company, urging them to take some nourishment and promising rescue. In the end, the centurion's desire to save Paul was the basis for the rescue of all.

Once in Rome Paul is allowed to set up his own living arrangements, guarded by a single soldier. Three days after arriving, he invites the leaders of the Jewish community (28:17), who duly respond to this summons and hear Paul's statement of his case. The Jewish leaders reply that they have heard nothing about him that would mar his reputation. About "this sect" they are eager to learn from him, as it has a bad reputation. This brief exchange calls for comment. Why should the elite of the Jewish community at Rome accept this invitation? Paul's contention that he was "delivered into the hands of the Romans" (28:17) is quite diplomatic but not quite true. More interesting is the Jewish leaders' reference to "this sect," about which Paul had said nothing. In fact there were believers in Rome at this time, of which not only Paul's letter to the Romans is proof, but also Acts 28:15. The heads of the Jewish community could have interviewed them at any time to learn about "this sect." Once Paul arrives in Rome he becomes, as in Ephesus, the effective founder and head of the community.

As it was in the beginning, so it is at the end. As in Pisidian Antioch, Corinth, and Ephesus, so also in Rome Paul offers his message to the Jews first. When most choose not to believe, he pronounces a judgment upon the entire group and states that the gentiles will listen. This is not history, not only because history is rarely quite so artistic, but also because it shows the apostle to the gentiles as a missionary to the Jews even when he is in Roman custody. Few readers have failed to find the close of Acts disappointing. They wish to learn here what came of Paul's legal difficulty. In their support they can note that this subject has been the primary concern of the book since 21:27. Luke's decision to end Acts at this point does not, however, conflict with the standards of some types of historiography.

The purpose of this review has been to demonstrate how historically shaky the narrative of Acts is. It is not the story of the earliest church, nor even the story of the gentile mission. Acts is not even, by any account, simply the story of Paul. Apart from its use of patterns and formulae, the book is very difficult to use as a firm historical resource because of its many gaps and improbabilities. The issues are not limited to matters about which Luke was uninformed, or even misinformed. At a number of points it is apparent that Luke knew more than he said or better than what he reported. The majority of the problems identified in this chapter—and it is by no means a complete catalogue—evidently stem from authorial decisions.

Please note that miracles or other supernatural phenomena have not entered into this discussion. Wonders were a part of Luke's world. Those who are suspicious of divine intervention as a solution to problems will find themselves in a large company today, and intervention from on high is a card that the author of Acts plays more often than any type of historian probably should; but miracle has been, by and large, left out of the presentation of historical problems. The question of miracle in Acts belongs rather to the author's philosophy of history and to his theology. On the subject of miracle there are two clear differences between Acts and ancient historians in general.

The first involves the nature and quantity of the miraculous in the narrative. The tradition of ancient historiography was rather open to various portents and omens, especially those of political significance, but Greco-Roman historians would incline to view most of the wonders in Acts as either the unlikely claims of a dubious cult or as the alleged activities of individual practitioners, few of whom were highly admired. Secondly, ancient historians often placed distance between themselves and reports of wonders either by attributing them to a source that is cited without judgment ("some people say"), or by offering two accounts, one "miraculous," the other "natural," leaving readers free to pay their money and take their choice. Both of these tactics relieve the author of responsibility for questionable material.

For Reference and Further Reading

The most detailed modern account of historical problems in Acts is the commentary of Ernst Haenchen. (See p. 25.)

Note also Richard I. Pervo, *Acts*. Hermeneia. Minneapolis: Fortress, 2008.

For a detailed effort to resolve almost every issue in favor of historicity see Colin Hemer, *The Book of Acts in the Setting of Hellenistic History*. Ed. Conrad J. Gempf. Winona Lake, IN: Eisenbrauns, 1990.

Charles Talbert seeks to present a balance sheet of problems and resolutions in *Reading Acts: A Literary and Theological Commentary on the Acts of the Apostles*. New York: Crossroads, 1997, 237–54.

Endnotes

1. This table is based upon that of John Hurd, *The Origin of I Corinthians* (2nd ed. Macon, GA: Mercer University Press, 1983), 38–39.

Chapter Eight

Some Historical Problems in Acts II

Chronology and Characterization

Chronology

Two other topics relating to history deserve attention. The first is the matter of chronology. Even the strongest defenders of Luke as historian regard as a defect his lack of attention to chronology. The word has two uses. One relates to the chronological findings of modern researchers based upon data in a work, the other to the ancient author's attempts to date the events under consideration. Acts exhibits no example of the latter, although Luke's gospel contains a famous instance that also serves as an illustration of the difficulties of reckoning time in the ancient world:

> In the fifteenth year of the reign of Emperor Tiberius, when Pontius Pilate was governor of Judea, and Herod was ruler of Galilee, and his brother Philip ruler of the region of Ituraea and Trachonitis, and Lysanias ruler of Abilene, during the high priesthood of Annas and Caiaphas, the word of God came to John son of Zechariah in the wilderness. (Luke 3:1–2)

Ancients often employed regnal dating, such as "the fifteenth year of Tiberius." A difficulty with this system is that one emperor may have taken office on 11 May and another on 14 November, so that the beginning of a particular ruler's "year one" may not coincide with other systems of dating. In addition, different localities employed different systems. At Rome, for example, each year was identified by the names of the annual consuls. Synchronisms like that in Luke 3 constituted one attempt to coordinate and specify dates that would be intelligible to those using different systems. There is nothing like it in Acts. Firm chronological markers are quite meager. Other data come from names that pop up in the narrative, such as that of Gallio, the proconsul of Greece (18:12) or Felix and Festus, successive procurators of Judea (23:26; 25:1), all of whom held office in the 50s. For Luke these persons are participants in the story rather than pegs with which to anchor the story by date; therefore only when it is possible to determine their terms of office can a date for that episode in Acts be proposed.

One further note: Ancients often (but not always!) used "inclusive reckoning." If you are going to be out of your office from Tuesday noon until Thursday noon, you are likely to say, "I'll be gone for the next two days." Ancients would be likely to say "three days," counting Tuesday as the first and Thursday as the third. The most familiar example is Easter, which is dated "after three days," whereas we would say "two days later" than Good Friday. The bottom line is that "three years" could be as little as two years and one day.

Luke's data are vague and infrequent. Acts 1:3 suggests that Jesus ascended forty days (thirty-nine?) after Easter. Acts 1:15 is the first of several occurrences of "in those days" (6:1; 9:37; 11:27), which is more of a narrative introduction than a chronological indicator; that is, it is not much better than "once upon a time." Acts 2:1 refers to the day of Pentecost. Luke may have understood this as fifty days (= seven weeks) after Passover. (Christians now celebrate this as the fiftieth day of Easter). All of the events narrated up to 11:26 could have taken place within a few months. There is no indication that the story has reached the year 31 CE. (The base for these calculations assumes that Jesus was crucified around Passover in the year 30.) Acts 11:26 indicates the duration of an entire year. Chapter 12 takes place around Passover. Internally, on the grounds of Acts alone, this could be the Passover of 32, but 33 would be more likely. Acts 11:28, which speaks of a coming famine that took place during the reign of Claudius (41–54), is in line with this, as it looks toward the future.

Yet those who work with external data are likely to place Acts 12 in the year 44, rather than 33, since "King Herod" is normally identified with Agrippa I (41–44), whose death the chapter relates (see pp. 101–6). If in fact chapter 12 relates events that occurred in 33, then in the subsequent chapters time flies by very rapidly.Acts appears to imply that Paul can establish a community within a few weeks, if not days. He remains in Corinth for more than a year and a half, a stay so lengthy that it is justified by a revelation (18:10–11), and then the very next verse introduces Gallio. Therefore the year can be no earlier than 51. That is another shock: though it is twenty-one years after the crucifixion, the related events seem to reflect at most one half of that time. Then Acts 19:10 mentions another long mission, a two-year stay in Ephesus preceded by a long overland journey. Chapter 20 consumes a number of months. Once Paul has been arrested, things move rapidly once more. In 24:11, during the second of his four trials, Luke has Paul state that less than a fortnight had elapsed since his arrival. Chapters 23–24 introduce three historical figures: the procurators (a title for governors of sub-provinces) Felix and Festus and the high priest Ananias. The last held office c. 47–58. Felix begin to rule in 52; Festus died while in office in 62, but the year when he took up his office is uncertain—proposals range from c. 56 to c. 59. Acts 24:27 refers to a period of two years. This may apply to Felix, but most take it to refer to two years of custody. Paul's arrest would then have taken place between c. 54 and c. 57. The trip to Rome began a good two years after his arrest at some time in the late summer and was completed the next spring. Acts thus spans three decades in external history, from c. 30–c. 60, but the internal data give the impression of a decade at most. Luke was evidently quite indifferent to this matter, and his indifference creates problems for historians and raises questions about his purpose.

In summary: scholars make regular use of chronological data derived from Acts, but not always, as previously noted (chapter Five, p. 81), with sufficient attention to the context. Judging by the use that many scholars make of the references to Festus or Gallio, one might conclude that Luke has carefully attended to chronology. He has not. It is not legitimate to hold—on the basis of names dropped in the narrative, or of references to the famine "under Claudius" in 11:27–30, or the same emperor's expulsion of Jews from Rome— that Luke should receive high marks for his provision of chronological data. Those who attempt to elaborate a Pauline chronology must do so almost in spite of Acts, and the results of these enterprises are not uniform.

The Characterization of Paul

One of the enigmas of Acts identified in Chapter Two is that Paul is Luke's hero, but that the Paul of Acts is often at odds with the Paul revealed in his letters. Historically speaking, there has been a battle over "the real Paul" for more than 150 years. Premodern thought focused more upon content than upon method—or, more accurately, historical-critical method. From this perspective the data from Acts were blended with the data from all of the letters. This mix gives priority to Acts. All of the data in Acts were assumed to be correct, and information from the letters was used to expand upon that data, or to fill in gaps. The battle over Paul focused upon whether the Paul

identified by Reformers through their interpretation of his principal
letters was to be the center of theology, or whether Paul should be
understood in the light of other scripture (and tradition).

With early modernism (c. 1800) came an emphasis upon the application of critical method to content. The modern Paul has been the
object of various quests and numerous squabbles. The sharper edge
followed a trail like that once blazed by *Marcion. The canon of
scripture, long the Protestant bulwark against ecclesiastical tradition,
was found to be contaminated by later tradition. The "real Paul" had
to be distilled out of a solution that had confounded him with various *Deutero-Pauls. One task was to identify the post-Pauline letters,
such as 1–2 Timothy and Titus. More or less simultaneously came the
discovery that there were major tensions between Acts and the genuine epistles. The Paul of Acts was not the real Paul, but a creature
of compromise. Historians must give primary weight and attention
to primary sources. By the late twentieth century a liberal consensus held that the primary sources were seven undisputed epistles:
Romans, 1–2 Corinthians, Galatians, Philippians, 1 Thessalonians,
and Philemon.

The task had not ended, for the formation of the Pauline corpus,
as the collected letters are called, was itself a post-Pauline activity. The
earliest known collections included some *Deutero-Pauline letters
and sometimes Hebrews. Some of these, most notably 2 Corinthians,
quite possibly Philippians, possibly 1 Corinthians, and, according to
some, 1 Thessalonians, were composite texts assembled from two or
more letters. In addition, the edited corpus may contain a number
of glosses (explanatory notes) and interpolations, the extent of which
is widely debated. As the Pauline corpus continued to deconstruct
under the critical knife, a debate began about the center and consistency of Pauline theology. Although conducted largely among
scholars of Protestant heritage, this quest raised a challenge to the
cornerstone of Reformation theology, that the center of Pauline (and
New Testament) thought is justification by faith alone.

Conservatives did not readily accept these conclusions. Opponents
of the liberal trend continued to insist that Acts was a primary source,
written by an eyewitness, and that the Paul of Acts is therefore the
real Paul. Many conservatives also rejected the idea that the Pauline
corpus included letters not written by Paul, viewed partition hypotheses (that is, efforts to demonstrate that some epistles were composite) with considerable suspicion, and showed strong distaste for the
notion that the letters contain interpolations. In its most undiluted

form, then, the conservative response to the liberal tradition rejected the presence of *Deutero-Paulinism in the New Testament.

These are the hard edges. Moderate conservatives may agree that 1–2 Timothy and Titus were, in part or whole, not written by Paul. They may express doubts about Ephesians and agree that 2 Corinthians may be a composite of at least two letters. Critics of this general orientation are also willing to admit that Acts may contain some errors. They minimize conflict between Acts and the epistles but tend to give the letters priority. Whereas earlier generations of Luke's admirers may have held that Paul's message was identical to that attributed to him by Luke, moderate conservatives today seek to show that Luke says the same as Paul. Moderate liberals, for their part, treat Acts as an often reliable secondary source. They are willing to debate, for example, whether Paul might have circumcised Timothy (Acts 16:1–3) or whether he would have been willing to undergo the vow proposed in chapter 21. In summary, premodern thought did not see much tension between Acts and the letters, whereas modern methods lead to various contrary conclusions, all based upon arguments supported by the application of critical methods.

The entry of postmodernism into the scholarly arena has underlined the growing recognition that all of the Pauls who have been derived from various sources and constructed by various means are "real Pauls" in one sense or another, and at the same time that none of them is real because each represents no more than fragments of the apostle's life and thought—immediate, contingent, and particular in the case of the letters, more distant and general from the perspective of Acts. Although relatively few Pauline scholars are card-carrying postmodernists, many have come to question the validity of seeking to construct elegant syntheses. Paul has become fragmented. Even the Paul of Acts is no monolith, as becomes apparent in reading the various discussions in a long-ranging debate. The thesis of this book is that the Paul of Acts belongs to a *Deutero-Pauline world because Acts is a secondary source that belongs to the history of Pauline thought, or as many today would say, to the history of the reception of Paul.

At one time classification of a letter as non-authentic was tantamount to saying that it should not be in the Bible. This gave the debate an urgency that it no longer possesses. Much of the fire has cooled. Yet from these dead ashes have risen several important gains. The several *Deutero-Paulinisms can now be seen as attempts to apply the apostle's earlier words and thoughts to different situations, to bring him up to date by stating what Paul would say if he were faced with the challenges of a later era. *Deutero-Paulinism is thus a kind of flattery, for it recognizes that Paul had made contributions of enduring worth.

No important thinker has escaped such revisions. A few examples are Plato, Aristotle, Augustine, Aquinas, Luther, Calvin, and Marx. An example closer to home, so to speak, is Jesus, whose practice of teaching in parables was so successful that it inspired numerous revisions and imitations. Luke's Paul is one representative of many neo-Paulinisms, and by no means the first entrant into the field. Luke's actual "sin" was not that he presented a revised Paul, but that his effort was so successful that to dislodge it from its privileged position is extremely difficult.

One doubts that the author of Acts would have found a great deal in common with Mae West, but he would have appreciated her sentiment that "too much of a good thing is WONDERFUL!" There is no better one-sentence summary of Paul's résumé in Acts, which includes *three*, count 'em, three sets of glittering credentials: Jewish, Greek, and Roman. Each deserves to be savored in its own right. The Jewish qualifications will receive first consideration. All of what follows is based upon the data of Acts.

Although born in Tarsus, Paul was reared in Jerusalem and then educated by Gamaliel, whom Acts regards as the premier Jewish thinker of his time. In that school Paul learned the strictest form of observance and deep commitment to *Torah (22:3). In that observance he never wavered. As for partisan affiliation, he was a Pharisee, "the strictest sect of our religion" (26:5). He was no latecomer to this party; his membership card was inherited (23:6). The Paul of Acts never burned that card; he was a Pharisee to the end (23:6). His Jewish learning is particularly manifest in his knowledge of the scriptures, which constitute the basis of his argument from beginning (cf. 9:22) to end (28:23). Despite his conversion of and association with gentiles, Paul was always very pious, undertaking vows (18:18; 21:26) and visiting Jerusalem to observe major festivals (cf. 21:16). His accomplishments met with due recognition. Although born in the Diaspora, Paul became a member of the Sanhedrin, as implied in 26:9–10, where he could cast votes in favor of executing followers of Jesus. In Rome the most prominent members of the Jewish community come at his bidding (28:17). Paul was a Jew of very high status, but that is not all.

His Greek credentials were no less impressive, and he had the skills to match. Paul was a citizen of Tarsus, one of the oldest bastions of Hellenic culture in "Asia," with Greek roots than ran wide and deep. In making that claim to citizenship, Paul employed a familiar figure of eloquence, litotes (a "not unimportant city," instead of "an important city"). While in Athens he used a religious dedication as his "sermon text" and supported his case just as ably with a citation from Greek poetry as he had from Hebrew scripture (17:23, 28). Paul's performance in Athens is, not surprisingly, a showpiece of his Greek culture. Like Socrates, he engages in dialogue with other philosophers in the civic center. Like Socrates he is "tried" on the charge of introducing new gods (17:17–19). The Areopagus, probably the most prestigious court in the Mediterranean world, deigns to hear him. Indeed, he converted one of their members, Dionysius. That sentence alone (17:34) speaks volumes.

Other than the ease with which he can enter into cultured conversation and relationships with the elite, as in Athens, Ephesus (19:31), and Caesarea (24:24–25), it is Paul's oratorical skill that marks him as a man of culture. In the trial before Felix his accusers were obliged to retain the services of a Greek orator, but Paul was able to speak for himself (24:1–21). The most remarkable demonstration of rhetorical prowess was not, however, before a Greek audience. In Jerusalem, battered as he was, Paul was able to still a raging mob with the power of his presence. In the Greco-Roman world that ability was the mark of a truly great speaker, and, of course, a very useful quality to possess. These are two quite impressive sets of credentials, one upper-class, educated, and Jewish, the other Greek, cultured, and elite. With those two sets of qualifications most would have been gratefully content, but Paul had yet one more passport in his pocket.

In terms of clout this was the most prestigious of all his credentials. Paul was a Roman citizen, and not a humble citizen of servile origin. (Many became Roman citizens through emancipation from slave status by Roman masters.) When his captor, Lysias, noted that citizenship had cost him a pile, Paul could reply that his own was inherited (22:28). In Paul's time only the inner circle of the Greek elite could hope to receive the privilege of a grant of citizenship. That was doubtless one reason why he was in such good standing with Asiarchs in Ephesus (19:31) and could engage Roman proconsuls (governors of the senatorial class) with facility (13:6–12; 18:12–17), let alone mere procurators, such as Felix and Festus, who were of Equestrian status (a step grade beneath senatorial rank).

The climactic presentation of this multi-cultural prowess and standing comes, fittingly, in Acts 26, the climax of his legal struggle. There Paul delivers a brilliant oration before an audience including

Jewish royalty, Roman officials, and representatives of the provincial Greek upper crust. He argues from scripture, cites a Greek proverb, displays overwhelming erudition and an astute mixture of deference with a refusal to pull punches, aptly employs a standard claim from the philosophical repertoire to refute the claim that his "great learning has driven him mad," and in the end convinces the entire audience of his innocence while deeply impressing King Agrippa. With these varied credentials went, naturally, the assumption of wealth (24:26). Finally, Paul topped his résumé with great physical strength and courage (14:18–20; 21:35; 27:21–44), great good foresight and sense (20:3; 27:9–11), a mastery of seamanship (chapter 27), and last but not least knowledge of a craft and willingness to labor so arduously at demeaning activity that, even while engaged in missionary enterprises, he could support not only himself but also his staff (20:34).

This is all splendid, but it is too much of a good thing. Paul may have been born in Tarsus, and he had been a Pharisee, but he could not have received both the Jerusalem education of which he boasted and spent the time in Tarsus required to receive citizenship there. The Jerusalem background is dubious, and the claims of citizenship at Tarsus are unlikely. Was Paul a Roman citizen? It is possible, but not certain. More importantly, he was not likely to have been a citizen of the high standing presented in Acts, where his possession of the franchise works as a "get out of jail free" card that is never played before the last possible minute (if then) and not played at all where one expects it—as grounds for an appeal to Caesar.

The single credential that was most important to the historical Paul is denied him, however regretfully, by Luke. This is the title of "apostle." The historical apostle was a Hellenistic Jew with some Greek education (it cannot be demonstrated that he knew Hebrew, but he evidently knew Aramaic) and more than an unusual share of genius. He did practice a craft, but Roman governors and elite Greeks did not hang around with tent-makers. The purpose of Luke's portrait is clear. Paul is certainly heroic, multi-cultural and omnicompetent, but Luke did not wish simply to paint a larger than life character. His "Renaissance man" is a universal figure, the all-but-perfect representative of an aspiring world religion that would clothe its Jewish message in Greek finery and conquer the Roman world. History would show that Luke was an insightful portrait painter.

This and the preceding chapter have set forth data to show that Acts is replete with historical implausibility, an almost non-existent chronology, and a quite improbable characterization of its leading personality, none of which elements serve history and all of which serve the purposes of the author. A great deal of evidence has been gathered and sifted. The hour is coming and is now at hand for that final chapter, during which everyone gathers about a table and listens as the expert reveals the solution to the mystery.

References and Further Reading

For a rounded and detailed description of the Jewish, Greek, and Roman elements in Acts there is Henry J. Cadbury, *The Book of Acts in History*. New York: Harper & Brothers, 1955, especially 32–135.

On the character of Paul see John C. Lentz, Jr., *Luke's Portrait of Paul*. SNTSMS 77. Cambridge: Cambridge University Press, 1993.

Chapter Nine

Conclusion

The seven preceding chapters have set forth a large amount of evidence on one side of a case. They have sought to demonstrate that Acts is not a reliable history of Christian origins. One important point is that it does not attempt to be. Another is that the literary techniques employed are too artistic. The use of cycles, parallels, repetitions, melodramatic characterization, stereotyped scene construction, inventing or presenting stories that replicate biblical narrative, unbalanced narrative with evident symbolic import, and a balanced structure—all these raise insurmountable objections. History cannot be quite so symmetrical. In addition there are any number of historical problems.

The accusation, bluntly put, is that Luke murdered the history of the early church. This is a crime because he was an historian and thus obliged to narrate this story with a minimum of prejudice and a maximum of truth. One defense for this misdeed is that Luke was a poor historian. It may also be claimed that he was inadequately informed or even misinformed. Accusers vary in their assessments of the gravity of the charges. A goodly number of people consider Luke to be guilty of a few misdemeanors, while some regard his conduct as utterly felonious. The legal debate has enjoyed a good run, well over a century and a half, with no hope of a verdict in sight. The critical situation is a kind of mirror-image of Acts 21–26, for the more that is known about the legal situation, the less clear matters are. Moreover, Luke has not been without some very able defenders who have attempted to refute every charge leveled against him.

There have been, and still are, those who would place him near the top ranks of ancient historians.

This study has not attempted a review of the entire proceedings. It has largely ignored arguments for the defense while attempting to show that the prosecution has a formidable case, but it would be incorrect to conclude that the investigator works for the prosecution. He does not. His conclusion, which should come as no surprise, is that both prosecution and defense have overlooked a point worthy of note: the text of Acts provides no convincing evidence that Luke was attempting to compose a history of the early church or that he wished himself to be placed in the company of professional historians. Both those who seek to exonerate him of the foul charge of falsification and those who wish to prosecute him for his dastardly actions are dealing with a crime that never took place. These findings would not allow the case to proceed beyond a coroner's jury, for without a crime, there can be no indictment and no trial.

By our lights Luke is better regarded as a creative author than as an historian, for it is the expectation of our culture that historians will strive for objectivity, that, while they may argue a thesis and seek to make a good case for it, they will not falsify data or ignore other points of view or interpretations. Luke had no interest in objectivity. He wrote as an insider, passionately committed to the Christian movement. Insider perspectives are vital resources for historians, but they rarely serve as historiography's finished product. The memoirs of politicians and other important figures are cases in point. Readers expect that books of this sort will be self-serving. These works may be of great interest, but only the highly partisan or the unfortunately gullible will take them at face value. Even ancient historians often attempted (or pretended) to show both sides of a debate and reflect upon alternatives. Luke does nothing of the sort.

The purpose of Luke and Acts was stated in Chapter One: to demonstrate the legitimacy of Pauline gentile Christianity. To accept this view—and it is rather widely held—is to recognize that "history" may be a misleading designation for Acts. Luke does not try to accomplish his goal by composing a treatise, but by telling a story. Treatises defending Christianity were written by apologists, such as *Justin. Luke wrote two volumes of narrative, the first of which looks and reads like a biography, while the second resembles an historical monograph. These appearances can be somewhat deceiving, especially when modern notions about historiography and biography come into play. Luke the Evangelist who wrote the third gospel was no less of an evangelist when he wrote Acts. Evangelists are, by definition, proclaimers. The truth in which they are interested is not identical to the truth of the detached observer. Good historians are skeptical by nature; they do not believe everything that they read. Acts was written neither by a skeptic nor for skeptics.

In short, it is erroneous to propose that if Acts is not good history it is not a good book. Acts *is* a good book, but it is not history in the normal and narrow sense. This statement does not mean that Acts does not contain history, but that history is secondary to its main purpose, just as history is secondary to the Gospel of Mark and the Epistle to the Galatians, although both include valuable historical data—as does, come to think of it, John Steinbeck's *The Grapes of Wrath*. It is not possible to deny that Acts omits much of importance, that it includes data that contradict primary sources, including some known to the author, and that it forces those stories it chooses to tell into molds and patterns that exceed the bounds of probability. Acts is good story but not, all in all, good history.

The core of this book has been the illumination of how Acts tells its story. Very little of this exposition is in any way novel. Entire monographs have been devoted to this or that item of the emperor's wardrobe, and many scholars have taken note of much of the ensemble. Those who uphold the tradition of Luke the Historian recognize at least some of the cycles, etc., and usually concede that the author composed the speeches. They state, or imply, that these are no more than accessories, and note that some of them, in particular the speeches, are accessories favored by historians. The thrust of my argument is that following this line of argument results in an emperor who is wearing little if anything other than accessories.

A second goal of this work has been to underline the implications of these common findings. Acts is a precarious source to use for early church history. Its outline is unreliable, and the episodes include many dubious features. The conventional practice of gleaning this or that historical datum from a passage and using that finding as the cornerstone of an historical argument is open to strong methodological objections. Acts presents a linear development of the Jesus movement with smooth, well-insulated transitions. The moderate critical tradition has tended to doubt that the transitions were quite so smooth but to accept the main outline. However much it is diluted by skepticism or drained of color by generalization, any outline of primitive church history based upon Acts will amount to a picture of linear progression.

For the real story of Christian origins, a string of atomic reactions will provide a better analogy than that of linear progression. The Jesus movement induced a number of explosions in Jerusalem, Galilee, Antioch, and many other places. These explosions had different triggers, ranging from the reform of synagogue life to the foundations of a new religion that worshipped Jesus as its heavenly sovereign. From the earliest time these eruptions reacted against one another, exchanging neutrons and electrons, as it were, as well as forming new elements or compounds. In addition, some vigorous collisions ensued. Of these strange and wonderful events Acts provides no more than vague clues, since its purpose was to deny that they had taken place and show instead the happy unity of the movement from its origins onward.

To fault Luke for his failure to detail conflict and diversity is fruitless. To pretend that he touched upon everything that is important is indefensible. Luke's achievement is remarkable and deserves honor even though in fashioning his construction he utterly obscured the story of Christian origins. Luke was often able to have his cake and eat it too. That luxury is not available to modern historians, who must acknowledge the severe limitations of Acts and be very cautious about the attempt to pick historical fruit from its elegant and well-trimmed branches. This thesis brings to the surface yet one more axiom worthy of analysis.

That axiom is the claim that history is written by the winners. Nowadays the appearance of this sentence is nearly tantamount to an announcement that what follows will be an attempt to write history from the perspective of the losers. But while it amounts to an apology for the paucity of data, the axiom is a valuable statement about the role of power in the preservation of historical data. One may place the story of Acts under its umbrella with two qualifications. The first of these is not especially remarkable. Acts is a story written from the perspective of those who would *become* the winners. It is also a bit more. Luke's story was so cogent that it helped to *create* the perspective that would emerge victorious and enduring. That observation returns the argument to where it began: Luke fashioned "the foundation myth of Christian origins."

Chapter Two took up the topic of Lucan "triumphalism" from a critical perspective. Triumphalism began to acquire dysfunctional features as soon as the church was established in the Roman Empire, a process that dominated the religious life of the fourth century. This means, to reiterate, that a book written to support a beleaguered collection of small sects cannot be taken at face value when those sects have become the dominant form of religious life and wield considerable political power. A painful example is the hostility toward the Jewish people that characterizes much of Acts. At the time Acts appeared this amounted to little more than a puny David taunting a Goliath. The results of the failure to take change into account have created an ineradicable blot upon Christian history.

Some seek to deal with these issues by arguing that Luke is not a triumphalist and that he was not anti-Jewish. Some support can be gleaned for these views, but even when offered in good faith the arguments work more harm than good. For behind them lurks that anachronistic view of history discussed earlier (p. 43). The scriptures, to quote an old Evangelical dictum, were written *for* us, not *to* us. The positive elements of Luke's myth of Christian origins are its message of hope, its conviction that no situation is utterly hopeless because God has the last word, and its vision of expanding possibility.

Furthermore, there are places and cultures where beleaguered Christians may still take nourishment from Luke's triumphal orientation. To pretend that Western, particularly American, civilization is the only culture that counts is sheer imperialism. As post-Christian orientations continue to grow, believers in the West may someday find Acts once again offering a useful and encouraging message.

Finally, the success of the author of Luke and Acts in addressing challenges facing the Jesus movement of his day should not be overlooked. He was able to integrate Pauline Christianity with other understandings of the faith and to maintain links with Israelite history and scriptures, links that were in danger of being abandoned. It is entirely possible that Christianity would not have survived without a myth like that provided by Luke. Even stronger is the likelihood that Luke played a significant role in the preservation of the Pauline heritage, including the letters. In any case, Luke's myth succeeded, for better and for worse. Both of these adjectives require critical attention.

For my part, thirty-five years devoted largely to the study of Acts have brought changes of mind on many issues along with continual surprise at the discovery of things overlooked. Such discoveries, along with attendant disappointments and failures, will continue. About one conviction, however, my mind has not changed. That is the belief that a full appreciation of Acts is not possible until one has accepted its limitations as a work of history. Luke the historian is an impediment to one's appreciation of Luke the author and theologian, as well as an impediment to the task of reconstructing the story of Christian origins. These convictions have been a sub-text of this little book, the major purpose of which has been to call attention to those limitations. Deriving history from Acts is an enterprise fraught with difficulty. I firmly maintain that Luke the Historian has very little to wear and have striven to demonstrate the point, but I shall not close without acknowledging my admiration (and even envy) for the splendid outfit worn by Luke the author. In that costume lurk mysteries galore, and because of it the story of Christian origins is more mysterious than ever.

Appendix

The Sources of Acts and Its Literary Genre

Source

There is general agreement that Luke used sources in writing the book of Acts. The Gospel provides one basis for observing how Luke utilized sources. For that work there were two major sources, one known and the other semi-known, as it were. The known source was an edition of the Gospel of Mark; the other a sayings gospel known as "*Q."[1] Mark was the major source and provided Luke with his basic outline. In contrast with Matthew, who also used Mark and Q, Luke tended to stick with one source at a time and to preserve its order. Other Greco-Roman authors also made use of sources. Writers were not obliged to name their sources, but were expected to rewrite them in their own style. This practice makes both the identification and the delineation of sources a tricky business. Without Mark, for example, it would be very difficult to reconstruct it from the text of Luke.

There is also general agreement that the matter of the sources of Acts is very different from that of the Gospel, not only because of the lack of comparable texts—there are no Acts written by the authors of Matthew or John, etc.—but also because the nature and extent of the sources were quite different. Before attempting to identify and isolate sources for Acts, certain questions must be addressed. Chief among these are the following: What would have been the purpose and function of a particular source? and, in a similar vein, What were

Note. These examinations are far more technical than those in the body of this book. It is not inaccessible to the average reader, but it does examine a number of scholarly theories in rather condensed form.

the genres of these sources? Suppose for a moment that minutes were taken at the "Apostolic Council" described in Acts 15. Luke could have read these, summarized the debate, reported the highlights of the speeches by Peter and James, and transcribed the letter in full. All would be neatly explained. But is it likely such minutes would have been taken? Did the early Jerusalem community envision itself as a formal organization? Luke so describes it, but his depiction is most unlikely. It is worth noting that Paul does not offer the Galatians a copy of those minutes.

For some decades scholars argued for the existence of one or more "Jerusalem sources" from which Luke drew his material for chapters 1–5 (or more). This argument is no longer made. One reason for its loss of favor is that nobody can point out what purpose such sources would have served. Similar questions must be put to a proposed "Hellenist Source" for chapters 6–8, a tradition that would have recounted the actions of early Greek-speaking believers and their mission. After setting aside the authorial summaries, one notes that Acts 1–12 prominently feature stories about the deeds ("acts") of leaders, especially Peter. For these a model is near to hand: the canonical gospels, which relate many deeds of Jesus.

Why tell similar stories about the followers of Jesus? One possibility would be to show that the work went on, that the benefits brought by Jesus continued through the activities of his disciples. But if that were the case, it would do just as well to record healings by Simon the zealot, Matthias, and others listed in chapter 1. Why spotlight Peter? Was there perhaps a collection of Petrine miracles? For reasons set forth below, that hypothesis is unlikely.

The general limitation of this franchise to Peter suggests another purpose. It is not only in early Christianity that personal names often stand for movements (witness such names as Lutherans, Stalinists, and Freudians). Those who wished to bolster Peter's views—or what were believed or desired to be the views of Peter—might well tell stories that showcased his power and prominence. Central items of their platform were moderation, balance, and synthesis. The name of Peter stood for efforts to celebrate the new without abandoning the old, to achieve a synthesis among divergent trends and to unite Jewish and gentile believers. This moderation is already apparent in Galatians 2 and is prominent in Matthew. 1 Peter is another example. (Others would kidnap Peter and put him under the authority of James, but that was a "deviant" and later trend. See *Jewish Christianity and *Pseudo-Clementines.)

The comparison with stories about Jesus also highlights differences. One is that if collections of the "sayings of Peter" (and/or others) existed, Luke did not preserve them. There is no "Apostolic Q" in Acts. The contrast is notable. Jesus' deeds were often invoked in support of principles. By healing a paralytic he demonstrated that humans could pronounce sins forgiven (Mark 2:1–12), and changes in Sabbath observance could likewise be justified by a miracle (Mark 3:1–6). These and similar issues might also be resolved by simple pronouncements (Mark 2:23–28). In Acts, however, the only person who possesses such authority is James (15:19; 21:18–24), and his power is not linked to miraculous vindication.

Mark 7:1–23 (cf. Luke 11:37–41) and Acts 10 illustrate the difference. Whereas in Mark Jesus pronounces all things clean, in Acts Peter comes very reluctantly to that conclusion only after a voice from heaven has demanded it three times (10:9–16). Luke's stories about the deeds of various missionaries do not establish moral and religious principles. An important exception to this "rule" is the *Torah-free gentile mission, but this exception supports the "rule," for in effect the holy spirit made the pronouncement (Acts 10:44–48). Another important difference between the canonical gospels and the various Acts of apostles can be found in this theological, authority-based realm. Instead of pithy sayings of Peter or crisp pronouncements of Paul, the various Acts offer lengthy speeches delivered by their central characters.

A known type to which the hypothetical Jerusalem Source(s) would be related is the "Foundation Legend." Foundation legends follow a loose pattern. They relate how the cult of Serapis was established at Delos, or Judaism was nurtured in the royal family of Adiabene, or Christianity was planted in Philippi. In Christian contexts there quickly emerged the need to trace one's origin to an apostle or other early figure. So Thomas founds the Church in India and Joseph of Arimathea goes to Glastonbury, establishing the Church in England (thoughtfully including the Holy Grail in his luggage). Whereas an "Act of Peter" would tell how he raised Tabitha and could be recited by anyone interested in Peter (or in an amazing story), a foundation legend may be the product and property of a local community, its story of "how we came to be." Luke does not wish to tell of the foundation of the Jerusalem Church from scratch, as it were, for the community began with those who had followed Jesus from Galilee (Acts 1:12–22). Pentecost is often regarded as the "birthday of the Church"—an epithet indicating that the Pentecost legend does not focus upon the Jerusalem community alone, since it has a strong international component (Acts 2:1–13).

Another hypothesis posits an "Antioch Source," which related the beginnings and early history of that community, in short, a foundation legend. This has been held as a primary source for Acts 6–15 and parts of subsequent chapters. Although the difficulties in envisioning both the purpose and limits of this source are substantial, it has retained a hold upon scholarship, and for good reasons. The chief of these is the apparent link in Acts between the work of the "Hellenist" missionaries and the foundation of the church in Antioch, manifest in the seam visible between Acts 8:4 and 11:19. Acts 13:1–3 almost certainly derives from a source. Its subject is neither Paul, nor Barnabas, but a mission authorized by the community at Antioch, in response to an oracle. This passage all but *must* have an Antiochene origin, and, since this is the case, much of the other material in Acts 2–15 may also stem from that same source. I shall return to this hypothetical document below.

The other major source proposed for Acts is an "itinerary," a list of the stations visited by Paul in Acts 16–21. One compelling element for positing this written source is the reference to a number of places en route where no missionary activity is noted. Acts 16:6–11 mentions the following localities: "Phrygian and Galatian territory," Asia, Mysia, Bithynia, Troas, Samothrace, and Neapolis, before the team arrives at Philippi and gets down to business. Discussions of this source debate the extent of other data it may have contained, such as (brief?) stories of missionary activity, names of converts, and so forth. What might have been the purpose of such geographical data? One possibility is that it provided information for other missionaries. This is possible, but not very likely. The itinerary information in 20:1–21:17 is similar in form but different in purpose. The same may be said of 15:3–4a. Finally, lists of stopping places appear also in Acts 27:1–28:14, but these cannot be attributed to the same type of source proposed for chapters 16–21. Luke uses an "itinerary style" when this seems suitable. It is not limited to a single source.

One element of the itinerary style is the presence of "we." For those who date Acts relatively early and view the author as a companion of Paul, usually the Luke of Philemon 24, "we" is proof that the author was present on the scene. As an occasional or frequent companion of Paul, Luke would have been able to garner first-hand information about events past and present. While Paul languished in custody at Caesarea his companion would have been able to speak with Cornelius and travel to Jerusalem for interviews with other key figures. From Mary the mother of Jesus he could have gained the information utilized to write Luke 1–2. Records of the Sanhedrin proceedings would have been available, as well as those of the Roman trials. By the time Paul was sent to Rome, Luke, who also accompanied him on that journey (never mind how and why), would have been well equipped to write the Gospel and fill in other gaps.

To me all of these hypotheses are pure fantasy, and not only because I date Acts much later. Trial records were not *verbatim*, nor were they available to the general public. Luke 1–2 and the balance of the material in Luke and Acts do not have the quality of eyewitness narration. Even a cursory examination of Luke 1–2 will expose the presence of discrete legends written from diverse viewpoints blended by an editor and the over-arching hand of an omniscient narrator. This material follows the forms of oral tradition, refined and shaped by community needs and interests.

The foregoing polemic does not dispose of the first-person plural accounts. Was there a "We-Source"? Better, were there we-sources not written by the author but preserved and incorporated into his narrative? The function of "we" in Acts is not a wee problem. There are clearly stylistic elements present. "We" tends to be used of travel (as it still is, in such expressions as "*we* took off two hours late and *I* didn't get into my hotel room until midnight"), and it is associated with the coastal regions in chapters 16–21. In 28:1–6 the we-narrator has omniscient qualities. The author of Acts may have had access to some material written in the first-person plural and may have extended or abbreviated the use of "we." One can gain some sense of the problems by reading through Acts 16–21 and 27–28 with attention to when "we" appears in and disappears from the narrative. "We" in Acts is best studied as a literary problem. Its major narrative function is to bring the readers into the story.

In addition to assuming more or less lengthy sources, commentators on Acts are likely to posit numerous traditions, many of which might have originally been oral. While such a suppositon is highly probable, it is also a convenient dodge. It is probable on general grounds: everyone and every entity recites traditions about what it was like when the grandparents came here from the old country or how it was in the old days; in particular because of specific stylistic and literary elements of Acts that suggest the use of antecedent material; and last but not least because of circumstantial details. Luke could not or would not simply have invented all of that detail—or so it is claimed. But this approach is a dodge insofar as it does not seek to account for the nature and form of the tradition or, more important, how the author came to learn of it. The sources of Acts remain an outstanding problem, one that will probably never find general resolution and consensus. The same statement may be made about the gospels of Mark and John, to be sure, but the case of Acts is more pressing because the question of sources is still embroiled in debates about their historical nature and value.

It is only fair that I summarize my own views. 1) Luke made use of a collection of Paul's letters. This is an old, long discarded hypothesis that is rapidly gaining new adherents at the present time. Whether circumstantial or otherwise, much of the information about Paul in Acts could have been derived from his letters. This is the most economical and probable solution, for it appeals to a known source that would have been accessible to the author of Acts. Furthermore, it is supported by specific words, phrases, and concepts, some of which are not characteristic of Luke.

2) Luke had access to some of the writings of *Josephus, in particular the last books of his *Antiquities.* That hypothesis also solves far more problems than it creates. Both of these proposals presume that Luke did not use these resources as a responsible modern researcher would, but selectively, sometimes carelessly, and for limited purposes. These techniques may offend modern sensibilities, but they conform to the general practice of ancient writers. In addition, as I have indicated, the Septuagint and the Gospel of Mark provided source material for Acts.

3) An "Antioch Source" is probable, but is probably a misnomer. The source I envision was an account of the origins of mixed Jewish-gentile Christianity. Antioch certainly played a major role in the source, which may well have originated at that place. It probably began with a charismatic experience, from which Luke derived the Pentecost story of Acts 2, re-located (probably) to Jerusalem, in which Peter played a key role. This was not a Pauline source. In fact, it probably justified the movement at Antioch upon which Paul eventually turned his back. This hypothetical tradition certainly looked back to founders who were the "Hellenists" from Jerusalem, subsequently supported by Peter. The decree of Acts 15:23–29 was a solution to the problem addressed in Galatians 1–2, a remedy that would not have been acceptable to Paul but which was a workable compromise weighted toward gentile believers but sensitive to those of Jewish background. Although Luke is responsible for the form of the decree, its provisions may have been formulated at Antioch. Much of the material about Peter in Acts may come from this document.

4) Luke may have had access to administrative and other letters of Paul that were still available (in copy) at Ephesus, but were not deemed suitable for the edition of collected letters. In particular, I propose an archive that included a letter written by Paul and/or by one or more of his companions about the reception of the collected funds raised for Jerusalem. Given the difficulties attending the Collection (see, for example, 2 Corinthians 8 and 9), a circular sent to the contributing communities to account for the fate of the money would have been wholly appropriate. Since the Collection was probably rejected, it is not surprising that this letter was allowed to disappear. Paul's followers would not have been eager to retain information about one of his failures, especially one so momentous as the fate of the Collection. That hypothetical source would have provided Luke with the data for Acts 20–21, and possibly more.

5) The story of the voyage to Rome is literature, certainly influenced by tradition, including the Bible and Homer. Luke may have used as his basis a "secular" (that is, non-Christian) story of a shipwreck, with suitable insertions. In any case, the distinctive material of Acts 27 is editorial. The strongest hint of an underlying "Christian" source for this passage is the evident assumption that the prisoners on the ship had already been found guilty, a viewpoint quite at variance with that of Acts.

An advantage of these source hypotheses is that they prefer the known to the unknown: Josephus to an unknown source who writes about the same matters with the same viewpoint, and known letters of Paul to proposed "traditions." They also prefer the more probable to the less probable. Early Christians produced numerous letters, whereas the "itinerary" would not become familiar in Christian circles until the fourth and later centuries, when there arose a market for travel reports arose among those who could not make the journey, and guides for those who could. In the face of these advantages some may wonder why the claims that Luke made use of Josephus and Pauline letters have been quite out of favor for the last eighty years. The major reason is, of course, history. If Luke did have these resources at his disposal, he would, as a proper historian, have written a different account. The presupposition to this incomplete syllogism is that Luke was an historian who should have made the kind of use of Paul and Josephus that a contemporary historian would make. That presupposition is invalid.

A more defensible approach is to make judgments about the historical value of Acts based in part upon the author's use of sources.

Negative conclusions about the historical value of Acts can be established by observing how Luke used Mark and the LXX. The question
then becomes why one should expect Luke to use Josephus and Paul
any differently. If the issue is to be argued on the grounds of how
Luke uses sources in Acts, the burden of proof lies upon those who
claim that he could not have had access to Paul and to Josephus. Let
the chips fall where they may. In summary, Luke's major detectable
sources for Acts were the *Septuagint, a collection of Pauline letters,
an Antiochene text describing the origin of the gentile mission from
its viewpoint, a letter about the Collection, and Josephus.

Genre

The preceding paragraphs indicate that questions of source and form
are often intertwined. The genre elected by an author influences the
nature and type of the sources that will be selected and, to a degree,
vice-versa. The bottom line of the genre question is where to put
a book on one's shelf. Reader expectation supplies one angle of
approach to the complicated question of genre. The proverb "You
can't tell a book by its cover" crystallizes the response of the disap-
pointed reader. Libraries and bookstores arrange their offerings by
genre so that people may find what they are looking for. To pursue
the question of the genre of Acts is therefore to ask where ancient
readers would shelve this book. A more learned way to frame the
question is to state that genre deals with comparability. Those seeking information about a particular book are likely to ask first what it's
about and then what it's like. The first question deals with content,
the second with comparability. "If you like Dorothy Sayers, I think
that you will like this," a helpful bookseller may say. Comparability is
less of a concern for the gospels, because there are four of them. They
may be read against one another or the vast amount of comparable
material in ancient biographical writings. This is not so in the case of
Acts, which, because it is unique, can pass as history—even though
comparison with Luke does not, as I have argued, promote the
expectation of historical reliability. Identification of the genre of Acts
is important because of this need for comparability. The enterprise is
difficult, for a number of reasons.

Chief among these is the lack of agreement about whether Luke
and Acts must belong to one genre, that of Luke-Acts, or whether
each book may be assigned to a separate category. Another is that
Luke was not bound by the generic conventions of *belles lettres*. His
audience did not insist upon close adherence to formal rules that
they may not have known and probably would not have appreci-

ated. The far from surprising result is that scholars have identified a number of proximate genres to Acts, and a few for Luke-Acts. All of these proposals have contributed valuable insights. The most useful generic model for Acts may well be a scheme that posits a number of circles representing those proximate models, some overlapping one another and Acts, while others stand at a greater distance from Acts and from one another. The argument would then focus upon which generic circle(s) most closely overlap that of Acts. It will be useful to keep such an approach in mind while evaluating various generic proposals. In addition, it is valuable to attend to both the strengths and weaknesses of the several theories, since scholars tend to emphasize the merits of the genre that they recommend and the weaknesses of alternate explanations, while neglecting the deficits of the preferred solution and the strengths of those they oppose.

The question of fact vs. fiction impinges upon, but is not determinative for, the question of genre. Nearly all agree that Acts lies at some point on a spectrum between absolute fact and pure fiction. The location of the arrow denoting the place of Acts on this spectrum will play a role in decisions about genre. Those who would place the marker very close to the pure fact side of the scale regard Luke as a fine historian and seek to *establish* this view. For them the genre of Acts is not a problem. Those who suspect or identify a good deal of fiction in the work seek to *explain* their views. For them, defining the genre of Acts is a means to explain a problem. My sympathies lie more with the explainers than with the establishers, for I believe that the fictions of Acts are too prominent and too numerous to be accounted for by denial and avoidance.

The path of denial is frustrating for both its proponents and its opponents. It seems stale and retrograde. Old arguments become threadbare from reassertion in successive generations, even if they are valid. Luke's defenders are inevitably involved in a series of rear-guard actions, abandoning one set of trenches to occupy another carefully prepared line. But these brilliant retreats do not add up to a victory. For an indication of the ground that has been lost contrast the ebullient opinions of Sir William Ramsay with the more reserved views found in the commentaries of F. F. Bruce and Ben Witherington III. This process of withdrawal must, by nature, be defensive.

The avoiders can present an apparently stronger case. They contend, in effect, that the best approach to the issue of genre is to compare the text, without judgments about accuracy, to other ancient writings. Acts indisputably narrates a story about the early Christian mission, a story about past events. Comparison with historiography is therefore inevitable. Acts has a little preface, linked to the slightly longer preface of Luke, and contains a number of speeches. Historians also used prefaces and were fond of speeches. Acts thus looks like a work of history. The next move seems equally axiomatic. Since Acts looks like history, its appearance lends weight to its accuracy, and since it looks more like history than anything else, it must possess considerable historical value. This pseudo-logic—a leap grounded upon an assumption—has largely dominated scholarship. It does not obviate the comparison of Acts to historiography, but it does require readers to exercise vigilance.

Ancient Greeks developed several different types of historiography, most of which have endured. Those who regard Luke as one of the best of ancient historians compare him to authors like Thucydides or Polybius, who focused upon a period in the history of various states. There are no strong grounds for this claim, which honors by an association that is difficult to establish. With the diffusion of Greek culture during the Hellenistic Era (c. 323–c. 31 BCE) other types of history became popular. With some inspiration from Herodotus, "the Father of History," ethnography, which included description of the social practices of exotic foreign groups as well as their histories, arose. The ethnographic tradition included much that was fabulous; this type already suffered from a poor reputation in antiquity, but one that did little if anything to diminish its popularity. The cosmopolitan nature of Hellenistic society promoted the production of "universal" histories, attempts to survey and integrate the stories of many nations. Diodorus of Sicily (c. 30 BCE), for example, trumped Genesis by beginning with the origin of the gods (and simultaneously claimed that his narrative was based upon personal observation).

Another type, known as "antiquities," traced the history of a state from its foundation. Dionysius of Halicarnassus wrote a work of this type about the Romans, followed by *Josephus' opus on the Jews. In addition, there were monographs—shorter works, usually a single book—devoted to a particular war or event. Finally, with the rise of monarchies, biography emerged as a prominent form. The stories of great men were appropriate to eras dominated by individual conquerors and rulers. And of course the biblical tradition of historiography should not be overlooked. Luke writes under the influence of Hellenism, without doubt, but a principal source was the Greek Bible. Finally, scholars take note of a *style* of historiography that emphasized the dramatic and emotional, and that often unfolded in episodic form. Such attempts to make history vivid also made it more entertaining. Eckhard Plümacher has sought to show the links between Acts and this style.

Scholars who follow David Aune in favoring the universal history paradigm understand that Luke did not wish to present his story as one chapter of the history of a small nation, but as a tale of world-wide impact, something that "was not done in a corner" (26:26). David Balch has looked to parallels with the *Roman Antiquities* of Dionysius of Halicarnassus, which explain the growth and devel-opment of a small entity (Rome) into a worldwide phenomenon. Valuable as the insights from these proposals are, they are limited by the subject and scope of Acts. Luke looks at the big picture, but his focus is upon a brief period and a single movement. The subject of Acts, or of Luke and Acts, was not the sort of thing that ancient historians regarded as suitable for an entire work. The history of a cult was not a proper theme for historical writing. The history of a philosophy, however, was.

Probably taking his lead from Josephus, Luke does portray nascent Christianity as a philosophical movement. This was not totally aber-rant, for what took place in Jewish synagogues and early Christian assemblies that met in halls or houses to hear authoritative texts and listen to lectures about these texts, did not conform to ancient notions of primary religious cults. Charles Talbert and Hubert Cancik have placed Acts within the tradition of institutional and intellectual history. Talbert views Luke's gospel as the biography of the founder of a movement and Acts as the story of Jesus' successors. Useful as these proposals are, they are not without difficulties. Luke, as this book has sought to demonstrate, is anything but clear and candid on the question of succession, and few readers of any era have viewed Acts as a specimen of intellectual history.

A more persuasive case for the link between Acts and historiogra-phy has been advanced by Gregory Sterling, who proposes that Luke-Acts represents "apologetic historiography," a type of writing that he has identified. Apologetic historiography, according to Sterling's analysis, has its roots in the Ionic (Herodotus) and ethnographic tra-ditions and was one form of response by proud old ancient cultures of the East to the dominance of Hellenism. This is a very workable category, sufficiently flexible and obviously compatible with the understanding of Luke and Acts as legitimating narrative. *Josephus is Sterling's chief complete model. His *Antiquities* has recognizably apologetic elements, and Josephus also wrote a two-volume apology, *Against Apion*. Sterling recognizes that Luke writes at a somewhat lower level than Josephus. His leading model for specific comparison to Luke and Acts is the work of one Artapanus, which survives only in fragments preserved by later writers. Sterling does not concentrate upon the question of how accurate this genre might be. Given the explicitly rhetorical title—apologetic is the Greek term for defense speeches—it seems justifiable to have guarded expectations for the reliability of apologetic history.

Many who assign Acts to a genre different from that of Luke look to the (historical) monograph. Their number includes conservatives, such as Martin Hengel and Darryl Palmer; liberals, including Hans Conzelmann; and more moderate exponents, notably Eckhard Plümacher. Monographs tended to be relatively short, carefully structured, and focused upon leading personalities. Although Acts *is* a monograph of sorts, the category is rather fluid. A genre that includes both the highly fictitious *3 Maccabees* and Tacitus' admired *Agricola* is, from the perspective of historical accuracy, quite capacious. The monograph is a tent under which creatures of many kinds may find shelter. Within that tent there is no peaceable kingdom. Ancient literary critics would not likely have viewed Acts as a contribution to genuine history; on the basis of its contents they would hardly have been moved to think of Polybius. In their eyes Acts would have been fiction or "false history."

The Greeks possessed a tradition of incredible history, including "tall tales," that went back to Homer. Criteria for distinguishing truth from fiction were rationalistic. A learned Hellene who examined Acts would have found it deficient by these criteria. The style would also have been found wanting, the speeches far too brief and inadequate, the preface inappropriate in wording and structure, and the subject quite unsuitable. Modern critics have some reasons for disagreeing with such elitist standards, but this putative opinion must be taken into account, especially by those who claim to judge Acts by the criteria of antiquity and its forms. Some subjects were suitable for historians; others were not. Style also played a crucial role, for different historical genres called for different styles.

A formal objection to the association of Acts with historiography is its reliance upon direct discourse. About 51% of the work consists of direct speech, a figure that has no comparison in ancient history. This factor alone makes the conventional link between Acts and ancient historiography questionable. Another, discussed in Chapters Four—Six, is that the text is too "artistic" in form. Narrative symmetry is at home in the world of the epic and the novel, that is, appropriate to fiction. When these various difficulties are taken together, the quest for other types and forms of comparison gains momentum. For these reasons some have turned to comparisons with ancient fiction. This enterprise differs from that of nineteenth century scholars who viewed Acts as fictitious because it was so tendentious in character. That approach, characteristic of the Tübingen school that followed Ferdinand Christian Baur (1792–1860), is close to the proposed view of ancient critics, that Acts should be labeled as "false history." This judgment was based upon content rather than form.

In summary, the leading impediments to classifying Acts as historiography are:

1. The *preface(s)* to (Luke and) Acts do not conform to those found in ancient historiography.
2. The *subject* (rise and expansion of a cult) is not a suitably overarching theme for ancient historiography.
3. The *speeches* are not consonant with the orations found in histories, for those tend to comment upon or explain decisions, but the speeches in Acts are usually part of the narrative, provoking action or advancing the plot. (In so far as they are commentary, they tend to be repetitious.)
4. The *quantity* of direct speech, c. 51% of the book, has no parallel in history or biography.
5. Narration is consistently *omniscient*. The narrator knows what characters think and can report private conservations, etc., in direct speech.
6. The nature and quantity of "supernatural" activity—miracles, visions, and divine guidance—differs in quantity, nature, and perspective from that found in Greco-Roman historians, who were inclined to place some distance ("people say") between their convictions and the prodigies they report.
7. The narrator of Acts makes *no claims to objectivity*. The author writes as a believer who does not seek to represent opposing views with any degree of fairness.
8. The book lacks a *chronological framework*.
9. The *style* falls below standards expected of historians. Josephus, for example, writes away from the LXX, improving its style, whereas Luke writes toward it, viewing the Greek Bible as an object worthy of imitation.
10. A number of the narrative techniques used in Acts are more common in ancient fiction than in historiography. These include modes of characterization, such as portraying lead characters as "supermen" with almost identical qualities and

assigning villains with black hats; and plot devices that include stereotyped scenes, invented episodes, and the overuse of parallelism and symmetry.

A moderate form of relating Acts to ancient fiction is by way of comparison to ancient historical novels. Lawrence Wills and I, among others, have examined Acts in relation to Jewish, Christian, and polytheist novels. Wills is a specialist in Jewish fiction, while I have taken a broad approach, looking also to the Apocryphal Acts and their successors. Critical reaction suggests that "novel" is too frightening a word, even when preceded by the adjective "historical." Dennis MacDonald has spent two decades developing the idea that much early Christian narrative is creative mimesis of the *Iliad* and the *Odyssey*. Beginning with the relatively obscure *Acts of Andrew*, he moved on to the Gospel of Mark, followed by Luke and Acts. Although he does not showcase the assumption, MacDonald regards Acts as an essentially imaginative creation of its author. Marianne Palmer Bonz also refers to epic, but views Luke and Acts as a Christian epic that follows the pattern of Vergil's *Aeneid*. Her underlying thesis, that Luke and Acts are heroic narrative of a foundational sort, is widely accepted. Bonz is the first to make a detailed and specific application to a particular epic tradition. (One might note that the conventional designation for an epic in popular prose is "a novel.")

The tension that governs the study of Acts is apparent in that few of the many who have jumped aboard the boat of narrative analysis bestow approval upon the work summarized in the previous paragraph, although it justifies that very approach. To put the case cynically, it seems acceptable to analyze Acts as if it were fiction so long as one does not use the word. Less cynically, the tug of history remains strong, and not only for such dubious reasons as the desire to cling to the idea that the Bible is historically if not scientifically true, or because of a belief that God would not inspire fiction. Since the relation between historicity and genre is not on the one hand firm, while on the other hand, decisions or conclusions about genre are strongly affected by views of the text's historical accuracy, the debate about the genre of Acts is not likely to be resolved in the foreseeable future.

What is important is that there *is* a debate about the genre of Acts. This is a clear and certain advance over the state of affairs that generally prevailed until the last decades of the twentieth century, when either the genre could be assumed or the question could be ignored. Study of Acts should henceforth take into account the proximate genres, including various types of historiography and especially "apologetic historiography," and the range of monographs and historical novels, including those in the LXX and the Christian Apocrypha, and various means for presenting intellectual and religious history. The goal of this summary is to urge readers to discover which of these proximate genres a particular critic views as central and why, and whether particular critics pay attention to other genres or simply reject their relevance.

Resources and Further Reading

Loveday Alexander, "Fact, Fiction and the Genre of Acts," *New Testament Studies* 44 (1998), 380–99.

_____, *The Preface to Luke's Gospel: Literary Convention and Social Context in Luke 1.1–4 and Acts 1.1*. SNTSMS 78. Cambridge: The University Press, 1993.

David Aune, *The New Testament in Its Literary Environment*. Library of Early Christianity 8. Philadelphia: Westminster Press, 1987, 17–157

David Balch, "The Genre of Luke-Acts: Individual Biography, Adventure Novel, or Political History?" *Southwestern Journal of Theology* 33 (1991), 5–19.

Marianne Palmer Bonz, *The Past as Legacy: Luke-Acts and Ancient Epic*. Minneapolis: Fortress Press, 2000.

Frederick F. Bruce, *The Book of the Acts. NICNT*. Rev. ed. Grand Rapids: Eerdmans, 1988.

Hubert Cancik, "The History of Culture, Religion, and Institutions in Ancient Historiography: Philological Observations Concerning Luke's History," *JBL* 116 (1997), 681–703.

Martin Hengel, *Acts and the History of Earliest Christianity*. Trans. J. Bowden. Philadelphia: Fortress Press; London: SCM Press, 1980.

Darryl W. Palmer, "Acts and the Ancient Historical Monograph," in B. W. Winter and A. D. Clarke, eds. *The Book of Acts in Its Ancient Literary Setting. The Book of Acts in Its First Century Setting 1*. Grand Rapids: Eerdmans, 1993, 1–29.

Richard I. Pervo, "Direct Speech in Acts and the Question of Genre," *JSNT* 28.3 (2006), 285–307.

_____, *Profit with Delight: The Literary Genre of the Acts of the Apostles*. Philadelphia: Fortress Press, 1987.

Thomas E. Phillips, "The Genre of Acts: Moving Toward a Consensus?" *CBR* 4 (2006), 365–96.

Eckhard Plümacher, "Die Apostelgeschichte als historische Monographie." In J. Kremer, ed. *Les Actes des Apôtres: Traditions, rédaction, théologie.* BETL 46. Louvain: Louvain University Press, 1979, 457–66.

_____, *Lukas als hellenistischer Schriftsteller.* SUNT 9. Göttingen: Vandenhoeck & Ruprecht, 1972.

William M. Ramsay, *St. Paul the Traveller and the Roman Citizen.* London: Hodder & Stoughton, 1897.

Gregory Sterling, *Historiography and Self-Definition. Josephos, Luke-Acts and Apologetic Historiography.* SuppNovTest 64. Leiden: E. J. Brill, 1992.

Charles A. Talbert and Perry Stepp, "Succession in Luke-Acts and in the Lukan Milieu," *Reading Luke-Acts in Its Mediterranean Milieu.* Leiden: Brill, 2003, 19–55.

Lawrence M. Wills, *The Jewish Novel in the Ancient World.* Ithaca: Cornell University Press, 1995.

Ben E. Witherington, III, *The Acts of the Apostles: A Socio-Rhetorical Commentary.* Grand Rapids/Cambridge, U. K. Eerdmans; Carlisle: Paternoster, 1998.

Endnote

1. The word "edition" intends to underscore the recognition that Luke and Matthew did not have before them identical copies of Mark or of Q. Manuscripts are rarely identical. In the period of Christian origins every copy of a work was effectively a new edition. Moreover, the Gospel of Mark was subject to frequent revision, and the same is likely of a work like Q, the very nature of which facilitates change.

Glossary

I Clement. This letter, about one and one-half times the length of Romans, was written by the church at Rome to the church at Corinth around 100. It forms part of the collection known as "the Apostolic Fathers" and was quite popular in early Christianity. Some manuscripts of the NT include *1 Clement.* The traditional author is one Clement, who was later regarded as an early Bishop of Rome.

Acts of Paul. One of the so-called "Apocryphal Acts of the Apostles," the *Acts of Paul* was written probably c. 175 in Asia Minor. In its original form the work covered Paul's career from his conversion to his martyrdom, but much of the book has been lost. One of its two complete sections tells the story of the woman missionary Thecla. The Paul of these Acts is more radical than his counterpart in the canonical book.

Acts of Thomas. One of the so-called "Apocryphal Acts of the Apostles," the *Acts of Thomas,* written in eastern Syria in the early third century, was probably composed in Syriac. This book, which exists in complete form, represents a type of Christianity that has affinities to "*Gnosticism."

Apocalyptic. Apocalyptic, from a Greek word for "reveal," is a type of *eschatology that constitutes a widespread phenomenon in the history of thought. It arises in many situations when the dissonance between expectation/promise and reality is too great to manage, when beliefs about what should be and actual conditions are at wide variance with one another. Apocalyptic opposes genuine to apparent reality. Its goals may be summarized in the petitions "Thy kingdom come; thy will be done, on earth as it is in heaven." Things are fine in heaven, the true and divine realm. Earthly affairs are the problem. There were strong apocalyptic currents in Judaism from the second quarter of the second century BCE onward. The Dead Sea Scrolls came from a community with a strongly apocalyptic orientation. The relation of Jesus' views to apocalyptic thought is debated. Paul had an apocalyptic orientation.

Apologists. A group of writers, mainly of the second half of the second century, who defended the Christian faith against political and religious opponents. Among them are Aristides, *Justin Martyr, Theophilus of Antioch, Athenagoras, and *Tertullian. The Christian apologists pioneered both philosophical theology, i.e., the use of ancient philosophy to explicate Christian thought, and the application of critical method.

Augustine of Hippo (354–430). Born in a period of imperial revival, Augustine lived to see the beginning of the collapse of the Western empire. He is the Latin theologian most honored by all varieties of western Christianity. His *City of God* and *Confessions* continue to be read and admired by many.

Clement of Alexandria (c. 150–215). Clement was one of the first highly educated Christian philosophical theologians, and among the first to call Acts by the name it now bears. He is noted for his use of the allegorical method of interpretation.

Collection, with an upper-case C, refers to Paul's activity of raising money from some of the communities he founded for delivery to believers in Jerusalem as a sign of unity and solidarity. The Collection was probably rejected by the Jerusalem leaders, with results that led to Paul's arrest.

Dame (or Lady) Wisdom. This is the personified Wisdom of Proverbs 1, 8, Sirach 24, etc. Dame Wisdom (or Sophia) was the agent through whom God created the world. By identifying Wisdom or Logos ("the Word") with Christ, early Christians were able to propound a "high" christology.

Deutero-Pauline. "Deutero," which means "secondary," is applied to letters written by successors of Paul as opposed to the *"Undisputed Pauline letters" (see below). These documents, produced by various movements, were intended to preserve and update the Pauline heritage. Acts is one example of "Deutero-Paulinism," since it represents an updated revision of Pauline thought and practice.

Diaspora. The Diaspora refers to places outside of the "Holy Land" in which Jews live. For about twenty-five hundred years the majority of Jews lived in the Diaspora. When historians of early Christianity refer to the Diaspora, they usually have in mind Greek-speaking Jews, although many Jews, most of whom spoke Aramaic, lived in lands to the East.

Eschatology. Derived from the Greek word for "last things," eschatology is a view about how the universe, the world, or the human race will end. Eschatologies may be scientific, secular, literary, or religious. Not all religions have a set of beliefs about the end.

Gnosticism or Gnosis. ("Gnosis" is a broader term.) "Gnosticism" is used with reference to religions such as Manichaeism, to movements within other religions including Christianity, and a religious philosophy or way of thinking. The most prominent feature of Gnosticism is a profound dualism that opposes the goodness of light or spirit to evil matter. Christian Gnostics therefore separated Creation from Redemption. The god who formed the material world was a lesser, not always benign, deity. Gnostics tended to use increasingly more elaborate myths to depict the gulf between God and the world and thus to explain the problem of evil. Opposition to Gnosis was a leading activity of such *proto-orthodox theologians as *Irenaeus and contributed to the prominence of doctrinal self-definition in Christianity (creeds), the development of a list of approved authoritative writings (canon), and the hierarchical organization of communities headed by a bishop who could demonstrate "Apostolic Succession." The use of quotation marks indicates that "Gnosticism" is too broad a concept for characterizing a single religion or thought system.

Ignatius of Antioch. A leader of the Christian community at Antioch. While on the way to Rome in the second quarter of the second century to be executed in the arena, Ignatius wrote a number of letters. He favored the governance of local churches by a single bishop, assisted by deacons and supported by *presbyters. Ignatius attacked views that he regarded as false.

Inspiration. The question of inspiration as a theological construct arose when the Hebrew scriptures were translated into Greek. (Aramaic versions and paraphrases had been made, but were not regarded as "Holy Writ" proper.) The Hebrew *Torah (and, in time, the Prophets and the Writings) were simply God's word. In Egypt and elsewhere Jews evidently knew no Hebrew. Their bible was in Greek, and to justify its standing Egyptian Jews like the philosopher and exegete *Philo propounded the thesis that all of the translators had produced identical versions, thus establishing the divine origin of the *Septuagint (LXX). Christians picked up this understanding (e.g., 2 Tim 3:16).

Irenaeus of Lyons (c. 130–c. 200). Irenaeus, Bishop of Lyons, constructed a synthesis of the theology that would become orthodox. Against *Marcion and various *"Gnostics" Irenaeus promoted the view that both the Third Gospel and Acts were written by a companion of Paul, Luke. This became the standard picture, and it still has many adherents.

Jewish Christianity. Almost every early form of Christianity, including the theology of Paul, could properly be called "Jewish Christianity." The expression is used technically to designate a number of texts and movements, including books like Matthew and James, that are sympathetic to Jewish practice and organization; communities who were observant of *Torah; groups such as the Ebionites, who had a low Christology and an ascetic bent; and the "Judeo-Christianity" found in works that venerate James and Peter but reject parts of the *Torah. (See *Pseudo-Clementines.) One element that unites this very disparate band is animosity toward Paul, whose name they refuse to mention but whose actual or reputed teachings they reject.

Josephus (c. 37–c. 100). Flavius Josephus was a Palestinian Jew of priestly ancestry who lived through, and participated in, the era of the First Revolt (66–73/74) and its aftermath. His writings include *The Jewish War*, a history of that revolt, *Jewish Antiquities*, a survey from creation up to the revolt, and an apology, *Against Apion*.

Justin Martyr. Active c. 150–160, Justin wrote two apologies (actually one and an appendix). He was executed, according to tradition, during the rule of Marcus Aurelius (161–180). Justin knew the Gospel of Luke, which he cites, although not by name. He did not mention either Acts or the letters of Paul, although he was familiar with the latter.

"Literal Interpretation." In fact, literal interpretation is almost impossible. Consider, for example, Ephesians 5:15 in the AV: "Walk circumspectly." Literally, this would mean that people should keep their eyes in motion as they strolled. The NRSV kills the imagery but communicates the meaning: "Be careful then how you live." "Literal" may refer (1) to concrete understanding or to what legal historians call "strict construction," and (2), in reference to biblical interpretation, to a criticism of the methods of symbolic or allegorical interpretation. (See p. 94.)

Marcion of Sinope (c. 90 [?]-c. 154). Marcion was a radical Paulinist, whose thought seems to have been influenced by *Gnosticism at some point. Marcion denied that the creator God of Israel was the same as the God who sent redemption through Jesus. He rejected the authority of Jewish scripture and put in its place a bipartite "Gospel" and "Apostle" (cf. Law and Prophets). The former was an edition of Luke, the latter a collection of Pauline letters. If Marcion did not "invent" the New Testament, he had a major impact upon the structure and contents of the Christian Bible.

Origen (c. 185–c. 251). Origen, originally from Alexandria, was a great Christian theologian and scholar, whose ideas fell under suspicion and were, in the form propounded by his successors, ultimately condemned (553 CE). Primarily a biblical theologian, Origen viewed scripture as multilayered, with the allegorical/spiritual as the highest level.

Philo of Alexandria (c. 20 BCE–c. 50 CE). Philo was a leader of the Jewish community in Alexandria and a philosopher who made contributions to the Platonism of his day. In addition to two works on political controversies, he wrote a number of treatises, most of which are allegorical interpretations of the *Torah. Philo had a profound influence upon many early Christian theologians.

Polycarp of Smyrna. Polycarp, bishop of Smyrna in Asia Minor, was active from c. 125–155. He received a letter from *Ignatius, wrote to the Philippians, and is the subject of a Martyrdom story. Polycarp was an admirer of Paul and an early opponent of *Marcion and other "heretics." His views have many similarities to the Pastoral Epistles (1–2 Timothy, Titus.)

Polytheist. This term is preferred to "pagan" or "heathen" to designate religious thought and practice that was neither Jewish nor Christian. Objections can be raised, but "polytheist" does not have the pejorative weight of "pagan" or "heathen."

Presbyter. This transliteration of a Greek word is preferred here to "elder," a term that has different meanings for various Christian bodies. Luke uses "presbyter" to describe the officers of local communities, always in the plural, with the implication that there was more than one in each place. He also uses the word for members of the Jewish governing council at Jerusalem, and apparently in the same sense for the Christian body in the place.

Pronouncement Stories. Also called "apophthegms," these brief narrative anecdotes centered upon a punch line (the "pronouncement"). Mark 12:13–17 ("Render unto Caesar . . .") is a good example.

Proto-orthodox. This term designates the forebears of views that would ultimately became orthodox, or catholic, in Christian theology, ethics, and polity. The "Apostolic Fathers," *Justin, and *Irenaeus are among those now called proto-orthodox. The views they opposed, including the system of *Marcion and various "*Gnostics," were condemned as "heretical."

Pseudo-Clementines. These writings are representative of an anti-Pauline "Judeo-Christianity." The *Recognitions* and *Homilies* are two editions of a novel that is a kind of "Acts of Peter," for, although subordinate to James, he is the central character. This novel, elements of which go back to the second century, was attributed to Clement of Rome. The *Recognitions* know and use Acts, giving it an anti-Pauline spin. They constitute a rival account of Christian origins to that of Acts.

Q. Q is a hypothetical source, based upon the large amount of material that Matthew and Luke have in common with one another but that is not found in Mark. Determination of the probable contents of Q is the result of a redaction criticism that was practiced before the text thus derived was given a name. Although Q does not exist as an independent text, its existence can be predicated in a manner like that used by scientists to postulate the existence of a particle of matter or energy based upon the behavior of other particles. Moreover, its genre *is* known from sayings collections in the Greek "Old Testament," including some in the Hebrew Bible, and, for example, the *Gospel of Thomas*. Since Luke more closely retained the wording and order of Q, Lucan enumeration is used to identify particular passages, i.e., "Q 7:36–50" = Luke 7:36–50.

Rule of Three. This is a principle of popular narration, often found in jokes ("A Roman Catholic Priest, a Protestant Minister, and a Rabbi . . ."). The first two items often establish, in the most economical fashion, a pattern. That a certain shoe does not fit one woman is no surprise. When two cannot squeeze into that slipper, it becomes clear that the foot in question is of more than average daintiness. The third instance is decisive.

Samaritans. From the sixth century BCE Samaritan Jews had rejected the centrality of the Jerusalem temple and its priesthood. Their worship centered upon Mt. Gerizim. During the first century of the common era relations between Jerusalem and Samaritan Jews were not good. Luke can use Samaritans as a primary example of "the other," e.g., Luke 10:29–37. (A small body of Samaritan Jews continues to exist in Israel.)

Septuagint (abbr. LXX). This is the traditional name for the most popular version of Jewish Scriptures in Greek. The name comes from a legend that a committee of seventy (or seventy-two) produced the translation. There was no Jewish "canon" of the LXX, for this undefined collection antedated the idea of an official list of biblical books. Included in the LXX are some books originally written in Hebrew (or Aramaic), such as Sirach (Ecclesiasticus), that did not become a part of the Hebrew Bible; others, such as Esther and Daniel, which differ from the Hebrew versions; and some composed in Greek, an example of which is Wisdom. The LXX, rather than the Hebrew Scriptures, was "the Bible" of early Christians and became their property.

Synoptic Gospels. Matthew, Mark, and Luke are called "synoptic" because they are similar enough in outline and content to be viewed in adjacent columns. Since antiquity it has been clear that there is a literary relationship among these gospels, i.e., that one or more of the evangelists used one or more of the other books. The dominant view is that Mark was the major source of the other two.

Tertullian (c. 160–225). This African theologian played a leading role in the translation of Greek thought into Latin. Puritanical, uncompromising, and anticlerical, Tertullian found much to oppose. Although he eventually separated from the catholic church, his writings were too valuable to be condemned. Among them is a work *Against Marcion* that maintains the traditional authorship and understanding of Acts.

Torah. This term often refers to the first five books of the Hebrew Bible, the Pentateuch. Here it is usually preferred to the translation "law," for Torah is also a way of life, and not simply a list of regulations.

Trope. In everyday speech "figures of speech" embraces both figures and tropes. Figures include rhetorical devices, such as alliteration and hyperbole.

Tropes refer to representations: simile and metaphor, which are based upon likeness, and synecdoche and metonymy, which relate to contiguity.

Undisputed Pauline Letters. All agree that Paul composed Romans, 1–2 Corinthians, Galatians, Philippians, 1 Thessalonians, and Philemon. These seven are therefore "undisputed." The authorship of 2 Thessalonians, Colossians, Ephesians, 1–2 Timothy, and Titus is a matter of controversy. The latter group is arranged here in order of scholarly consensus, from least disputed to most, i.e., more scholars consider 2 Thessalonians to be authentic than is the case for 2 Timothy. In this book all the disputed epistles are viewed as "Deutero-" or "Pseudo-" Pauline, i.e., not written by Paul. (Hebrews, although anonymous, was transmitted with the Pauline epistles.)

Bibliography

Alexander, Loveday, "Fact, Fiction and the Genre of Acts." *New Testament Studies* 44 (1998), 380–99.

_____, *The Preface to Luke's Gospel: Literary Convention and Social Context in Luke 1.1–4 and Acts 1.1.* SNTSMS 78. Cambridge: The University Press, 1993.

Aletti, Jean-Noel, *Quand Luc raconte. Le récit comme théologie.* Lire la Bible 115. Paris: Cerf, 1998.

Aune, David, *The New Testament in Its Literary Environment.* Library of Early Christianity 8. Philadelphia: Westminster Press, 1987.

The Apostolic Fathers. Ed. and trans. Bart D. Ehrman. 2 vols. Loeb Classical Library. Cambridge: Harvard University Press, 2003.

Balch, David, "The Genre of Luke-Acts: Individual Biography, Adventure Novel, or Political History?" *Southwestern Journal of Theology* 33 (1991), 5–19.

Barr, David L., *New Testament Story: An Introduction.* 2nd ed. Belmont, CA: Wadsworth, 1995.

Beker, J. Christiaan, *Heirs of Paul: Paul's Legacy in the New Testament and in the Church Today.* Minneapolis: Fortress, 1991.

Beutner, Edward F., ed., *Listening to the Parables of Jesus.* Santa Rosa, CA: Polebridge, 2007.

Bonz, Marianne Palmer, *The Past as Legacy: Luke-Acts and Ancient Epic.* Minneapolis: Fortress, 2000.

Brodie, Thomas L., "Toward Unraveling the Rhetorical Imitation of Sources in Acts: 2 Kgs 5 as One Component of Acts 8,9–40." *Biblica* 67 (1986), 41–67.

Brown, Raymond E., *Introduction to the New Testament.* New York: Doubleday, 1997.

Bruce, Frederick F., *The Acts of the Apostles.* 3rd ed. Grand Rapids: Eerdmans, 1990.

_____, *The Book of the Acts.* NICNT. Rev. ed. Grand Rapids: Eerdmans, 1988.

Bultmann, Rudolf, *Theology of the New Testament.* Trans. K. Grobel. 2 vols. New York: Scribner's, 1951–1955.

Cadbury, Henry J., *The Book of Acts in History.* New York: Harper & Brothers, 1955.

_____, *The Making of Luke-Acts*. London: SPCK, 1958 (original, 1927).

Campenhausen, Hans v., *Ecclesiastical Authority and Spiritual Power in the Church of the First Three Centuries*. Trans. J. A. Baker. Stanford: Stanford University Press, 1963 (original, 1953).

_____, *Tradition and Life in the Church*. Trans. A. V. Littledale. Philadelphia: Fortress, 1968 (1960).

Cancik, Hubert, "The History of Culture, Religion, and Institutions in Ancient Historiography: Philological Observations Concerning Luke's History." *Journal of Biblical Literature* 116 (1997), 681–703.

Clarke, W. K. L., "The Use of the LXX in Acts." In F. J. Foakes Jackson and Kirsopp Lake, eds., *The Beginnings of Christianity*. 5 vols. London: MacMillan and Co., 1922–1933, 2:66–105.

Conzelmann, Hans, *The Theology of St. Luke*. Trans. G. Buswell. Philadelphia: Fortress, 1982 (original, 1960).

Dibelius, Martin, *Studies in the Acts of the Apostles*. Ed. H. Greeven. Trans. Anon. London: SCM, 1956.

Goulder, Michael D., *Type and History in Acts*. London: SPCK, 1964.

Haenchen, Ernst, *The Acts of the Apostles*. Ed. and trans. B. Noble et al. Philadelphia: Westminster, 1971. ET of *Die Apostelgeschichte*. 14th ed. KEK. Göttingen: Vandenhoeck & Ruprecht, 1965.

Hemer, Colin. *The Book of Acts in the Setting of Hellenistic History*. Ed. Conrad J. Gempf. Winona Lake, Indiana: Eisenbrauns, 1990.

Hengel, Martin, *Acts and the History of Earliest Christianity*. Trans. J. Bowden. Philadelphia: Fortress; London: SCM Press, 1980.

Hurd, John C. Jr., *The Origin of I Corinthians*. 2nd ed. Macon, Georgia: Mercer University Press, 1983 (original, 1965).

Johnson, Luke T., *The Writings of the New Testament*. Philadelphia: Fortress, 1986.

Koester, Helmut, *Introduction to the New Testament*. 2 vols. New York: Walter de Gruyter, 1995–2000.

Konstan, David, *Sexual Symmetry: Love in the Ancient Novel and Related Genres*. Princeton: Princeton University Press, 1994.

Lentz, John C. Jr., *Luke's Portrait of Paul*. SNTSMS 77. Cambridge: Cambridge University Press, 1993.

Lüdemann, Gerd, *The Acts of the Apostles: What Really Happened in the Earliest Days of the Church*. Amherst, NY: Prometheus Books, 2005

MacDonald, Dennis R., *Does the New Testament Imitate Homer: Four Cases from the Acts of the Apostles*. New Haven: Yale University Press, 2003.

_____, "Luke's Eutychus and Homer's Elpenor: Acts 20:7–12 and *Odyssey*, 10–12." *Journal of Historical Criticism* 1 (1994), 5–24.

_____, ed., *Mimesis and Intertextuality in Antiquity and Christianity* Harrisburg, PA: Trinity Press International, 2001.

_____, "The Shipwrecks of Odysseus and Paul." *New Testament Studies* 45 (1999), 88–107.

Mayes, A. D. H., "Deuteronomistic History." In John H. Hayes, ed., *Dictionary of Biblical Interpretation*. Nashville: Abingdon, 1999, 1:268–273.

Neyrey, Jerome, *The Passion according to Luke: A Redaction Study of Luke's Soteriology*. New York: Paulist, 1985.

Palmer, Darryl W., "Acts and the Ancient Historical Monograph." In B. W. Winter and A. D. Clarke, eds., *The Book of Acts in Its Ancient Literary*

Setting. The Book of Acts in Its First Century Setting 1. Grand Rapids: Eerdmans, 1993, 1–29.

Parsons, Mikeal C. and Richard I. Pervo, *Rethinking the Unity of Luke and Acts* Minneapolis: Fortress, 1993.

Pervo, Richard I., *Acts. A Commentary*. Ed. Harold W. Attridge. Hermeneia. Minneapolis: Fortress, 2008.

_____, *Dating Acts: Between the Evangelists and the Apologists*. Santa Rosa, CA: Polebridge, 2006.

_____, "Direct Speech in Acts and the Question of Genre." *Journal for the Study of the New Testament* 28 (2006), 285–307.

_____, *Luke's Story of Paul*. Minneapolis: Fortress, 1990.

_____, *Profit with Delight: The Literary Genre of the Acts of the Apostles*. Philadelphia: Fortress, 1987.

Phillips, Thomas E., "The Genre of Acts: Moving Toward a Consensus?" *Currents in Biblical Research* 4 (2006), 365–96.

Plümacher, Eckhard, "Die Apostelgeschichte als historische Monographie." In J. Kremer, ed. *Les Actes des Apôtres: Traditions, rédaction, théologie*. BETL 46. Louvain: Louvain University Press, 1979, 457–66.

_____, *Lukas als hellenistischer Schriftsteller*. SUNT 9. Göttingen: Vandenhoeck & Ruprecht, 1972.

Powell, Mark Allan, *What Are They Saying about Acts?* Mahwah, NJ: Paulist, 1991.

Praeder, Susan M., "Jesus-Paul, Peter-Paul, and Jesus-Peter Parallelisms." In K. H. Richards, ed., *Society of Biblical Literature Seminar Papers 1984*. Chico, CA: Scholars Press, 1984, 23–39.

Rackham, Richard B., *The Acts of the Apostles*. 2nd ed. London: Methuen & Co., 1904.

Radl, Walter, *Paulus und Jesus im Lukanischen Doppelwerk: Untersuchungen zu Parallelmotiven im Lukasevangelium und in der Apostelgeschichte*. Bern: Peter Lang, 1975.

Ramsay, William M., *St. Paul the Traveller and Roman Citizen*. London: Hodder and Stoughton, 1897.

Reardon, Brian P., ed., *Collected Ancient Greek Novels*. Berkeley: University of California Press, 1989.

Sterling, Gregory, *Historiography and Self-Definition: Josephos, Luke-Acts and Apologetic Historiography*. SuppNovTest 64. Leiden: Brill, 1992.

Talbert, Charles H., *Literary Patterns, Theological Themes, and the Genre of Luke-Acts*. SBLMS 20. Missoula, MT.: Scholars Press, 1974.

_____, *Reading Acts: A Literary and Theological Commentary on the Acts of the Apostles*. New York: Crossroads, 1997.

_____, and Perry Stepp, "Succession in Luke-Acts and in the Lukan Milieu." *Reading Luke-Acts in Its Mediterranean Milieu*. Leiden: Brill, 2003, 19–55.

Tannehill, Robert, *The Narrative Unity of Luke-Acts: A Literary Interpretation*. 2 vols. Minneapolis: Fortress, 1986, 1990.

Williams, Charles S.C., *The Acts of the Apostles*. HNTC. New York: Harper, 1957.

Wills, Lawrence M., *The Jewish Novel in the Ancient World*. Ithaca: Cornell University Press, 1995.

Witherington, Ben E. III, *The Acts of the Apostles: A Socio-Rhetorical Commentary*. Grand Rapids/Cambridge, U. K. Eerdmans; Carlisle: Paternoster, 1998.

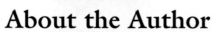

Richard I. Pervo began his research on Acts in the 1970s with a Harvard dissertion on its literary genre. He taught at Seabury-Western Theological Seminary and the University of Minnesota. He is the author of several books on Acts including *Profit with Delight: The Literary Genre of the Acts of the Apostles* (1987), *Luke's Story of Paul* (1990), *Rethinking the Unity of Luke and Acts* (with Mikeal C. Parsons, 1993), *Dating Acts: Between the Evangelists and the Apologists* (2006), and *Acts: A Commentary* (Hermeneia, 2008).

CPSIA information can be obtained at www.ICGtesting.com
Printed in the USA
LVOW101742201212

312633LV00017B/1025/P